THE REALM OF
REDEMPTION

THE REALM OF REDEMPTION

Studies in
the Doctrine of
the Nature of the Church
in Contemporary
Protestant Theology

by

J. ROBERT NELSON
A.B., B.D., D.Theol.

WIPF & STOCK · Eugene, Oregon

Wipf and Stock Publishers
199 W 8th Ave, Suite 3
Eugene, OR 97401

The Realm of Redemption
Studies in the Doctrine of the Nature of the Church
in Contemporary Protestant Theology
By Nelson, J. Robert
Copyright©1951 Methodist Publishing - Epworth Press
ISBN 13: 978-1-5326-3064-4
Publication date 4/6/2017
Previously published by Epworth Press, 1951

Every effort has been made to trace the current copyright
owner of this publication but without success. If you have
any information or interest in the copyright, please contact the publishers.

DEDICATED
WITH
GRATITUDE AND AFFECTION
TO MY
MOTHER AND FATHER

ACKNOWLEDGEMENTS

THE FOLLOWING publishers and owners of copyrights have kindly granted permission to quote from their books, and the author wishes to make acknowledgements to them with genuine gratitude, inasmuch as this work would have been impossible without the extensive use of many current theological writings:

To Messrs. George Allen & Unwin Ltd. for Loisy's *The Birth of the Christian Religion*, the *Church, Community, and State* volumes entitled *The Kingdom of God and History* and *The Church and Its Function in Society*; to the Abingdon-Cokesbury Press for Clark's *The Small Sects of America* (Revised edition, 1949); to Mrs. J. Forsyth Andrews for Forsyth's *The Church and the Sacraments*, lately reprinted by the Independent Press Ltd.; to Messrs. A. & C. Black Ltd. for Schweitzer's *The Mysticism of Paul the Apostle* and Thornton's *The Common Life in the Body of Christ*, first published by the Dacre Press; to the Cambridge University Press for Burn-Murdoch's *Church, Continuity and Unity*, Dodd's *The Bible Today*, Hayman's *Worship and the Common Life*, Johnston's *The Doctrine of the Church in the New Testament*, Knox's *St. Paul and the Church of the Gentiles*, Manson's *The Teaching of Jesus*, and Whale's *Christian Doctrine*; to the Canterbury Press for Dillistone's *The Holy Spirit in the Life of Today*, Neill's *The Ministry of the Church*, and Taylor's *The Church of God*; to Messrs. T. & T. Clark for Barth's *The Doctrine of the Word of God* and Buber's *I and Thou*; to Messrs. James Clarke & Co. Ltd. for Barth's *The Church and the Churches* and Scott's *The Fellowship of the Spirit*; Messrs. Faber & Faber Ltd. for D. M. Baillie's *God Was in Christ*, John Baillie's *Revelation*, Eliot's *Collected Poems*, Hebert's *The Form of the Church*, and Jenkins's *The Nature of Catholicity*; to Messrs. Hodder & Stoughton Ltd. for Barth's *The Resurrection of the Dead*, *The Knowledge of God and the Service of God*, *The Church and the Political Problem of Our Day*, Cave's *The Doctrines of the Christian Faith*, Dodd's *The Epistle of Paul to the Romans*, *The Johannine Epistles*, *The Apostolic Preaching and Its Developments*, Dehn's *Man and Revelation*, Kirk's *The Apostolic Ministry*, Manson's *The Church's Ministry*, Micklem's *What Is the Faith? Congregationalism and the*

Church Catholic, Raven's *Jesus and the Gospel of Love*, and Scott's *The Epistle of Paul to the Colossians, etc.*; to Messrs. Longmans Green & Co. Ltd. for Bell and Deissmann's *Mysterium Christi*, Mascall's *Christ, the Christian and the Church*, Ramsey's *The Gospel and the Catholic Church*, Rawlinson's *Authority and Freedom, The Church of England and the Church of Christ*, and Thornton's *The Incarnate Lord*; to the Lutterworth Press for Brunner's *The Mediator, The Divine Imperative*, Heim's *Spirit and Truth*, Lecerf's *An Introduction to Reformed Dogmatics*, and Minear's *Eyes of Faith*; to the Macmillan Co. for Grant's *The Gospel of the Kingdom*, Mathews's *Jesus on Social Institutions*, and Wedel's *The Coming Great Church*; to Mr. John Murray for Headlam's *The Doctrine of the Church and Christian Reunion*; to Messrs. James Nisbet & Co. Ltd. for Dodd's *The Authority of the Bible, The Parables of the Kingdom*, Hodgson's *The Doctrine of the Trinity*, Niebuhr's *Beyond Tragedy, Faith and History*, Quick's *The Christian Sacraments*, Robinson's *The Christian Experience of the Holy Spirit*, and Van Dusen's *The Christian Answer*; to the Oxford University Press for Baillie's *And the Life Everlasting* and Barth's *The Epistle to the Romans*; to the S.P.C.K. for Brilioth's *Eucharistic Faith and Practice, Evangelical and Catholic*, and Goudge's *The Church of England and Reunion*; and to the Student Christian Movement Press for Brunner's *The Divine-Human Encounter, Revelation and Reason*, Dunkerley's *The Ministry and the Sacraments*, Newbigin's *The Reunion of the Church*, Phythian-Adams's *The Way of At-one-ment*, Scott's *The Church: Its Worship and Sacraments*, Stählin's *The Mystery of God*, Tomkins's *The Wholeness of the Church*, Visser 't Hooft's *The Wretchedness and Greatness of the Church*, and the Amsterdam volumes, *The Universal Church in God's Design* and *The Church's Witness to God's Design*.

PREFACE

IN AUGUST 1948, Christian leaders came from all parts of the world to participate in the historic assembly at Amsterdam which brought the World Council of Churches into being. No person present could fail to experience a sense of wonder at the spectacle of all these Christians, representing denominations of such diverse and often conflicting beliefs, worshipping together and mutually seeking the ways by which a higher degree of Christian unity may be expressed. There could be no doubt of the profound longing for unity and the sincere feeling of love which characterized this great meeting. But lurking behind the scenes, so to speak, and frustrating every facile scheme for attaining unity was the ancient theological question, now made more urgent than ever: *What is the Church?* So long as this problem remains unsolved, and until all Christians understand what is fully intended when the word, 'Church', is spoken, the efforts to realize the unity of the One Body of Christ will lead to only an approximation of the ideal.

The predicament of Christians who earnestly desire unity, but find difficulty in realizing it, is further intensified by the fact that so many persons, and even some leaders of the churches, do not really understand the nature of the fundamental issues which keep Christians in a state of schism. Such misunderstanding can often undo the constructive work which ecumenically-minded enthusiasts have accomplished. It is quite apparent, then, that everyone who has a genuine concern for the advancement of the Ecumenical Movement in our time should feel obliged to inform himself on the matters which are of essential importance to the various conceptions of the nature of the Church of Christ.

The study underlying the present book was undertaken for just this purpose. Finding that Protestant Christians have long suffered from geographical, linguistic, and denominational isolationism, I have attempted to bring together the views of the leading theologians and churchmen who belong to many communions and speak several tongues. The result is by no means to be thought of as a synthetic ecclesiology, which somehow comprises every viewpoint and permits no contradictions to persist. It is utterly unrealistic even to think that such a synthesis might be possible; and in the chapters which follow, the reader will find many references to doctrines which are obviously irreconcilable to one another. This work is intended to be a synopsis, not a synthesis, of the foremost ideas and beliefs concerning the Church which are now current. As such it may be considered at best as a guide-book for further study in each of the areas which are treated.

A word of caution, based upon my own experience in writing this book, might well be offered to the reader at this point. It is very easy to become so absorbed in the theological problems relating to the Church that one unconsciously ignores the plain fact that the Church is made up of people rather than of doctrines and traditions. These are the ordinary Christian folk in every land, who have little or no concern for problems of theology, but whose worship and work are indispensable to the existence of the Church in any locality. It is for their ultimate benefit, and not for the intellectual delight of the theologically-minded, that the questions posed in the course of this study need eventually to be answered.

It is only natural that I should want to express my sincere feeling of gratitude to all the persons who have helped me to complete this work, but the number of such friends is too large for all to be named. However, I must surely mention Professor Brunner and his colleagues at the University of Zürich, Dr. Nils Ehrenström of the Study Department of the World Council of Churches, and Principal R. Newton Flew of Wesley House, Cambridge, for the guidance they gave me during the time of research and writing. And for their positive, constructive criticisms of the original script, I am indebted to the Rev. Daniel T. Jenkins, the Rev. Oliver S. Tomkins of the Faith and Order Commission, and Dean Clarence T. Craig of Drew Theological Seminary. In retrospect, I feel that having the privilege of associating with these men was more meaningful to me than the study itself.

J. R. N.

URBANA, ILLINOIS

Easter 1951

CONTENTS

ACKNOWLEDGEMENTS vii

PREFACE ix

FOREWORD, by Emil Brunner xv

CHAPTER ONE

THE ORIGIN OF THE CHURCH

1 THE VIEWPOINT: HISTORY AND FAITH . . . 1

2 THE CHURCH'S ROOTS IN ISRAEL . . . 3
   The Israel of God, 4. Linguistic studies: *qāhāl* and *ekklēsia*, 6. Jesus Christ the new factor in Israel, 8. The primitive Church a Jewish sect? 9. The Remnant, 11. Eschatological faith of early Church, 13. Accommodation to continuing history, 14. Effects of Christians' belief in Church, 17.

3 THE RELATION OF JESUS TO THE CHURCH . . 19
   Jesus' intention for a community, 20. When did the community begin? 27. Interpretations of Matthew 16$^{17-19}$, 28. The Last Supper as beginning of Church, 34. Pentecost the decisive event, 35.

CHAPTER TWO

THE CHURCH AND THE HOLY SPIRIT

1 FAITH IN THE PERSON AND WORK OF THE HOLY SPIRIT . 37
   The Spirit and Christ, 37. The Spirit Person or 'power'? 39.

2 PENTECOST 41

3 THE HOLY SPIRIT AS GIFT IN THE CHURCH . . 45

xii   THE REALM OF REDEMPTION

4   THE WORK OF THE SPIRIT IN THE CHURCH . . 48
Making known the presence of Christ, 48. Calling men to faith and discipleship, 50. The 'fruit of the Spirit', 52. *Koinōnia*: its various meanings, 53. Summary of Spirit's work, 57.

5   *KOINŌNIA* IN THE CHURCH TODAY . . . 60
Personal community: 'I and Thou', 61. Communion with God, 62. *Koinōnia* and *agapē*, 64.

CHAPTER THREE

THE CHURCH'S RELATION TO CHRIST

1   THE 'BODY OF CHRIST' IN NEW TESTAMENT THOUGHT . 67
Meaning of *sōma*, 68. Suggested sources of Body-concept, 68: Gnosticism, 68; Eucharistic language, 69; Hebrew personification, 69. 'Body in Christ' in 1 Corinthians, 70. In Romans, 76. In Colossians and Ephesians, 77: Question of Pauline authenticity, 77; Figure of the 'building', 78; The 'Bride of Christ', 78; Meaning of the 'Body of Christ', 80.

2   THE 'BODY OF CHRIST' IN CONTEMPORARY THEOLOGY . 84
The phrase, 'in Christ', 86. Christ as 'Head' of the 'Body', 89. The 'extension of the Incarnation', 95. The Church as organism, 101. *Koinōnia* in the 'Body of Christ', 103.

CHAPTER FOUR

THE WORD OF GOD AS THE CHURCH'S AUTHORITY

1   THE NEED FOR AUTHORITY 105

2   WHAT IS MEANT BY THE WORD OF GOD? . . 106
The Word as preaching, 108. The Word as Scripture, 109. The Word is Christ, 112.

3   HOW THE WORD OF GOD IS THE CHURCH'S AUTHORITY . 113

CONTENTS xiii

CHAPTER FIVE

THE SACRAMENTS AND THE MINISTRY

Part One—The Sacraments of the Church

1 VERBUM VISIBILE 120
2 THE MEANING OF HOLY COMMUNION AND BAPTISM . 120
  Principles for agreement on Sacraments, 121. Problem of 'validity', 123. The Presence of Christ in Sacraments, 126. Confusion regarding Baptism today, 127. Infant Baptism, 129.
3 THE WORD OF GOD INCLUDES THE SACRAMENTS . . 133
4 THE WORD AND THE SACRAMENTS CONSTITUTE THE CHURCH 135
  Danger of objectivization, 137. Danger of subjectivization, 139.

Part Two—The Ministry of the Church

1 A MATTER OF FAITH OR OF ORDER? . . . 142
2 THE PRIESTHOOD OF ALL CHRISTIANS . . . 144
3 THE SERVANT OF THE WORD 147
4 APOSTOLIC SUCCESSION 150
  'High Church' claims, 151. Alternate ideas of Apostolicity, 156.

CHAPTER SIX

SALVATION IN THE CHURCH

1 THE PROBLEM FOR MODERN CHRISTIANS . . 160
2 THE 'VISIBILITY' AND 'INVISIBILITY' OF THE CHURCH . 161
  Lutheran interpretation, 162. Calvinistic view, 164. Misunderstanding of 'Invisibility', 166.
3 MEMBERSHIP IN THE CHURCH 168

4 THE CHURCH AND SALVATION 172
   Protestantism is not individualism, 173. The Church in the divine plan of salvation, 174. Problem of Election, 180.

5 RECOVERY AND REINTERPRETATION OF 'EXTRA ECCLESIAM NULLA SALUS' 183

CHAPTER SEVEN

THE CHURCH'S ESSENTIAL UNITY

1 RATIONALIZATIONS OF DISUNITY . . . 188
   A spiritual, invisible unity, 189. Sociological concept of Church, 190. Values recognized in diversity, 192. The 'branch theory', 193. Problem of sectarianism, 194. The whole Church is in schism, 199.

2 WHY THE CHURCH IS ONE 200
   The 'given unity' of the Church, 201. New Testament bases for unity, 202. The Church's catholicity, 205.

CHAPTER EIGHT

THE CHURCH AND ESCHATOLOGY

1 THE CHRISTIAN AND THE 'LAST THINGS' . . 211

2 THOROUGHGOING ESCHATOLOGY . . . 213

3 REALIZED ESCHATOLOGY 217

4 THE KINGDOM PRESENT AND STILL TO COME . . 223
   Time of the consummation, 225.

5 CONCLUSION 233

BIBLIOGRAPHY 235

INDEX OF NAMES 247

INDEX OF SUBJECTS 250

FOREWORD

SCARCELY any concept of Christian doctrine in the present time stands so greatly in need of clarification from the ground up as that of the 'Church'. During the past decade numerous historical-exegetical monographs concerning the *ecclesia* in the New Testament have appeared in America, England, Germany and the Scandinavian countries; and during the same period of time there has been built up from the side of systematic theology a new consciousness of the meaning of the Church. But unfortunately these efforts to comprehend the nature of the Church have developed all too often *next* to each other and without integral relationship with one another. And yet, just that interpenetration was necessary, especially in view of the Ecumenical Movement, which, with the formation of the World Council of Churches, has not indeed attained its goal, but has only reached a first stage on its way.

It is, therefore, a fact to be welcomed that Mr. Nelson has ventured in his present book to fix his eyes upon the problem of the Church from both sides—namely, from that of historical-Biblical research and that of theological reflection. It would be unwarranted if this book claimed to speak the conclusive word concerning the solution of the problem. This is not its intention. Essentially it is a circumspect and deliberate presentation of those previously produced writings which have worked out the questions sharply and taken a critical position towards the results. Therefore, it will be welcomed by all those who are participating in ecumenical discussions as a comprehensive survey of the whole area of contemporary study of the Church, doing justice to both Anglo-Saxon and Continental European research.

That this solid work, undertaken with an inner sympathy and mature understanding, was carried out under the auspices of the University of Zürich, and so has become a part of the American-European conversation on the Church, is a fact which brings particular pleasure and satisfaction to my colleagues and myself.

ZÜRICH

EMIL BRUNNER

September 1950

CHAPTER ONE

THE ORIGIN OF THE CHURCH

1. THE VIEWPOINT: HISTORY AND FAITH

THE NATURE of the Christian Church is not the same as the history of the Church. A scholar may indeed possess a thorough knowledge of ecclesiastical history and yet have very little understanding of the Church's essential nature. This statement does not imply that the immense volume of facts about the Church's long history has nothing to contribute to such an understanding. But it indicates that the unique genius of the Church is to be apprehended by other than historical method and information, that is, by actual participation in the life of the Church. There are, therefore, historians who know in detail the whole story of the historical development of the Church, but their relationship to the Church itself is that of scholarly detachment rather than participation in faith, and so they cannot apprehend its true meaning. On the other hand, literally countless faithful Christians have only a rudimentary, often distorted, knowledge of Church history, and yet they know personally that the Church is a reality in their lives to which nothing else in the world is comparable. For the detached historians the Church is just an important material in the total structure of civilization. For faithful Christians, it is the sphere in which God makes Himself known to them and gives them purpose and direction for living.

This distinction between the facts of history and the fact of faith must be borne in mind when we undertake any kind of study of the Church, and especially one such as this investigation into the doctrine of the nature of the Church. Even though it will be necessary to refer rather frequently to historical data in the course of this study, the problem itself 'is a realm which lies beyond the historian's grasp'.[1] The facts about the Church can indeed be considered as mere elements of man's history, but basically they belong to the province of theology.

[1] G. Johnston, *The Doctrine of the Church in the New Testament*, p. 1.

The importance of this distinction can be seen quite clearly when we attempt to solve the complex riddle of the origin of the Church. Following a purely historical approach to the sources, one hardly recognizes that a riddle exists. The loyal followers of Jesus gathered together some time after His death and organized a religious society for the purpose of propagating His teaching and proclaiming their belief in His divinity. Such a simple account may satisfy many people as both accurate and adequate. But it is surely not an adequate description of the Church's origin for the Christians who belong to this 'society' today. If the problem were so simple, there could be no reason for the vast amount of research which has been directed in this century toward the elucidation of the obscure beginnings of the Church. For the purpose of this research is not merely to find out how the Church began, but much more, to reveal why, and to what end, it took form.

All of the scholarship and intellectual energy which have been concentrated on the problem of the first Christians, their relationship to Judaism, and their faith concerning themselves and the risen Christ, would seem rather extravagant, and a little wasteful, if the objective were just to illuminate another little corner of ancient history. But the scholars who have dedicated themselves to this inquiry have done so because they are convinced that an understanding of the Church in our own time can be no better than fragmentary without reference to that first generation of believers.

It should be noted that hardly any of these men look for a model of Church order and activity which ought to be imitated today. There are certain aspects of that first form of the Church which, as we shall see, continue with only slight modifications to the present. But in view of the profound difference between first-century and twentieth-century society, primitive forms can hardly be considered binding upon the Church today, particularly when the Church is known as a religious, rather than a sociological, entity.[2] That the continuing Church is dynamic and changing, rather than static and changeless, in form hardly needs to be argued, even with those who hold most rigidly to the ancient traditions.[3]

---

[2] E. von Dobschütz, 'Die Kirche in Urchristentum,' *Zeitschrift für die neutestamentliche Wissenschaft, usw.*, XXVIII.118; cf. E. F. Scott, *The Nature of the Early Church*, p.6: 'We cannot revive the New Testament church, nor is this desirable.'

[3] cf. H. Sasse: '*Die Kirche des Neuen Testaments steht nicht im Sein, sondern im Werden.*' *Credo Ecclesiam* (H. Ehrenberg, ed.), p. 309.

Christian scholars today are indeed seeking an authority in the primitive Church, but it is not an authority of form or organization so much as an authority on which to rest their belief about the divinely-appointed role of the Church in the world. If it can be demonstrated that the Church occupies a distinctive position in God's plan of salvation, and that it was Jesus' intention to establish the Church for just this purpose, such a belief will be substantiated and vindicated.

Theologians and biblical scholars are, therefore, seldom free from prejudice when they undertake the study of the primitive Church, since they usually approach the task with some particular conception of the Church which they would like to see verified by historical evidence. Complete open-mindedness on the subject is rarely to be found, although dishonesty and irresponsible treatment of the source material are equally rare, since each man feels certain that both his point of view and his historical or exegetical method are true to his sincere belief. For this reason, devoted Christian scholars, pursuing the same problem and utilizing the same materials, often arrive at conclusions which are mutually irreconcilable. The origin of the Church and the apostolic authority of the ministry are two of the problems in which this dilemma is most clearly to be seen.

When one reads the contradictory reports of various scholars, one is tempted to abandon the whole field of inquiry as hopelessly obscure and incomprehensible. Strong as this temptation to surrender may be, the men who are to be discussed in this chapter have been able to resist it because of their belief, or at least hope, that a satisfactory solution to the riddle may yet be found. And the high degree of unanimity and agreement which has been attained in recent years is an indication that such belief, or hope, is not without justification.

II. THE CHURCH'S ROOTS IN ISRAEL

Many Christians today are unwilling to acknowledge the debt they owe to Judaism. They use the Old Testament for study and inspiration, to be sure, but do so unavoidably with a Christian bias. Particularly offensive to Christians is the apparently arrogant claim made by the Jews to be the 'chosen people' of God, an exclusive kind of dogma which, they feel, must relegate all non-Jews to a secondary position in the sight of God, though some Christians have turned the tables and made the same claim for themselves. Since the time of Marcion, in the second century, until the present, Christians have to a large degree preferred to remain aloof from Judaism and assert that the Christian Church is original and independent of previous influences.

On the other hand, the Jews have often revolted against the misuse of their Scriptures by Christian interpreters, many of whom have appropriated whatever materials could be made to substantiate the Christian faith and rejected the rest.

It is, of course, impossible for Christianity and Judaism to be completely reconciled with each other, unless each should deny the distinctive beliefs which constitute its identity. However, among Christian theologians today there is an increasing agreement, almost amounting to a consensus, that the Church cannot be understood without an appreciation of the belief of the Jews that they were the 'people of God'. F. W. Dillistone goes so far as to claim 'that the altogether significant movement of thought during the past century amongst both Catholic and Protestant theologians has been that which has made its concern the setting forth of the nature of the relationship between the historical experience of the old Israel and that of the new'.[4] His claim is well founded. Spokesmen for all strains of Christian thought and tradition have made this clear.

The basis for this movement was not a discovery, but a recovery of one of the dominant ideas of the primitive Church. Throughout the New Testament one finds this problem of the relationship of Christians to Israel in the foreground of discussion. Only once does Paul speak of the Church as 'the Israel of God',[5] but elsewhere he makes it plain that the Christians believed themselves to be the true continuation of the elect people. The argument he pursues in Romans 9–11 is particularly instructive. Here he insists that membership in God's people is not limited to those who are descended biologically from Abraham, as 'the children of flesh', but declares that membership is open instead to those who are spiritual descendants, 'the children of the promise'.[6] These latter are not members of Israel because they have received circumcision, but because they have lived wholly by faith in God.[7]

---

[4] *The Word of God and the People of God*, p. 41.   [5] Galatians 6^{16}.
[6] Romans 9^8.   [7] Romans 4^{12}; cf. Philippians 3^3 and 1 Peter 2^9.

That is why Paul had so firm a ground on which to stand when he opposed the Jewish members of the first Church who wanted to observe traditional ritual legalism and force all Gentiles to accept circumcision as well as baptism.[8] The distinction between the true and false members of Israel was not an original idea of Paul. He himself quoted Hosea—'Those who were not my people I will call "my people" '—and Isaiah—'Though the number of the sons of Israel be as the sand of the sea, only a remnant of them will be saved'—to strengthen his argument.[9] And the action of the council in Jerusalem by which the Jewish party agreed to admit Gentiles without circumcision, as well as the subsequent dissipation of Jewish ritual observance, is testimony that these first Christians came to believe that the heritage of Israel had passed from the Jews to themselves.

This idea has received much emphasis in contemporary writing about the Church, for it expresses not only the present universality of the Church's appeal to non-Christians, but also the continuity of the Church with the people whom God chose before the time of Jesus. Thus Karl Barth declares: 'The people of Israel was never identical with the Jewish people, as a natural entity';[10] therefore our thought today has to do 'with the connexion (even the unity) of the Church with the people of Israel, whose place and function the Church has taken, one might say, automatically with the putting to death and the resurrection of Jesus the Messiah'.[11]

Some may question the statement that this transformation of Israel occurred so 'automatically' as Barth maintains. Lacking the belief that such an occurrence was an action of God rather than a normal event of history, they point out how uncharitable the Christians were toward their Jewish predecessors, from whose religious inheritance they had taken so much. This is the judgement of Alfred Loisy, whose reading of the history of the origin of the Church is informed by a scepticism toward the customary Christian interpretations. He describes how the Christians claimed at first to be the realization of the long-awaited Kingdom of God, or at least the means by which it would be made perfect. But the Jews would not recognize Christ, nor believe that he should

---

[8] cf. Acts 15$^{1-29}$.   [9] Romans 9$^{25, 27}$.
[10] *The Knowledge of God and the Service of God*, p. 151.
[11] *The Church and the Political Problem of Our Day*, p. 6.

bring the Kingdom, so the Christians, angered by the intransigence of the Jews, appropriated for themselves the title of 'the community of God', the true Church. 'From that time onwards', Loisy charges, Christianity 'denied the claim of the Jews to the very attribute it had borrowed from them.'[12] Seen from this historical perspective, the Christian pretension to being the 'Israel of God' does appear to be an unjust theft of title. But criticisms of this nature can be acknowledged only upon the assumption that Jesus on the Cross was not the Christ of God, and that the faith of the first Christians concerning the destiny of their Church was another religious delusion.[13] Obviously there can be little chance for agreement on the centre of Christian faith. Thus Loisy's rather unfavourable judgement on the Christians illustrates how the attitude of faith and the attitude of historical criticism render interpretations of an event of history which are largely irreconcilable.

A more exacting and demonstrable basis for judging the attitude of the first Christians toward their relationship to Israel has been provided in recent decades by the philological research of biblical scholars. By comparing the words in Hebrew, Greek and Aramaic which designate the Church in ancient writings and the New Testament, the scholars of recent decades have traced out a pattern of development which seems to provide much support for the idea that the primitive Church regarded itself as the continuation and heir of Israel.

It has long been known that the men who translated the Old Testament into Greek, the Septuagint, usually, though not always, rendered the Hebrew *qāhāl* into the Greek *ekklēsia*. In the postexilic literature of the Old Testament, *qāhāl* generally expressed the meaning of 'the assembly of the Congregation of Israel'.[14] In a similar way, the Greek *ekklēsia* carried the simple meaning of 'the summoning of Greek citizens by means of the herald's trumpet to the assembly of the city'.[15] While agreeing that *ekklēsia* was just a secular word in Greek, many scholars interpreted *qāhāl*

---

[12] *The Birth of the Christian Religion*, pp. 285f.
[13] This point of view is manifest in Loisy's estimate of the entire development of the early Church: 'In the whole course of this remarkable evolution nothing happened which cannot be explained by the laws that govern human life, and this may be said with confidence in spite of the obscurity resulting from the conditions under which the movement went on its way.' ibid., p. 358.
[14] G. Johnston, *The Doctrine of the Church in the New Testament*, p. 36.
[15] P. G. S. Hopwood, *The Religious Experience of the Primitive Church*, p. 230.

as having a distinctly religious connotation, meaning the assembly or people of God. The obvious deduction to be drawn, then, is that the first Christians, so far as they wrote and spoke Greek and used the Septuagint, appropriated the name *ekklēsia* for themselves because by that time it too had the meaning of 'people called forth specially by God'. All language at best is inexact, and frequently ambiguous, for meanings are constantly being modified by usage. And although the scholars who accept the *qāhāl-ekklēsia* hypothesis cannot describe exactly how *ekklēsia* came to have a distinctly Christian application, they seem to have a strong clue in this fact of translation. It would be too simple to suppose that the Christians just decided at an early date that *ekklēsia* would be their name. It has been suggested that, since the language of Jesus (and perhaps of the earliest documents of the Gospels) was Aramaic, the Christians at first called themselves the *k'nishta*, which expressed not only the idea of the divine calling of the people (*ekklēsia*) but also the people in common assembly for worship (*sunagōgē*).[16] If Christianity had not shown itself so soon to have a universal destiny, and if Aramaic had not been so provincial a language, the Church might have been extensively known as the *k'nishta*, if this theory is correct. But Greek was the language by which the Gospel was to be proclaimed and recorded, and *ekklēsia* was the most accurate word to characterize the Christian belief about the character of the Church, particularly its being the true people of God. Furthermore, the word was satisfactory for two other reasons: first, it carried no Jewish nuances which would make it displeasing to Gentile Christians; and second, the word already was familiar because it had a scriptural authority.[17] In the light of this evidence, most contemporary scholars confidently assume that the meaning of *ekklēsia* in the New Testament is based firmly upon the Old Testament *qāhāl*.

Almost alone in taking exception to this widely accepted theory is J. Y. Campbell. In the Old Testament he finds little substantiation for the definition of *qāhāl* as the divinely chosen

---

[16] cf. F. Kattenbusch in *Festgabe für Harnack*, pp. 166f., and K. L. Schmidt, Article *Ekklēsia*, *Theologisches Wörterbuch zum Neuen Testament* (ed. G. Kittel), hereafter abbreviated *TWNT*, III.528. Against the use of *K'nishta* may be noted W. G. Kümmel, *Kirchenbegriff und Geschichtsbewusstsein in der Urgemeinde und bei Jesus*, p. 23, and A. V. Ström, *Vetekornet*, p. 434.

[17] cf. G. Johnston, *The Doctrine of the Church in the New Testament*, pp. 43f.

people: instead, he claims, the word means simply a meeting or assembly of some kind, much as the secular meaning of *ekklēsia*.[18] The word which occurs frequently to express the idea of the people as a whole, whether assembled or not, is *'edah*, but this was generally rendered into *sunagōgē* in the Septuagint. Having studied exhaustively the uses of these words in the Old Testament, Campbell concludes that they afford little basis for the Christians' employing *ekklēsia* to mean Israel, the people of God.[19] If he is correct, therefore, the philological argument outlined above is invalid. But as yet his attack upon the widely-held view has been neither supported nor rebuffed.

At any rate, it is clear that within a few years after Pentecost the Church began to be known as the *ekklēsia*, and the word's use was well established by the time Paul wrote his letters—and clothed in a religious meaning, the word did express comprehensively the self-identity of the Church.

If the Christians considered themselves to be the true Israel, it may seem justifiable to some to assume that they were most arrogant, stealing the birthright of the Jews and denying them any part of it, because of the conviction that they were exclusively the people of God. This is the assumption which Loisy apparently holds, but it is invalidated by the New Testament itself. In Acts we see the Christians continuing to worship in the temple,[20] and Paul declares that, for all the Jews' unwillingness to believe in Christ, it is his heart's desire that they shall be saved.[21] Thus, Hopwood observes that 'it is to misinterpret the facts to infer that the primitive Church was aware of itself as the New Israel, for the essential fact of its self-consciousness here is its sense of belonging to Israel, with an urgent mission to Israel, but with no thought of being apart from Israel'.[22] The Christians preserved their continuity with Israel, and yet there was surely something altogether new in their concept of being God's people.

This new factor, which gave the Church its sole foundation for the claim of uniqueness, was Jesus Christ. Before Him, indeed, Israel was called to be the Church, the *ekklēsia*, but its history right up through the day of the crucifixion was an endless

---

[18] 'The Origin and Meaning of the Christian Use of the Word *EKKLĒSIA*' in the *Journal of Theological Studies*, XLIX(1948).133.
[19] ibid., p. 136.
[20] Acts 2^{46}, 3^1, 5^{21}.
[21] Romans 10^1. [22] *The Religious Experience of the Primitive Church*, p. 231.

repetition of rejections of the call. Some will go so far as to say that the Church had its origin as far back as the time when God called Abraham, not only to seek a new country, but to enter into a covenant relationship with Him.[23] So Abraham's descendants in their flight from the slave-masters of Egypt are called 'the militant Church of the wilderness',[24] and the subsequent decisive events in the history of Israel are considered points of time at which God's dealings with His Church are most clearly manifest.[25] In all the centuries of this colourful history of the people, who time and again disobeyed God by monstrous sins, only to return to worship Him, there was proclaimed by the leaders and prophets the message that the destiny of Israel would be fulfilled on the day when the Lord God would reveal Himself. And for the Christians that revelation was in Jesus Christ, the promised Messiah, the risen Lord.[26] Any interpretation of the history of the first generation of the Church in the years just after Pentecost cannot possibly be accurate if the full tradition of Israel's history is not recognized as a determining factor. The first Christian believers, as their words and actions in the accounts of Acts decisively portray, were thoroughly Jewish in thought and emotion. The religion and history they had received, to whatever degree of knowledge, were those of the chosen Israel. Therefore, they could not have known at the outset that their new faith in the risen Christ would eventually necessitate a divorce from the religion of their fathers, a break which none of them really desired.

Because they remained entirely within the bounds of their native Judaism at first, they gave the general appearance of being just another Jewish sect. Indeed, the Jewish hierarchy and the Roman rulers specifically referred to the Christians as such,[27] for outwardly they seemed to be nothing more than a small band of Jews with some religious ideas peculiar to themselves, often called simply 'the Way'. Even modern readers of their history have received such an impression, and E. F. Scott asserts that the

[23] F. J. Leenhardt, '*Realité et caractères de l'Église*' in *La Sainte Église Universelle*, p. 61.
[24] F. W. Dillistone, *The Word of God and the People of God*, p. 67.
[25] C. T. Craig, 'The Church of the New Testament' in *The Universal Church in God's Design*, p. 32.
[26] R. N. Flew: 'If we lay all the stress on the continuity of the new community with the ancient People of God, it would seem incorrect to use the phrase New Israel at all. But the claim to be the true sons of the covenant, the legitimate heirs of the promises, is dominated by the conviction that the Messianic Age had already dawned and that the last days were at hand.' *Jesus and His Church*, pp. 102f.
[27] Acts $24^{5, 14}$, 28^{22}.

Christians' 'chief anxiety' in the beginning was to be recognized as a legitimate sect.[28]

But the idea of their being only one sect among others fails to contain the elements of newness and uniqueness which were characteristic of their belief in Jesus Christ, with all the soteriological and eschatological implications of that belief, which made them altogether distinct from their co-religionists, even while remaining a part of Judaism. So the original disciples could not have held the view that they were just a sect, declares R. N. Flew. 'A sect is a party or school within Israel', he writes: 'But the disciples *were* Israel. They were the Church or People of God. They did not separate from Israel. They could not. It was the rebellious sons of Israel who forfeited their covenant by rejecting Christ.'[29] This attribute of being uniquely the true Israel, by possessing in Christ the fulfilment of all previous hopes, may not have been apparent to the Jews, who beheld the insular social organization of the Christians as well as their participation in the worship at the temple. One must appreciate the fact that these people were taking part in a remarkable transition which must have been very confusing to them, since the concept of being a new people did not come to them fully formulated. They were in a state of flux, wherein their very thought-forms and words had to be reorientated to the new situation of faith.[30] Just like the few members of a family who in some instances are singled out to inherit a great fortune, while the majority receives none, these few believers retained a family relationship with their ancestors of Israel; they offered to share the treasure with their brothers and sisters, who had disinherited themselves by rejecting Christ, but they could not fail to recognize that the inheritance had suddenly made them a distinctly different kind of people. And what is this priceless inheritance which makes them new? It 'lies in the Spirit which informs the community', writes C. A. A. Scott, 'in the changed attitude and relation to God, in the fact of possessing what the Church of pre-Christian days had only hoped for, and in the unexpugnable conviction resting on the death and resurrection of Christ that sin was forgiven'.[31]

---

[28] *The Nature of the Early Church*, pp. 30f.
[29] *Jesus and His Church*, p. 101; cf. A. G. Hebert, *The Throne of David*, p. 238; (F. C. Grant, *An Introduction to New Testament Thought*, p. 270).
[30] O. Michel, *Das Zeugnis des Neuen Testaments von der Gemeinde*, p. 15.
[31] *The Fellowship of the Spirit*, p. 82.

THE ORIGIN OF THE CHURCH 11

Inevitably in this discussion of the Church's continuity with Israel one has to refer to the Old Testament concept of the Remnant; nor can it be gainsaid that the Christians of the New Testament were conscious of being in some sense the living embodiment of this favoured few. So the Apostle Paul assured the Roman Christians that, just as God had saved seven thousand faithful persons who would not worship Baal in the days of Elijah, so He was gracious to choose such a Remnant in their own time.[32] And although 'Israel failed to obtain what it sought', the Remnant of the elect, those chosen and summoned by God to know Jesus Christ, had attained it.[33] It is plain to see how very adaptable the Remnant-idea was for Paul's explanation of the Church, not merely as an analogy, however, but as a veritable identification of the Church with the Remnant which the prophets had described and foretold.[34]

It is indeed questionable whether Jesus Himself consciously applied the idea of the Remnant to the people who gathered around Him and became His disciples. Some have suggested that when Jesus refers to His 'little flock' or to 'the lost sheep of the house of Israel', He implies that they are the Remnant, which is already saved and has the purpose of mediating salvation to others.[35] The reasons for such interpretation, consisting chiefly of parallels to passages in the Old Testament, are conclusive enough for proponents of this idea, despite the fact that at no time does Jesus personally refer to the Remnant as such. So it is not at all clear that Jesus held the same view which Paul espoused concerning the relation of the *ekklēsia* to the Remnant. As N. A. Dahl concludes: 'The group of disciples is for Jesus not the object of a special theological reflection.'[36]

Although it is dubious that Jesus definitely identified His followers with the Remnant, a number of New Testament interpreters in recent years have attributed to Jesus Himself the function of bearing the continuity of the Remnant through the critical passage from the old aeon of Israel to the new. Expressed

[32] Romans 11$^{1-5}$, 9^{27}; cf. 1 Kings 19^{18}.
[33] Romans 11^7.
[34] cf. A. E. Garvie's statement that the Jewish Church was born when Isaiah gathered the Remnant about him (Isaiah 8^{16}): *The Holy Catholic Church from the Congregational Point of View*, p. 33.
[35] cf. R. N. Flew, *Jesus and His Church*, p. 39; F. R. Barry, *The Relevance of the Church*, p. 69.
[36] *Das Volk Gottes, usw.*, p. 161f.

simply, the interpretation runs as follows: During the course of Israel's history the number of those belonging to the true Israel steadily diminished because of faithlessness and apostasy. Finally the Remnant had disappeared, except for Jesus, who bore its destiny alone. Thus we see His death on the Cross as an Atonement for the disobedient Israel. 'Jesus alone was the true Remnant,' writes T. A. Lacey; 'before Caiaphas, before Pilate, Jesus stands absolutely alone as the true seed of Abraham.'[37] And in the same line of thought: 'When Jesus Christ climbs toward Golgotha, He *alone* is the people of God. He bears the whole weight of God's work for this world. At that moment there was not even a Remnant, but only a Man who obeyed even unto death on the Cross.'[38]

The whole people of God is thus narrowed down to one person, the Christ, and after His resurrection the people begins to increase again in the Church, which continues and sustains the Remnant.[39] This view, though pertinent to the discussion of the Church's relation to Israel, is not self-evidently valid, and it is difficult to grasp without a corresponding faith in the Church as the Body of Christ, a concept which must be considered in another context.[40]

It was obviously not possible for the early Christians to think of Christ and the Remnant of Israel except in close connexion with their belief in the Kingdom of God and the breaking forth of the eschatological order, the long-awaited Messianic Age. Even when we make ample allowance for the eschatological character of the synoptic gospels, we tend to underestimate the intensity of the primitive Church's conviction that they lived in the critical 'last days', when history was being transcended by the reign of God.[41] This is convincingly set forth in the first two

[37] *The One Body and the One Spirit*, p. 52.
[38] W. A. Visser 't Hooft, *The Wretchedness and Greatness of the Church*, p. 15; cf. D. M. Baillie, *God Was in Christ*, p. 207; A. G. Hebert, *The Throne of David*, p. 238; A. M. Ramsey, *The Gospel and the Catholic Church*, p. 21.
[39] This idea is developed by T. W. Manson in terms of the 'Son of Man' of the gospels. He believes that the Son of Man is none other than the Israel of God, declared and described in the 'Remnant' of Isaiah, the 'Servant' of Deutero-Isaiah, the collective 'I' of certain Psalms, and the 'Son of Man' of Daniel. These related conceptions were fulfilled in Jesus. 'He sets out to create in Israel that Son of Man. But not many can be found to go with Him any part of the way, and none to follow Him to the end. The last part of the way He travels alone: and at the Cross He alone is the Son of Man, the incarnation of the Kingdom of God on earth.' *The Teaching of Jesus*, p. 235.
[40] Chapter 3.
[41] cf. W. G. Kümmel, *Kirchenbegriff und Geschichtsbewusstsein in der Urgemeinde und bei Jesus*, pp. 18f.

chapters of Acts, in which the disciples witness the ascension of Christ, hear the promise of His coming, receive the outpoured Spirit of God, and begin preaching repentance and faith in the resurrected Christ because the time has been fulfilled.

Their eschatological belief, which was so integrally a part of their faith that Jesus had risen from death, gave both content and urgency to the apostolic preaching. And this preaching was of incalculable importance to the constituting of the *ekklēsia* itself, inasmuch as it informed and propagated the faith in Jesus Christ which was indispensable for the Church.

To explain the origin of the Christian *ekklēsia* in terms of a natural banding together of those persons who were loyal to the memory of Jesus and desirous of trying to practice His teaching, to make the Church 'and the inbreaking Kingdom belonging to it trivial by allegories',[42] is to treat the records dishonestly and to misunderstand the motivating power which was all-important to the Christians. For them, Jesus was the long-awaited Messiah, whose mission was to redeem Israel.[43] His death was first seen as the defeat and destruction of their hopes for Him, but His resurrection more than compensated for the temporary feeling of defeat, and the authenticated testimonies of those who had seen the Lord were sufficient to convince the believers that they lived in apocalyptic days. The experience on the day of Pentecost was further evidence that their expectation was not an illusion. The Holy Spirit's descent was their 'guarantee', as Paul later described it,[44] that God's reign, as announced by Jesus, was a present reality and that the great consummation could not be long delayed.

What this meant for their conception of the Church is not really evident. At such a critical time, when the familiar patterns of life and thought were being shaken and transformed, they could not be expected to hold any well-defined doctrine about the infant Church of which they were members. Neither were any of them, prior to Paul, systematic thinkers, who could attempt to reflect upon their situation and make coherent judgements. To be sure, such theological reflection, even if it had been within their capacity, would have seemed needless and irrelevant in their time of upheaval. The essential elements of a doctrine were

---

[42] R. Otto, *The Kingdom of God and the Son of Man*, p. 375.
[43] Luke 24^{21}.   [44] 2 Corinthians 1^{22}, 5^5, or 'earnest'.

present in their minds: the messianic belief about Jesus, the fact of the resurrection, the wonder of Pentecost, and the long-held tradition of the Remnant of Israel; but there was no inclination on their part to formulate it.

Of course, the consummation as they expected it did not come to fruition, and we can only surmise how deep their disappointment was, as the years passed on and their brightest hopes constantly faded. We can imagine also how bitterly some of the believers must have been scorned and ridiculed by those who had heard their preaching but had sceptically refrained from joining their ranks.

The wonder is that the faith of the Christians was not so completely shattered that they themselves fell away in disillusionment. But the faith which was able to survive this disappointment was shared by many of the Christians, and was so strong, that they were not aware of having betrayed their belief when they modified their idea of the Kingdom of God and began building up the Church. Some may have observed rather sardonically, as Loisy did in our own time, that Jesus preached the Kingdom of God but the Church came instead.[45] However, the fact that a definite eschatological hope continued to be held by the Christians even after the Church became well established,[46] and that the hope is by no means dead today, indicates the persistency of this theme in Jesus' preaching.[47]

Various scholars in recent years, spurred by the thoroughgoing interpretation of New Testament eschatology, have submitted the biblical material to fine analysis, and have produced some illuminating results, which help our understanding of the situation of the first Christian generation.

In his scrutiny of the sermons, or proclamation (*kērugma*) of the apostles, C. H. Dodd has observed that the primary emphasis, the main burden, of their preaching was that the Kingdom of God was already an accomplished fact.[48] The second coming of Christ is specifically proclaimed in only one recorded sermon, Acts 3^{20-1}; other sermons fail to make any explicit reference to it. Why is this? Because, Dodd asserts, the first Christians looked upon the

---

[45] '*Jésus annonçait le Royaume de Dieu et c'est l'Église qui est venue,*' quoted by M. Goguel, *Le Problème de l'Église*, p. 22.
[46] cf. 1 John 2^{18}: 'It is the last hour.'
[47] Further discussion of eschatology and the Church today in Chapter 8.
[48] *The Apostolic Preaching and Its Developments*, p. 33.

facts of the Lord's resurrection, exaltation and second coming, not as a series of eschatological events, but as one single event. The final, decisive event, the fulfilment of the messianic hope, had already happened. Therefore, 'it was not an *early* advent that they proclaimed, but an *immediate* advent. They proclaimed it not so much as a future event for which men should prepare by repentance, but rather as an impending corroboration of a present fact: the new age is already here, and because it is here men should repent.[49] This was the pristine Christian eschatology of apostolic belief, which endured in an unmodified form for only three or four years after Pentecost. By that time, the disappointment could no longer be denied, and the readjustment of their faith was necessary. It was this necessity, Dodd concludes, which was 'a principal cause for the development of early Christian thought'.[50]

A different interpretation has been propounded ably by Oscar Cullmann, who sees evidence in the early eschatology for believing that the revelation in Jesus Christ had, in effect, brought a new dimension of time: *die Endzeit*, the time of the end or *eschaton*. As he regards this history, Pentecost was the '*endzeitliche*' beginning of the Church, the fulfilment of the People of God in the *eschaton*.[51] The Church had existed as the People of God prior to this event in the Israel of the Old Testament. But the coming of Christ annulled what was past. In Christ is the 'new creation', unique and distinct from the old.[52] The believer who has become a 'new man' in Christ has therefore been translated into a new order of time. This time in which the Church lives is the Reign of Christ, which Cullmann distinguishes from the Reign of God, the former being anterior to the latter and serving a preparatory function. The obvious clues which Cullmann follows to reach this theory are Pauline, expressed most completely in 1 Corinthians $15^{24\text{-}8}$, and Philippians $2^{9\text{-}11}$ and $3^{20\text{-}1}$.

[49] *The Apostolic Preaching and Its Developments*, p. 33.
[50] ibid., p. 34f.
[51] *Königsherrschaft Christi und Kirche im Neuen Testament*, p. 20; cf. his *Christus und die Zeit*.
[52] cf. R. Bultmann's interpretation: The Christian community was conscious of solidarity with Israel and its history. But the relationship is a dialectic one, since the history of Israel and Christian history were not really continuous, but broken by the eschatological event in Christ's coming. This was not a discontinuity in *Heilsgeschichte*, however, but only of secular history, for the history of redemption is continuous. *Theologie des Neuen Testaments*, pp. 95-6.

But however attractive and plausible the idea may be, that historical time has been superseded by the new dimension of time, it has not been widely accepted by theologians and biblical scholars. Flew regards this kind of speculation as out of harmony with Jesus' own teaching about the Kingdom, since there is no basis in the Gospels for construing the divine order to be beyond the historical time we all experience: 'New Testament "eschatology" . . . assumes that men and women are living in the last age of human history.'[53] In this age it is still proper to speak of present and future. And though the eternal Kingdom has come in the person of Jesus, so that those who have faith can participate in its blessings, the final consummation is still to be anticipated.[54] How long that period of expectation shall be can not be determined, and for the truly faithful person it should make no difference whether the time of waiting should be measured in years, centuries, or millennia. We need only consider how relentlessly the stream of time has flowed over scores of millenarians and chiliasts to appreciate this conception of eschatology.

Thus, the Church was not obliged to forget its hope in the consummation after the first note of urgency vanished. But during the following decades, we know, the eschatological element of the faith persisted. Both Schweitzer and E. Lohmeyer regard the Pauline concept of the *ekklēsia*, the community of God, as that of the eschatological fulfilment of the Jewish people: the people of the Church were called by God to be the community of the Messiah in his reign.[55] Paul often reminded the Christians of this in his letters, and encouraged them to live worthily of their great destiny.

The general effects of the inflation and deflation of this primitive hope upon the self-consciousness of the Christian community are well summarized by Hopwood in five paragraphs.[56]

(*a*) The fact that the 'Church came into being out of the experience of a grand failure' resulted in the Christians' coming to know the significance of Jesus more than ever for the effect His personality, as remembered and repeated orally, had upon their own living.

---

[53] *Jesus and His Church*, p. 33n.
[54] ibid., p. 32.
[55] A. Schweitzer, *The Mysticism of Paul the Apostle*, p. 104; E. Lohmeyer, *Grundlagen paulinischer Theologie*, p. 175.
[56] *The Religious Experience of the Primitive Church*, pp. 246-50.

(b) When the *eschaton* failed to appear, as expected, they became more and more conscious of the part which the Church must play for the redemption of the world, and the Kingdom came to be thought of in terms of a present possession.

(c) The centre of Christian hope moved away from the idea of an apocalyptic consummation of the heavenly order on earth toward the more serene belief in eternal life. This appears as the emphasis in the Gospel according to John, late in the first century, to the virtual exclusion of the Kingdom of God, as proclaimed in the Synoptics. It also gave to the Christians a characteristic, which, as A. M. Ramsey declares, distinguishes them as much as anything else from the old Israel; namely, the faith to consider death as no longer a baffling problem.[57] The tremendous fact of the witnessed resurrection of the Lord was proof for them that resurrection need no longer be a matter for debate and speculation, nor even a matter of hopeful belief. It is a certainty.

(d) The Church soon came to realize, according to Hopwood, that the apocalyptic concepts—'Kingdom, Messiah, Last Days, signs and portents, the Judgement apparatus, angels, archangels, demons, Messianic woes, etc.'—in which their first hopes had been clothed were really accidental elements, which obscured the leading ideas of the Gospel and hindered them in their apprehension of the 'new life' in Christ.

(e) Finally, the very extremity of their eschatological belief had so freed the Christians from the encumbering restraints of daily cares, prudence, and common-sense concern for social advantage, that they were better able to bring the new life to full expression.

These observations would appear either inadequate or slightly inaccurate to some scholars, according to their several points of view. But, on the whole, they indicate rather well how the Church, as the messianic People of God, was able to change its attitude toward the *eschaton*, without losing the sense of being the bearer of the true marks of Israel, and gaining in the process a clearer idea of what life on earth can be when lived in the power of the Spirit. So, far from suffering loss of their faith, the members of the community found that their faith in the sufficiency of Christ's revelation was actually strengthened.

It was just this element of faith which was determinative for the decision which the Church soon had to make with regard to the

[57] *The Gospel and the Catholic Church*, p. 18.

matrix of Judaism into which it was born. In the years just after Pentecost the Church existed, or rather, the Christians believed it existed, as both a definite part of Israel and a unique fulfilment of the hopes of Israel. Having experienced the radical transformation which none but those who knew the Christ could appreciate, the Christians' existence was paradoxical and necessarily unstable. In such an ambiguous position they could not long remain, however, and they eventually had to move toward one of two alternatives: either assimilation by traditional Judaism, or excursion on a course of their own. That they would have to take the second alternative was evident at a very early date, even when Peter professed before the high priest and elders that there is no salvation except in Christ, 'for there is no other name under heaven given among men by which we must be saved'.[58] Confident that this condition of faith is essential to the constitution of the Church, the Jewish Christians relinquished their hold on their former religion, though not without some longing, backward looks,[59] and then boldly proceeded under the conviction that the blessings and responsibilities of being the Israel of God were theirs.

In view of this early belief in the Church as the true People of God, it is worth noting the effects which the belief had upon the communal life of the Christians. These effects, which have been remarked by various scholars, demand little examination, since they are hardly controversial, though they are of real importance to our understanding of the Church's self-consciousness in these earliest times.

First, this concept of being truly Israel furnished the first Christians with a sense of historical identity, giving them at the same time defence against the polemics of their critics and the corruptions of faith which soon threatened to dilute the Gospel of Jesus Christ with elements of Greek philosophy and pagan religions.[60] Having the knowledge that they were the elect people of the One God of Israel, the Father of Jesus Christ, they resisted such influences, even though not always successfully.

Secondly, the Christians were provided with a strong feeling of solidarity, which may be traced to their understanding of Israel. The community of the first believers, expressed in terms of their own kind of fellowship, will be treated in the next chapter.

[58] Acts 4^{12}.
[59] Romans 9$^{3-4}$.
[60] C. A. A. Scott, *The Fellowship of the Spirit*, p. 78; cf. Colossians 2$^{8-23}$, Romans 14$^{1-5}$, and 1 Corinthians 8.

What should be noted here is, that the social unity which became so distinctive of Christians depended to a large extent upon the fact that the individual goodness and piety of the people did not constitute Israel, but rather that membership in Israel was itself the ground for their enjoying God's favour. 'It is the group that sanctifies, not vice versa.'[61] The equating of the Church with Israel thus helped to prevent Christianity from becoming an atomistic religion.

In the third place, an ethical responsibility was laid upon the Christians which was of greater weight by far than that they would have borne without the Israel-consciousness. The same prophets who had proclaimed the Remnant had set forth vividly the divine demands for righteousness and mercy which Israel must obey. And the risen Lord, who was the focal point of their faith, had given them both the commandment and the example of the love (*agapē*) by which they were to live as a people. Great promises had been made concerning the fulfilled state of Israel. Now the people's task was 'to become what it is, to live on the level of the promise'.[62] And to the extent of their actual living according to Jesus' principle of extreme love, they demonstrated to the world that the power of God's people lay just there, in the divine gift of love.

To underestimate the importance of the early Church's consciousness of being in the full sense the Israel of God inevitably means to eliminate one of the basic elements of Christian belief about the nature of the Church. Therefore, as Emil Brunner declares, when 'we no longer take seriously the idea of a people of God, chosen by Him', we miss the whole point of Paul's theology. 'Paul takes this idea absolutely seriously,' Brunner continues, 'and he was able to carry out his idea. But he takes it seriously in the idea of the universal Church. . . . The *ekklēsia* is the people of God . . . exactly like the people of Israel in the Old Testament, the object of the Divine Will of revelation.'[63]

III. THE RELATION OF JESUS TO THE CHURCH

One of the major results of the school of biblical criticism, which had as its goal the reconstruction of the true picture of the

---

[61] B. S. Easton, 'The Church in the New Testament,' *Anglican Theological Review* XXII(1940).157.
[62] W. A. Visser 't Hooft, *The Wretchedness and Greatness of the Church*, p. 17.
[63] *The Mediator*, p. 587.

'historical Jesus', free from later dogmatic embellishments, was the thesis that between Jesus of Nazareth and the Church bearing His name there existed no organic connexions. The idea was thrown confidently into the faces of orthodox biblical scholars, who had long believed on scriptural authority that Jesus intended to establish the Church in order to continue His ministry in the world, and that the 'Rock' upon which he built the Church was the disciple Peter. Between these extreme views there can be no thorough reconciliation, but exegetes and theologians of the past three decades have expended much energy in formulating theories about the relation of Jesus to the Church which would make some sort of compromise, and so avoid the unwelcome implications of either extreme. By examining and contrasting these various views, we may be able to appreciate the significance and complexity of the problem for Christians today.

Some writers have frankly maintained the position that the problem of the connexion between Jesus' thoughts and words and the founding and organizing of the Church is really not an important one. One of these, A. J. Mason,[64] points to the writing of Paul and his contemporaries as evidence that even then there was no real concern to probe the intention of Jesus on this matter or try to explain exactly how and why the Church came into being. Mason asserts: 'To them the unity between Christ and the Holy Spirit was so perfect—they were so vividly conscious of being guided by the Spirit of Jesus—they were so confident that the work which went on under their hands was the work of God —that it was a matter of comparative indifference to them at what stage in His career the Lord had given the first impetus to the movement.' If this was the position of Paul, then, Mason implies, the problem had little bearing upon Paul's doctrine of the Church.

Others find it necessary for us to give closer attention to the kind of questions we usually pose when we consider Jesus and the Church. Dietrich Bonhöffer, for example, addresses himself to those who ask whether Jesus began a new religion and religious community: 'Essentially Jesus Christ was just as little a founder of the Christian religious fellowship (*Religionsgemeinschaft*) as He was the founder of a religion.[65] But to speak in these terms is not

---

[64] 'Conceptions of the Church in Early Times,' in *Essays on the Early History of the Church and the Ministry* (H. B. Swete, ed.), p. 5.

[65] *Sanctorum communio*, p. 82.

to speak of the Church. 'The reality of the Church is the reality of revelation;'[66] and just as a religion differs from God's revelation, so a religious fellowship of one kind or another differs from the Church. We will save ourselves difficulty, he observes, if we avoid thinking historically of the Church as a 'religious fellowship' and of Jesus as the original leader and founder of it.[67] We should be prepared to ask instead, how Christ, as the Revelation, and the unique Church are related in the scheme of God for mankind. Thus, Bonhöffer infers that the entire question has meaning only when approached with certain presuppositions of faith.

In his significant book on this whole matter, Flew also suggests the necessity for clarifying our thoughts before we approach the problem, but his specific recommendation is just the reverse of Bonhöffer's. 'Instead of asking, "Did Jesus found the Church?" or "Did Jesus organize a Church?" we should ask whether Jesus directed His ministry to a particular community, and whether His ministry had in view the formation of a community as one of His dominant aims.'[68] Instead of allowing theological presuppositions about the Church to influence our inquiry, we should be able to find objectively in the teaching of Jesus the answer to this question. When Flew speaks of 'Church' in connexion with Jesus, then, he wishes to separate from that term all the associations of meaning which became attached to it in later years. What he means by 'Church' in this context is 'a new religious community, with a new way of life, a fresh and startling message, and an unparalleled consciousness of inheriting the divine promises made to Israel of old'.[69] It is only by limiting the definition of 'Church' to these attributes, he believes, that we can hope to find it at all in the teaching of Jesus, even though it must be conceded that the word for us has a much wider meaning. Much misapprehension about the particular claims and judgements of scholars can be avoided if the reader knows beforehand whether he means by 'Church' the distinctive sphere of revelation, as a definite theological concept, or the simpler idea of a religious community.

[66] *Sanctorum communio*, p. 65.   [67] ibid., p. 64.   [68] *Jesus and His Church*, p. 19.
[69] ibid., p. 18. Even this moderate statement is unacceptable to W. G. Kümmel, however. He contends that the messianic mission of Jesus precluded any idea of a continuing society. 'Jesus saw the presence of the reign of God only in his person and work, and he speaks only of a fellowship of those grouped about him as the coming Messiah, but not of a new community.' *Verheissung und Erfüllung*, p. 85.

Very often it is the former meaning of the Church which is in the minds of those who deny that Jesus thought at all in terms of it. The words of M. Goguel are a fitting example of this widely held point of view: 'Jesus neither instituted nor foresaw the Church. He did not believe that His disciples would have to wait long for His return. The Church as such began to exist on the morrow of the passion.'[70] By the phrase, 'Church as such', we assume that he has in mind the developed institutional form which it began to take after the disciples realized that Christ's second advent was to be long delayed. So Goguel is satisfied to conclude that the Church was neither instituted by Jesus nor created by the Apostles, but that 'it owes its origin to the dynamic force of the personality of Jesus. In this way it is the outcome of His life.'[71]

Another authority on the New Testament, E. F. Scott, reached a similar conclusion, after exploring the biblical evidence. 'Jesus himself laid down no directions as to how his followers were to order their society. He only gave them a task to fulfil, and left them to discover for themselves how they might do so most effectually.'[72] The statement to the effect that Jesus' only legacy to the disciples was a 'task to fulfil' seems to leave the question of His intention about a new community unanswered. However, Scott goes on to assert that the essential constitution of the Church rested on the disciples' 'allegiance' to Jesus.[73] It may be said then, he infers, that the Christians looked back to Jesus as the source and principle of their community, but that Jesus personally had nothing to say about this community.

Adverse judgements about the institutional church have prejudiced the convictions of theologians and laymen alike in the present time. More radical opinions can hardly be found than the two following, though both come from spokesmen within the Church of faith. First, a biblical scholar, following carefully the critical principle of radical eschatology, writes: 'The Church as the official organ of His faith and the future form of organization for His following never figured in the religious outlook of the historical Jesus. In fact, the idea of the Church contradicts the whole of his religious outlook.'[74] While a group of Indian laymen

---

[70] *Le Problème de l'Église*, p. 29.
[71] In *The Ministry and the Sacraments* (R. Dunkerley, ed.), p. 325.
[72] *The Nature of the Early Church*, p. 6.
[73] ibid., p. 28.   [74] W. E. Bundy, *The Religion of Jesus*, p. 299.

confess this remarkable idea: 'The Church as we know it was not in the scheme of Jesus. It came into existence only when the Holy Spirit ceased to be a reality (!) and the sense of His immediate direction evaporated.'[75]

In fairness to the former, however, it should be noted that his judgement was not derived altogether from a lack of appreciation for the Church. Another important factor, upon which much of the thought in harmony with his view is based, was Jesus' proclamation of the imminent, apocalyptic coming of the Kingdom of God. The arguments for this eschatological interpretation of Jesus' mission and teaching need not be discussed here. It is sufficient to acknowledge, as Easton does, that in such sayings as, 'there are some standing here who will not taste death before they see the Son of man coming in his kingdom',[76] there is ample reason for considering the continuing Church in the world as incompatible with the mind of Jesus.[77] Whether Bundy and Easton would change their position if they took the word 'Church' in the sense of Flew's usage, is a matter for conjecture. But Flew shows that Jesus not only preached the coming of God's *basileia*, but that He had every intention of instituting the community of the New Covenant, to live under this divine sovereignty.[78] More and more do we see how conceptions of the Church are inseparably bound to, and informed by, the viewpoint and method of exegesis.

The denial that Jesus had anything at all to do with the idea of a community of believers or a Church is an extreme one; and not many persons hold this position in the present. A somewhat modified view, which has gained considerable currency, is that, although Jesus did not actually found or establish the Church, the idea of the *ekklēsia* was really present in His teaching and work. Such is the position of E. von Dobschütz. Insisting that Jesus was not a *Kirchengründer* or *Religionsstifter*, but the Messiah of His people and the fulfiller of prophecy,[79] he still regards the Church

[75] From *Rethinking Christianity in India*: quoted by A. J. Appasamy, *The Gospel and India's Heritage*, p. 201.
[76] Matthew 16^{28}.
[77] cf. B. S. Easton, 'The Church in the New Testament,' *Anglican Theological Review*, XXII(1940).167: Jesus could not have used the word *ekklēsia* in Matthew 16^{18}, 'for it is wholly irreconcilable with Jesus' teaching about the Kingdom, whether present or future'.
[78] *Jesus and His Church*, pp. 20-4, 25.
[79] '*Die Kirche im Urchristentum,*' *Zeitschrift für die neutestamentliche Wissenschaft, usw.*, XXVIII(1929).114.

as implicit in the very activity of Jesus and His disciples. Jesus preached the Gospel and taught His disciples, He gave them a prayer for collective worship, and on occasion they joined in singing a hymn.[80] And despite the fact that the burden of Jesus' preaching was the imminence of the Kingdom, and the urgent ethical appeal to prepare for it, Dobschütz sees strong evidence that Jesus wanted His disciples to preserve the distinctive kind of community they already had. The disciples, according to this view, were not yet the Church, but the forerunners of it.[81] However, when they and their converts did become the Church, after the resurrection of Jesus, they were conscious of being in complete harmony with the mind of Jesus.

Among the many scholars who have written on this persistently puzzling issue are those who feel that, whatever the idea of the Church one holds, it is not a legitimate question to ask whether Jesus *founded* the Church at all. This question, they urge, implies that the concept of a people of God, existing since the ancient times of Israel, is only a myth or delusion. If the evidence already cited, to the effect that God was calling a people for Himself in the history of Israel, is at all credible, then it is a direct contradiction in terms to speak of this people, or the Church, as being established by Jesus. Thus Hermann Sasse concludes: 'It was not so that a new religion emerged in history through Jesus Christ. But in the history of revelation the already prepared Church became a reality through Jesus Christ.'[82] The same point of view is expressed by H. L. Goudge, quoting Ephesians 1²² as his authority: 'Let us then keep the scriptural language,' he writes: 'Our Lord did not found the Church, for the Church was in the world long before He was. Rather, as St. Paul says, "God gave Him to be Head over all things to the Church".'[83] This interpretation is not far from the thought connoted by Johnston's

---

[80] '*Die Kirche im Urchristentum,*' *Zeitschrift für die neutestamentliche Wissenschaft, usw.*, XXVIII(1929).114. p. 113.

[81] So also O. Cullmann. *Königsherrschaft Christi und Kirche im Neuen Testament*, p. 22. Cf. N. A. Dahl, *Das Volk Gottes, usw.*, p. 166, in which he proposes that Jesus himself incorporated the People of God in his personal nature and experience. His baptism, temptation, and transfiguration repeat, in a sense, the experience of Israel, and prefigure the life of the Church. '*Der Sohn ist der eschatologische Antitypus der Volkes.*'

[82] In *Credo Ecclesiam* (edited by H. Ehrenberg), p. 304.

[83] *The Church of England and Reunion*, p. 94; cf. J. B. Bernadin: 'So may it well be said that Christ found the ancient Church of God and refounded it on the foundation of faith in himself.' 'The Church in the New Testament,' *Anglican Theological Review*, XXI(1939).170.

aptly chosen phrase, 'an adoptionist ecclesiology',[84] meaning that the pre-Christian people, or Church, was taken into a new relationship with God when Christ was made its Head. What these quotations suggest as the actual relation of Jesus to the founding—as they prefer, refounding—of the Church, can hardly be challenged, if one holds to the belief that a direct, unbroken line of continuity runs from the people of the Old Covenant to the Church of the New. How else could the primacy of Christ be introduced into this continuing Israel of God, if not by a reconstituting of the faith of the people of Israel unto a recognition of Him? There are two alternatives to this thesis: either, that Jesus had nothing to do with any such community as the Church, or that the Church was intended, and possibly instituted, by Jesus as something new and unprecedented. The former makes the Church an accidental consequence of Jesus' ministry, and renders invalid any claim that the Church exists to fulfil the work of redemption which Jesus initiated. The second alternative virtually ignores the idea that the Israel of the Old Covenant was in some sense the people of God. Between such incompatible positions is the plausible and widely accepted conviction, not that Jesus founded the Church, less that He ignored the Church, but that He redeemed the already existing Church.[85]

A careful weighing of the biblical passages which are pertinent to this problem reveals no one, indisputable solution. For this reason, many persons are content to admit that the beginning and original nature of the Church are so shrouded in darkness, that we should cease such fruitless speculation, which all too often treats the historical and biblical material with denominational bias. J. van Holk presses this idea by insisting that any talk of God's willing the Church, or of Christ's founding it, is nothing more than metaphor, which endeavours unsuccessfully to describe and substantiate a strictly *a priori* concept of the Church.[86]

The temptation to surrender to this idea, and so to abandon any hope of knowing more fully what Jesus' actual relation to the Church was, is indeed strong for those who either regard the matter as irrelevant to their personal faith or lack the required equipment for pursuing an exhaustive research in the written

---

[84] *The Doctrine of the Church in the New Testament*, p. 56.
[85] cf. C. T. Craig, in *The Universal Church in God's Design* (W.C.C), p. 33.
[86] 'The Nature of the Church,' in *Christendom*, V.1(1940).39.

records. But the doctrine of the Church ceases to have any importance for the Christian faith if it is not grounded in some kind of relationship to Jesus Christ, its Lord. To an even greater degree than other doctrines or principles of ethics, it defies easy authorization on the basis of scriptural proof-texts; and so it can be clarified only with a large measure of patience, scholarship, and faith.

Having taken this brief look at the conflicting theories regarding the thought of Jesus and the existence of the Church, we should proceed to give closer attention to the writings of those who are convinced of the Church's vital connexions with Jesus and his ministry. These deserve special attention because they represent the great majority of scholars who interest themselves in this problem, and their positive position has enjoyed, and still enjoys, the widest acceptance. On certain points their opinions diverge and clash, such as on the interpretation of Matthew 16^{17-19}, where the use of the word *ekklēsia* is first ascribed to Jesus, or on the question of the exact time when the *Christian* Church, as distinguished but not divorced from the old Israel, took form. Even though such particular disputes are unavoidable, because of diverse types of exegetical thought, there is a growing feeling of certainty among Protestant theologians with regard to Jesus' desire to have a community of believers following Him. 'The origin of the community . . . ', declares Karl Heim, 'is nothing other than a work of the historical Christ, who, as the Perfecter with super-spatial and super-temporal power, further extended and continued His life's work.'[87] C. C. Morrison's conviction is even stronger than the Lutheran Heim's; he writes: 'Above everything that Jesus said or did, this stands as his supreme achievement, that he formed an organic community to carry forward in history the revelation of God which had been made in Israel.'[88] That this idea can be expressed and receive extensive support in a decade which is barely removed from the time when the existence of the Church was considered by many to be irrelevant to the attainment of an individual's full Christian life, is indicative of the grave seriousness with which more and more Christians are regarding the necessity of the Church for the completion of Christ's work in the world.

---

[87] *Der evangelische Glaube und das Denken der Gegenwart*, III.242.
[88] *What is Christianity?* p. 108.

THE ORIGIN OF THE CHURCH 27

But when did this 'supreme achievement' of Jesus take place? At what stage of His ministry did He consciously begin to form a community, which would eventually be called the *ekklēsia*? It seems quite obvious for some scholars that this took place when Jesus selected His inner circle of twelve disciples during the first months of His public ministry. In these simple followers of Jesus, the living kernel of the coming Church was formed by a 'mysterious act of begetting',[89] and they became a living organism which was destined to grow up through a process of maturation. They appear in history as the social product of the action of God in Christ, destined to be the first to recognize that God has entered the temporal, spatial world of man, the first to proclaim the advent of the expected Messiah.[90] Jesus disclosed to them the ethical content of God's will, in all its radical perfection, a teaching which 'presupposed a new community, and the power to fulfil the new demands'.[91] As the Messiah, sent by God, He could not stand alone, but needed a messianic people to carry out the divine redemption of sinful mankind, so that 'under the leadership of the Son of man the fulfilling of the promise should be experienced'.[92] Having designated the disciples as His community, Jesus sent them on a preaching mission, whereon they not only proclaimed the urgency of repentance, but discovered to their amazement and joy that the spiritual power which was in Jesus was also granted to them.[93]

The concurring reports of the first three Gospels concerning the calling and the sending of the disciples surely give strong support to the contention that they then became the special new people, or community, or Church of the Messiah.[94] Against this theory stands the aforementioned idea that Jesus Himself embodied the true Israel, the Church, during His earthly life. But must this mean that the disciples have no significance as a

[89] F. Heiler, *Im Ringen um die Kirche*: 'Einen geheimnisvollen Zeugungsakt.' Quoted by E. Foerster, 'Kirche wider Kirche,' *Theologische Rundschau* (1932), p. 132.

[90] R. D. Grützmacher, '*Die alt- und neuprotestantische Auffassung von der Kirche*,' *Neue kirchliche Zeitschrift*, XXVII(1916).486.

[91] N. Flew, *Jesus and His Church*, p. 35.

[92] Anton Fridrichsen, '*Église et sacrament dans le Nouveau Testament*,' *Revue d'histoire et de philosophie religieuses*, XVII(1937).342.

[93] Luke 9¹, 10¹⁷.

[94] cf. M. Boegner: 'By the choice of the disciples, Jesus constituted the kernel of the new Israel, and organized a cell of the new humanity.' Quoted by R. Will, '*La conception protestante de l'Église considérée comme le corpus Christi*' in *Revue d'histoire et de philosophie religieuses*, XII (1932).470

community of followers of Jesus? So it would seem at first glance. However, a suggestive solution to this problem has been offered by A. V. Ström, among others, who declares that the disciples are the *ecclesia designata*, the Church-to-be, who really become the *ecclesia revelata*, the Church-manifest, only after Jesus' resurrection.[95] For those who cannot agree, this scheme may seem to be a facile but imaginary construction. But it does have much merit in that it retains without compromise the two elements—Jesus as the bearer of Israel, and the disciples as a community—which many consider to be the true relation of the disciples and of Jesus to the Church.

Ström's interpretation also harmonizes in one respect with the viewpoint of those who consider the words in Matthew 16[17-19] as an authentic saying of Jesus. In this passage Jesus says: 'I will build my *ekklēsia*.' The future tense of the verb, *oikodomēso*, seems to preclude the idea that the disciples are already the Church. But if they are the *ecclesia designata*, Jesus can still speak of their being built as a Church in the future time, after His crucifixion and resurrection. If Jesus already considered the disciples as constituting that community, it is hardly conceivable that He would have spoken of the Church's being built in the future.[96]

The validity of this argument, however, must depend wholly upon the interpretation given to the whole passage in question. And few words of the New Testament have been the cause for so much exhaustive study and involved debate as these remarks which Jesus is alleged to have made to Peter, after Peter had made the momentous confession of Jesus' messiahship at Caesarea Philippi.

Interest in this debate has long been stimulated by the implications for the Roman papacy, which bases its claim to authority upon these verses, as well as upon the reading of history which views Peter as the first pope. The general understanding is that Jesus singled out Peter as the foundation stone for His Church, giving to him full authority of 'the keys of the kingdom of heaven', and that Peter, so armed with authority,

---

[95] *Vetekornet*, p. 436; cf. G. Johnston, *The Doctrine of the Church in the New Testament*, p. 48.
[96] cf. O. Cullmann, *Königsherrschaft Christi und Kirche im Neuen Testament*, p. 22. But E. Lohmeyer interprets the future tense to mean the day of the 'coming of the Messiah', the *eschaton*, and not an event in time. *Grundlagen paulinischer Theologie*, p. 158.

eventually came to Rome as its first bishop, and hence the first of the continuing line of infallible popes.

Even if this were a true exposition of the text, however, there should be no need for anxiety over such an argument in support of papal authority. Apart from all questions of textual criticism, Karl Heim declares that the obvious meaning of these words can be nothing other than that to Peter was given the role of foundation stone, second only to Jesus, and this was a position which could not be delegated or transmitted to successors.[97] If Peter ever received such an honorific blessing, it would have died with him.

Nevertheless, the contention over the authenticity and meaning of this passage continues among present-day scholars, and the facts of the debate are of importance to our discussion of the nature of the Church, since upon them must rest our estimate of the first of only two sayings in which the word *ekklēsia* is ascribed to Jesus.[98] Could the passage be shown to be a genuine saying, no further disputation concerning Jesus' intention of having a Church would make sense. But if the words should be adjudged unauthentic, scholars would have to exclude this evidence from the body of material supporting their conclusions about Jesus' relation to the Church.

Before considering the problem of the authenticity of Matthew 16[17-19] in more detail, we shall do well to heed the warning of J. Y. Campbell, that there is a much deeper problem here than that of the validity of the Greek text as a report of Jesus' saying. For even if these are the original words of Jesus, translated into Greek, 'we have no means of determining what Aramaic word he used; whatever it was, it would inevitably be translated *ekklēsia* as soon as that had come to be the accepted name for the Christian church,' he writes.[99] This acute observation does not show the great amount of scholarly inquiry directed toward this passage to be valueless or even insignificant for the understanding of the origin of the Church. But it does remind us that the idea of Jesus' willing the Church does not stand or fall with His address to Peter.

[97] *Spirit and Truth*, p. 55f.
[98] The other passage, Matthew 18[17], is less important and has far less claim to authenticity.
[99] 'The Origin and Meaning of the Christian use of the word EKKLĒSIA,' *Journal of Theological Studies*, XLIX(1948).141.

In this context only a summary of the argument *pro* and *contra* authenticity can be given, since few competent New Testament scholars have refrained from entering the dispute, and the writing on it during the past thirty years has been voluminous.

Taking the negative side first, we find that five major factors are generally emphasized, involving both textual and historical considerations.[100]

(*a*) First is the so-called 'argument from silence'. Neither Mark nor Luke reports these words as the sequence to Peter's confession. Why do they omit them? If they knew of the significant instance in which the fact that Jesus was the Messiah was professed and not denied, how could they have failed to know about Jesus' answer? The conclusion seems to be inevitable that the writers of Mark and Luke either did not know these words, or else that they knew them but omitted them intentionally because they deemed them spurious.

(*b*) Another familiar objection to the passage is that which is based upon the eschatological character of Jesus' teaching: how could Jesus proclaim the imminent and catastrophic coming of the Kingdom of God and at the same time make provision for building a continuing Church?

(*c*) Bultmann takes special care to show that these words must have been a later insertion into the text of Matthew, reflecting an attitude toward Peter and the Church which developed after Jesus' lifetime. In the synoptic gospels as a whole there are no distinctively ecclesiological words employed which belong to the original sources of Jesus' teaching, and *ekklēsia* is therefore foreign to the words of Jesus.

(*d*) Two other important passages contradict the idea that Jesus would single out one disciple as the uniquely authoritative person in the Church. In responding to the request of James and John for the places of privilege beside Him, Jesus asserts that such privilege is not His to give.[101] And at another time Jesus declares that *all* the disciples shall have places of glory.[102] The authenticity of Matthew 16[18] is called into question, therefore, on the basis of consistency with Jesus' other teaching.

(*e*) Moreover, the singling out of Peter seems all the more

---

[100] For good summaries of this view, cf. R. Bultmann, *Theologische Blätter*, XX (1941).265ff.; T. W. Manson, *The Sayings of Jesus*, pp. 201-3.
[101] Mark 10[40].
[102] Matthew 19[28].

dubious when one reflects upon the known facts of Peter's personality and life. In no sense was Peter a 'rock' of a man: rather, he was an undependable, vacillating, and inconsistent person, who denied his Lord, forsook Him in crisis, and later caused disharmony in the Church because of his insincere attitude toward the keeping of Jewish laws.[103] To this observation about Peter's character may be added the fact that in the Jerusalem Church his position was not that of primate, for although he was an apostle and leader of the community, it is apparent that James held a position of equal, or surpassing authority.

On the strength of these arguments from text and history, a good many contemporary scholars have taken the view that these verses were never spoken by Jesus, but are the product of literary imagination and Christian faith. Easton undoubtedly exaggerates the extent to which this antagonistic position is held when he writes of the passage: 'That it is secondary is now universally admitted.'[104] However, it is obvious that the rejection of Matthew 16[17-19] has gained wide approval, and the arguments listed above must be treated with respect by those who do not agree to them.[105]

On the other hand, an interested student can find even more recent authorities who are persuaded for various reasons that the words of Jesus to Peter are not only consistent with the main strain of His teaching, but that they are to be accepted as an authentic saying. Some of these have taken their position according to the results of Harnack's earlier studies of the problem.[106] But more recently the most influential advocates have been F. Kattenbusch and K. L. Schmidt, who have gone much farther than Harnack went in their belief that the passage is not only authentic, as Harnack thought, but that the literal meaning

[103] cf. Mark 14[54-72], Galatians 2[11-14].
[104] 'The Church in the New Testament,' *Anglican Theological Review*, XXII(1940). 167.
[105] To the names of T. W. Manson and R. Bultmann may be added these other scholars who share the view that the words are not authentic:
P. Althaus, *Die christliche Wahrheit*, II.292.
C. J. Cadoux, *The Historic Mission of Jesus*, p. 308f.
B. S. Easton, *loc. cit.*
F. J. Foakes-Jackson, *The Beginnings of Christianity*, I.1.329n.
M. Goguel, *L'Église Primitive*, p. 191.
K. Holl, *Gesammelte Aufsätze zur Kirchengeschichte*, II.45.
G. Johnston, *The Doctrine of the Church in the New Testament*, p. 49n.
W. G. Kümmel, *Die Eschatologie der Evangelien*, p. 16; *Kirchenbegriff und Geschichtsbewusstsein in der Urgemeinde und bei Jesus*, p. 21.
[106] '*Der Spruch über Petrus als den Felsen der Kirche*' in *Sitzungsberichte der preussischen Akademie der Wissenschaft* (1918), pp. 637-54.

applies to the Christian *ekklēsia*, which Harnack did not admit.[107]

In a brief summary of the arguments in favour of authenticity,[108] we encounter both refutations of the contrary points listed above and new bits of evidence which have been brought to the case.

(*a*) As to the text itself, K. L. Schmidt reports that no ancient manuscripts known to us fail to include these words;[109] and Manson admits that they belong to the original text of Matthew.[110] But what about the omission of the three verses in Mark and Luke? It is argued by A. Oepke and others that such an appeal to the silence in other synoptic gospels carries little weight, for it is a common observation that such omissions were frequently made, and if the authenticity of verses and single words were made dependent upon parallel reports in other gospels, some of the most important of Jesus' sayings would be adjudged not genuine.[111]

(*b*) The criticism of the passage in the light of Jesus' expectation of the coming of the Kingdom of God is more serious so far as the plausibility of Jesus' intending the Church is concerned. If, as is now generally acknowledged, the major emphasis in Jesus' preaching was the proximity of the Kingdom of God, how could He speak also of the Church? This argument is valid, of course, only when the *ekklēsia* itself is considered as a strictly temporal institution. But such cannot be readily admitted. Therefore, Schmidt asserts that the *ekklēsia* itself is eschatological and is so meant in Jesus' words.[112] Because the thought of Jesus was so deeply rooted in the concept of the People of God, observes Oepke, the Church in this passage must be understood as that People, gathered about the Messiah in anticipation of the imminent Reign of God, and not as the organized Church of later generations. According to this interpretation, the future tense of the verb 'to build' means that the building of the Church is also an eschatological event.[113] It is very significant that

[107] Harnack thought the words referred to Peter rather than the Church, and 'the gates of hell etc' meant that Peter would not die.

[108] cf. the surveys of H. Windisch, '*Urchristentum*,' *Theologische Rundschan* (1933), pp. 239-58, 289-301; and A. Oepke, '*Der Herrenspruch über die Kirche* Matthew 16$^{17-19}$ in der neuesten Forschung,' *Studia Theologica*, II.11(1948).110-65.

[109] *Festgabe für Deissmann*, p. 291f.

[110] *The Sayings of Jesus*, p. 202. As additional evidence, the decidedly Semitic colour of the diction and the metrical rhythm of the lines are adduced by Schmidt, Windisch, and Oepke.

[111] Oepke, op. cit., p. 149.

[112] Article *Ekklēsia* in *TWNT*, III.525.

[113] E. Lohmeyer, *Grundlagen paulinischer Theologie*, p. 158n.

immediately after saying these words, Jesus began to tell His disciples of His impending passion and resurrection on the third day, both events being eschatologically connected with the Kingdom of God. Rather than recognizing a contradiction between Jesus' preaching of the Kingdom and the idea of His building an *ekklēsia*, therefore, these scholars see a natural and essential connexion between them.

(*c*) Another point at issue is the position of Peter in this context and in the actual history of the early Church, considered apart from its eschatological character. If Jesus had really given Peter such a sweeping commission of authority, why was no appeal ever made to it? Why did Peter not enjoy the primary position in the early Church? Why was he so far from being a 'rock' in his personal life? And how can we possibly conceive of Jesus' delegating to one man the power of the keys, by which he could admit or exclude persons from the Kingdom? No easy answers to these questions may be found so long as the authenticity of the passage is defended, but some plausible explanations have been offered. To the question about Peter's character and faith, Schmidt replies with the analogy of Israel: God's own People were entrusted with the revelation about Himself, and yet they repeatedly showed their weakness, perversity, and unworthiness.[114] This, to be sure, is a familiar Roman Catholic defence of Peter, and it does exhibit the belief that God works with whom He pleases, regardless of moral qualifications.[115] Moreover, it is offered as a solution of the problem that the 'rock' in verse 18 does not refer to Peter personally, but rather to the *confession* of faith in Jesus' Messiahship, the faith which is fundamental to the participation of men and women in the messianic community.[116] Consistent with this interpretation is the conviction that the power of the 'keys' really means the grace given to the disciples to unlock the mystery of the Scriptures and to recognize the Christ, and that this power and the authority derived from it were given not to Peter alone, but to all the disciples, of whom Peter was the representative.[117]

---

[114] In *Festgabe für Deissmann*, p. 291f.
[115] cf. F. M. Braun, *Neues Licht auf der Kirche*, p. 83.
[116] cf. T. H. Robinson, *The Gospel of Matthew*, p. 141; F. J. Leenhardt in *La Sainte Église Universelle*, p. 68.
[117] cf. C. Gore, *The Holy Spirit and the Church*, p. 50; F. Kattenbusch, *Theologische Studien und Kritiken*, XCIV.(1922).121; R. Otto, *The Kingdom of God and the Son of Man*, p. 365; and R. N. Flew, *Jesus and His Church*, p. 95.

In such ways have the scholars sought to explain the embarrassing implications of Matthew 16[17-19] without surrendering to the judgement of their more severe colleagues that the words are a part of later tradition.[118]

It is obvious from a survey of contemporary writing on the problem that no universally acceptable interpretation has been found. But this need not have so profound an influence upon one's view of Jesus' relation to the *ekklēsia* as some might think. For although the problem of authenticity and explanation looms large in the thinking of many scholars, this passage is surely not the ultimate basis of appeal for those who maintain that Jesus desired to have a worshipping community for the continued proclamation of the Gospel and of the Kingdom. Furthermore, with respect to the point in time when the disciples were really constituted as the *ekklēsia*, another event in Jesus' lifetime has drawn more support than Peter's confession at Caesarea Philippi.

According to a well-known theory of Kattenbusch, the disciples became the Church when they gathered with Jesus in Jerusalem to eat the Last Supper with Him.[119] It was then, in the breaking of bread and sharing the cup, that the true form of the *qāhāl* in its glorified condition was made. Kattenbusch understands the Last Supper as a preamble to the heavenly feast of the Messiah, which shall take place in the coming Kingdom. Therefore, this was a truly eschatological event, and the disciples were entering the state of preparation as a community of faithful ones. Although the view has been seconded by K. L. Schmidt[120] and others, there have been some adverse criticisms of it in recent years,

---

[118] Among the well-known men who have defended the originality of the text are:
A. T. Cadoux, *The Theology of Jesus*, p. 225.
O. Cullmann, *Königsherrschaft Christi und Kirche im Neuen Testament*, p. 22.
R. N. Flew, op. cit., p. 13.
C. Gore, op. cit., p. 47.
P. G. S. Hopwood, *The Religious Experience of the Primitive Church*, p. 235.
A. Juncker, In *Neue Kirchliche Zeitschrift*, XL(1929).183.
F. Kattenbusch, op. cit., p. 98f.
F. J. Leenhardt, op. cit., p. 68.
E. Lohmeyer, *Grundlagen paulinischer Theologie*, p. 158.
O. Michel, *Das Zeugnis des Neuen Testaments von der Gemeinde*, p. 10f.
A. Oepke, *Studia Theologica*, II.11(1948).163.
R. Otto, op. cit., p. 364.
K. L. Schmidt, In *Festgabe für Deissmann*, p. 291f.
A. Schweitzer, *The Mysticism of Paul the Apostle*, p. 103.
H.-D. Wendland, *Die Eschatologie des Reiches Gottes bei Jesus*, p. 172f.
H. Windisch, In *Theologische Rundschau* (1933), p. 253.

[119] *Festgabe für Harnack*, pp. 169ff.
[120] *Festgabe für Deissmann*, p. 295.

THE ORIGIN OF THE CHURCH   35

based largely upon new research into the meaning of the Holy Communion for the early Church.[121]

There remains for consideration one more point in time when the disciples, as the nearest to Jesus, were constituted as the *ekklēsia*. This was Pentecost, which must be inseparably linked to the resurrection and the appearances of Christ. Writing for many of his contemporaries, Edwin Lewis states that 'there was in any profound sense no Church until Christ had finished His work of conquering sin and death. The resurrection is at one and the same time the consummation of the Incarnation, the completion of the Atonement, and the creating of the Church.'[122] Prior to this momentous out-pouring of the Holy Spirit, 'whereby the new life of the risen Christ was precipitated into his community,'[123] the disciples had had a degree of fellowship with Jesus and among themselves. But only after they knew the terror of the crucifixion and the miracle of the resurrection could their fellowship as the Church be actualized, bound together in common faith in their Lord and in the unity of the Spirit.[124] This is not to ignore the reality of what has been discussed heretofore: the members of the Old Israel were in a sense the Church; and the disciples, when gathered about Jesus, were in a sense the Church. But in the *full* sense, it is urged, the Church should be reckoned from the days of Easter and Pentecost. So Johnston recommends that the use of *ekklēsia* and Church 'should be reserved for the society which gathered itself into a vital fellowship as a result of the Resurrection, inspired and called by God'.[125] The important thing to stress here is not the gathering of the disciples, so much as God's calling of those to whom the great sign of the resurrection had been revealed. This divine action in Jesus Christ, which created faith and was itself the content of faith, was the true inauguration of the Church, the refounding

[121] cf. N. A. Dahl, *Das Volk Gottes, usw.*, p. 163; H. Lietzmann, *Messe und Herrenmahl*; M. Goguel, *Le Problème de l'Église*; O. Cullmann, 'La Sainte-Cène dans le Christianisme Primitif,' *Revue d'histoire et de philosophie religieuses* (1936), pp. 1-22. G. Gloege, *Reich Gottes und Kirche im Neuen Testament*, p. 411, sees no adequate basis for Kattenbusch's theory and charges that it localizes and makes static the action of God, which is dynamic toward the Church.

[122] In *The Ministry and the Sacraments* (R. Dunkerley, ed.), p. 478.

[123] L. S. Thornton, *The Common Life in the Body of Christ*, p. 190.

[124] D. Bonhöffer, *Sanctorum communio*, p. 81; cf. O. Cullmann, *Königsherrschaft Christi und Kirche im Neuen Testament*, p. 20; A. M. Ramsey, *The Gospel and the Catholic Church*, p. 6.

[125] *The Doctrine of the Church in the New Testament*, p. 56. Supported by C. K. Barrett, *The Holy Spirit and the Gospel Tradition*, p. 137.

of Israel. These writers feel that no other time or action could so adequately account for the content of the apostolic faith of the first Christians nor initiate the kind of community life which they had in distinction to all others.

From the foregoing discussion it should be rather clear that the problems connected with the origin of the Church have commanded the attention and labour of some of the most prominent biblical authorities and theologians of the past three decades. With regard to the Church's inheriting the characteristics of the pre-Christian Israel and appropriating the heritage as the faithful Remnant, the agreement has been nearly unanimous. As to the eschatological role of the *ekklēsia* with respect to the preaching of Jesus, there have been various interpretations, but with few sharp or absolutely exclusive differences. A greater variance can be seen among those who believe that Jesus did have a definite intention for the Church and those who believe He did not; but their differences are traceable in large part to the differing concepts of the meaning of the *ekklēsia*, as either a people called by God to be His own, or as an institutionalized religious cult.

Finally, it is evident that at least four theories have been advanced as to the time when the Church was actually constituted, or refounded, as some prefer to say. While some see the real start of the Church within the historic life of Jesus, many others are convinced that there was no real Church until after the concomitant events of the resurrection and Pentecost. But whatever the actual point in history was when the divine and human elements coalesced, so to speak, to become the Church, the doctrine of the nature of the Church may be more profitably considered from a study of its other aspects.

CHAPTER TWO

THE CHURCH AND THE HOLY SPIRIT

I FAITH IN THE PERSON AND WORK OF THE HOLY SPIRIT

'Anyone who does not have the Spirit of Christ does not belong to him. . . . Now the Lord is the Spirit.'[1]

'Where the Spirit of the Lord is, there is the one true Church, apostolic and universal.'[2]

These two forthright declarations, the first from the Apostle Paul and the second from a modern ritual, express a conviction which is of the highest importance for the Christian faith. That the New Testament does not develop a systematic and coherent doctrine of the Holy Trinity may be readily admitted, but that the faith of the apostles and the early Christians can be treated in ignorance of the Spirit may not be.

Of course, our knowledge of the Spirit, as our knowledge of God, is fragmentary at best; limited by our creatureliness, since we are far from being divine. Whatever language we employ to describe the identity and nature of the Spirit must also reflect the imprecision and finiteness of our knowledge. Nevertheless, such imperfection on the part of human beings cannot be interpreted to mean that the Holy Spirit is only a myth or fiction of the religious imagination. Our knowledge and imagination are not the same thing. What we understand of the initial origin and the continuity of life is very rudimentary, nor can we describe with exactness the processes of the mind nor identify the character of the soul. We know, however, that they are *there*, that they are realities for which no satisfactory formal explanations can be constructed, but which are none the less the primal facts of our existence.

It is surely unnecessary to cite passages of the Bible to prove that the evangelists and apostles, following the thought of Jesus Himself, considered the Holy Spirit with the utmost seriousness and reverence. One can hardly understand the Gospels and

[1] Romans 8:9, 2 Corinthians 3:17.   [2] *Ritual of the Methodist Church*, U.S.A.

Epistles without perceiving that the faith in the Spirit is inseparably bound to the lives of persons and to the whole Church. We should be justly astonished, then, to find any Christians endeavouring to discuss the nature of the Church without giving extensive consideration to the relationship of the Holy Spirit to the *ekklēsia*, whether in the first century or the present one.

In some of the most influential theological works of the present time, the reality and centrality of the Spirit have been treated with very deep earnestness. Whereas most theologians who followed the tradition of Ritschl's liberalism have been satisfied with a concept of the Spirit which makes little distinction between the Holy Spirit and the spirit of man, the trend in more recent years has been leading toward a sober recognition of the Third Person of the Trinity in terms of New Testament faith. This does not mean that Christians have advanced so far in this direction that with much confidence they can speak familiarly of the Spirit. A feeling of speechless awe and mystery must still control us when we ponder His nature and work, a feeling which is well described by Barth in his commentary on Romans 8[2]: 'For the description of other possibilities we possess a large vocabulary, but we have no single word which we can make use of to define the impossible possibility of our lives. Why, then, are we not silent concerning Him? We must also be silent; but none the less we must bear in mind that our silence compromises Him no less than our speech. We do the Spirit no greater service by our silence. The Spirit remains the Word whether we proclaim Him in silence or in speech.'[3] Thus, with the mixed, paradoxical sense of hesitancy and urgency, we must regard the Holy Spirit.

So far as the Church is concerned, it is progressively coming to be realized that the effective presence of the Spirit is no less essential to its life than the continuing presence of Christ is. The *ekklēsia* apart from Jesus Christ is no longer the Church in any true sense. Neither can it exist without the Spirit, since the very faith which is implicit in one who belongs to the Church is, according to the New Testament, the work or gift of the Spirit—'No one can say "Jesus is Lord" except by the Holy Spirit.'[4] Likewise, it is urged by Paul that the unity into which all were

---

[3] *The Epistle to the Romans*, p. 273.
[4] 1 Corinthians 12[3]; cf. Romans 8[14], John 16[13].

baptized, the individual talents by which the Church is served, and the power of the new life are all direct results of the work of the Spirit.[5] In truth, the Church without the presence and the work of the Holy Spirit is inconceivable.

When reading Paul's letters, one is inclined to interpret his references to the Spirit as a virtual identification of the Spirit and Christ. The unconscious facility with which Paul slides from 'the Spirit of God' to 'the Spirit of Christ' to the Spirit by Himself easily causes confusion to the reader.[6] And as we noted in the words from 2 Corinthians, Paul even declared that 'the Lord (Christ) is the Spirit'. However, biblical writers, Paul included, cannot be considered as meticulous dogmaticians, nor should they be judged by exacting and definite canons of modern scholarship. The ardent religious impulses which motivated their writing, and the evangelistic purpose for which they wrote, determined the inspirational character of the New Testament and prevented it from becoming a textbook of doctrine.

Thinking of the Holy Spirit and Jesus Christ as identical in every respect, basing our thought on what Hodgson calls 'the certainty of a possible exegesis of an obscure phrase', we do violence to the total New Testament witness to the nature of the Spirit.[7] When Paul uses such seemingly confusing terms, he is not in a strictly theological sense identifying the Son and the Spirit, observes Dodd, but he is acknowledging 'his virtual identification of the experience of the Spirit with the experience of the indwelling Christ', and this is something different.[8]

What the consequences for the Christian faith would be if the Holy Spirit be not distinguished at all from Jesus Christ are well described by H. Sasse: 'Either the historical Jesus becomes a mere symbol and, in antithesis to the actuality of the Holy Spirit, loses all independent significance, or the Holy Spirit recedes into the background and becomes a mere "power", a *motus in rebus creatus*, "a created motion in creatures".'[9] But neither the historicity of Jesus nor the real Person of the Spirit can be neglected, much less denied, in Christian belief without doing intolerable violence to much of the witness of the New Testament. To be sure, the trinitarian doctrine of the three 'Persons' in the

---

[5] 1 Corinthians 12:4, 11, 13.   [6] cf. Romans 8:3-11.
[7] *The Doctrine of the Trinity*, p. 83.   [8] *The Epistle of Paul to the Romans*, p. 124.
[9] In *Mysterium Christi* (G. K. A. Bell and A. Deissmann, eds.), p. 117.

Godhead is not coherently formulated, but only prefigured, in the New Testament. Within the first century the Christians did not go to much trouble about defining their concept of the Spirit. They were usually content to make their reverent and often joyful testimonies to what the Spirit had accomplished in their lives. When describing the Spirit's effects, they had as evidence their own personal experience. Not only were there the essentially moral fruits of the Spirit, so that men could live and walk by His guidance,[10] but their own consciousness of being sons of God was due to the work of the Spirit as He bore witness to God.[11] The Spirit was not only the communicator of divine power, therefore, but also, like Christ, the means of God's self-revelation.

Attitudes regarding the nature of the Spirit are hardly free from contradiction in the New Testament, however. While the Spirit is often presented only as a 'power' in some passages, He is elsewhere spoken of distinctly as a Person. Bultmann finds this dual conception of the Spirit running through the Testament, with the same writer taking at times the impersonal view and at times the personal.[12] To read all references to the Spirit in terms of the personal view exclusively is just as unfair to the text as to regard all references as expressions of the impersonal conception.

Christian faith has not been content to tolerate such a dualistic, self-contradicting idea of the Holy Spirit, however, and so the speculations of post-biblical theologians concerning the distinct Person of the Spirit in unity with the Father and the Son have become the accepted statement of the trinitarian mystery. While the formulators of the doctrine of the Spirit departed from certain impersonal, or dynamistic concepts of the New Testament, they did not arrive at the orthodox, personal concept by way of sheer philosophizing or mystical imagining. F. C. Grant, who is very critical of attempts to read back the trinitarian doctrine into the New Testament, affirms that it was necessary for the Christian faith to develop such a doctrine of the Spirit in order 'to safeguard the truth of revelation', to explain the nature of God's saving relationship to men.[13] In other words, in view of the fact that Christian faith holds God's dealing with His creatures to be personal rather than mechanical and impersonal, the acting

---

[10] Galatians $5^{22\text{-}5}$.   [11] Romans $8^{15\text{-}16}$.
[12] *Theologie des Neuen Testaments*, p. 153f.
[13] *An Introduction to New Testament Thought*, p 112.

Spirit of God must also be thought of as a divine Person, as a 'He' rather than an 'it'.

The belief in the Trinity, in the three personal modes of the unity of God, has always been perplexing for most Christians. And ultimately the path of intellectual inquiry leads to the dark abyss of mystery, where the ultimate answers to all problems of deity lie hidden. To acknowledge this mystery does not mean to deny the Trinity, nor does it remove the basis for faith in the three Persons. But to regard the Third Person as just a 'spiritual power', or a mechanical instrument of God's power is to make nonsense of the doctrine. So Micklem declares that the Holy Spirit who gives new life to men is distinct from 'the general providential government of the world by God', which is not of a personal character.[14] Such a distinction is fundamental to Christian thinking about the Holy Spirit, however strongly the personal nature of the Spirit is emphasized in the various shades of interpretation of this belief among Christians today.[15] Not a vague sort of 'spiritual power' in men's lives, nor even God's creative and sustaining power which keeps the world going is meant when many modern theologians speak of the Holy Spirit in relation to the Church. Rather, they mean God Himself as He is present and actively effective in His aspect or 'Person' of Spirit. Christians in the present, as in the past, regard the Spirit as such an expression of the reality of God's love and power, and so is He to be regarded in respect to the Church.

II. PENTECOST

The inseparability of the Church and the Holy Spirit is nowhere made more clear than when we consider that, in the belief of many Christians, the same day of Pentecost was of unique and critical importance for both. It was on this day that the actual constituting of the *ekklēsia* took place. At the same time, the Spirit was given, or 'poured out', to the disciples. And

---

[14] *What Is the Faith?* p. 131.

[15] For the strongest emphasis upon the Person of the Spirit see the discussion by L. Hodgson, *The Doctrine of the Trinity*, pp. 80-3, as well as his controversy in the Appendix, pp. 226-8, with such theologians as H. W. Robinson, who are more cautious in stressing the personality of the Spirit. cf. A. G. Hebert, *The Form of the Church*, pp. 21f., and L. S. Thornton, *The Incarnate Lord*, p. 324. In *The Faith of the Christian Church*, p. 256f., G. Aulén shows how excessive stress upon the conception of the Spirit as Person can lead to 'tritheism'.

the latter event was the cause and manifestation of the former.

Critics may dispute the meaning of the related account in John 20$^{22-3}$, where at Easter the risen Lord breathed upon the disciples, just as God had breathed life into Adam, and said to them: 'Receive the Holy Spirit.' In an earlier connexion in John it was said that the Spirit had not yet been given during Jesus' ministry (7^{39}), and in the farewell discourse Jesus had promised the future coming of the Spirit, the Paraclete (14$^{16-17}$). The impartation on Easter was the consummation towards which these earlier passages looked. But whether this event was simply a preparation for Pentecost, as some hold, or a strictly Johannine tradition which must either be accepted in place of Pentecost or rejected in favour of it, as others hold, we cannot now decide. Surely the intention in each account would be the same: namely the description of the way in which the disciples received the Spirit and became transformed men, though the differing details could perhaps lead to variant interpretations of the Spirit's nature.[16]

Christian tradition has, nevertheless, almost unanimously preferred Luke's report of Pentecost to John's, perhaps because there is no mention of the receiving of the Spirit in the Easter stories of the three Synoptic Gospels, as Flew observes.[17] Teachers of the Bible in our time have often experienced both confusion and embarrassment in trying to explain the phenomenon of Pentecost. It is evident to the modern mind that the circumstances of the event in Acts 2 seem very crude and unedifying, and the story itself is anything but satisfying, with the rushing wind, the tongues of flame, the miraculous speaking of strange languages, etc. Yet, these bizarre elements can be magnified beyond their importance, and usually are. The advice of Hodgson is sound: namely, that we ought to regard the intensely emotional manifestations, as well as the legendary physical appearance of the Spirit, as of such minor importance in comparison with the real significance of the day as to be negligible. He adds that 'only those are to be accepted as true manifestations of the Spirit which are consonant with the acceptance of Jesus Christ as the revelation of God and (we may add) bear fruit in a life which is

---

[16] cf. R. H. Strachan, *The Fourth Gospel*, p. 329; G. H. C. MacGregor, *The Gospel of John*, p. 365; E. C. Hoskyns, *The Fourth Gospel*, p. 547.

[17] *Jesus and His Church*, p. 105.

a recognizable imitation of His character'.[18] And such manifestations were undoubtedly to be seen in the individual and corporate nature of the Christian life which appeared in the Church after Pentecost.

But this new kind of life which is the Spirit's gift ought not to be regarded as merely the result of man's inspiration to be a better person. There is little to stop a non-Christian psychologist, for example, from explaining the whole incident in terms of hallucination and moral idealism, and such has often been attempted—and not always with the opposition of some theologians. However, if the fact of Pentecost could be justified by psychology alone, the Spirit as a Person of the Trinity and even as active power would be necessarily negated. 'That the Spirit inspired the apostolic circle seems a strangely inadequate verdict for scholarship to pass on one of the greatest moments in the history of religion.'[19] The conviction of the apostles that Pentecost was an actual encounter between men and the Divine Spirit is not to be treated lightly. Barth's words about the Spirit, that 'He is invisible, outside the continuity of the visible human subject and beyond all psychological analysis',[20] repeats in technical language the unsophisticated faith of those who first testified that the prophecy of Joel was fulfilled in the outpouring of the Spirit to men.

But can it really be maintained that the Spirit was *first* given at Pentecost? This question is vital for support of the belief that the Church may look to this day as its new beginning; for if the event were nothing unique for the Spirit, the Church could make no special claim for Pentecost. It is well known, of course, that 'Spirit' (*ruach*) appears a great many times in the Old Testament to represent the Spirit of God. But to urge that the numerous witnesses to the work of the Spirit in pre-Christian writings are not true experiences of divine power is to place a limitation upon the action of God which is so narrow as to be blasphemous. On the other hand, to admit no difference in kind between the disciples' experience of the Spirit and that of the people of the Old Testament is to invalidate the witness of Jesus Himself and the faith of the Church.

[18] *The Doctrine of the Trinity*, p. 53; cf. F. J. Foakes-Jackson, *The Acts of the Apostles*, pp. 10-12.
[19] R. N. Flew, *Jesus and His Church*, p. 106.
[20] *The Epistle to the Romans*, p. 158.

An understanding of the eschatological belief of the earliest Christians, as demonstrated in the New Testament, is our key to this problem. For the gift of the Spirit to men was seen to be an indispensable aspect of the coming of the new, messianic aeon, against which the old aeon before Jesus Christ was contrasted. C. K. Barrett sees much significance in the fact that the synoptic gospels do not speak of any disciples receiving the Holy Spirit, but only of Jesus' having the Spirit.[21] The Spirit could be known and experienced only in the messianic kingdom itself, into which the first Christians felt themselves to have been delivered. As to those living before the time of Christ who testified to the experience of the Spirit of God, it may be submitted on this basis of belief that they had not yet entered into full possession of the Spirit. Just as there were persons who only anticipated the Christ, but did not recognize Him when he finally came in the flesh, so also there were perhaps those faithful people who received an unfulfilled promise, an earnest, of the Spirit prior to Pentecost. But the newness of the life in the Spirit for the disciples after Pentecost was visibly different from the life they had lived as daily companions of Jesus. The Johannine observation, then, that the Holy Spirit was not given because Jesus was not as yet glorified by the resurrection, is the expression of historical fact and not only of theological principle.[22] Assuming the historicity of most of Acts, we encounter testimonies which are wholly inexplicable apart from the recognition that a new departure had been made in the intercourse between the Spirit and human beings, a new and unique relationship of power and response, which Paul calls 'the first fruits of the Spirit',[23] and which apostolic tradition dates from the day of Pentecost, and not before.

An implication of Pentecost which is of great importance for the Church, and which indeed is integral to the Church's existence, is the fact that the Spirit was given to the whole community of believers as a group, and not to isolated individuals. The individual knew that his own life was changed and transformed, and that the transformation took place because of his participation in the community.[24] In such a way, Pentecost is interpreted by

---

[21] *The Holy Spirit and the Gospel Tradition*, p. 160.
[22] L. Hodgson, *The Doctrine of the Trinity*, p. 182.   [23] Romans 8[23].
[24] cf. H. W. Robinson, *The Christian Experience of the Holy Spirit*, p. 149: 'The Holy Spirit creates a new individuality in the believer, but the very content of the new individuality is social, issuing in a new consciousness of fellowship.'

T. O. Wedel: 'The Holy Spirit is henceforth a corporate, not an individual possession ... the Spirit dwells in the Body. Apart from this corporate community there is no gift of the Holy Spirit.'[25] The idea of the organic structure and nature of the *ekklēsia* was not something added by theological speculation at a much later date, but was inherent from the beginning, when the disciples became 'filled' with the Spirit. Then they found themselves indissolubly united in a new kind of fellowship, into which they entered unconsciously and almost imperceptibly, without the constitution or agreements of ordinary social groupings. In the first century, and in every century, the Spirit has come and has been received within the community of Christ's followers. Every person who by faith wills to be grasped by the Spirit stands in the community, and no one who stands within it is a stranger to the presence and power of the Spirit.[26]

III. THE HOLY SPIRIT AS GIFT IN THE CHURCH

It is customary in the present time to speak of the Spirit as a 'gift' of God to man. There is adequate New Testament precedent for such usage,[27] and the word denotes a divine action which is inseparable from our concept of the Spirit. The Spirit is not a given part of creation, any more than God is identical with nature, as the pantheists believe. The idea of the 'gift of the Spirit' is that He comes from outside the natural order of creation in which man lives, breaking into this order to confront man and be received by man. The Bible refers to the giving of the Spirit in much the same way as the free giving of divine grace: something offered by God to man as a testimony and expression of His love, or *agape*, which man cannot earn nor merit by anything he does. In view of the belief that the Spirit, like grace, is given freely by God as an act of His *agapē*, we can well understand the indignation of the martyr, Stephen, when he charged the Jews with having resisted the Holy Spirit,[28] and even more, the wrath of Peter toward the magician, Simon, who thought that the gift of God could be purchased with silver.[29]

From the day of Pentecost onward the gift of the Spirit was

---
[25] *The Coming Great Church*, p. 60.
[26] D. Bonhöffer, *Sanctorum communio*, p. 86.
[27] cf. Luke 11^{13}, John 3^{34}, Acts 2^{38}, 8^{20}, 10^{45}, 11^{17}, etc.   [28] Acts 7^{51}.   [29] ibid., 8^{19}.

frequently associated with the rite of baptism. The people standing about and hearing the preaching of Peter asked what they should do in the light of the revelation he described. 'Repent,' replied Peter, 'and be baptized every one of you in the name of Jesus Christ for the forgiveness of your sins; and you shall receive the gift of the Holy Spirit.'[30] Some scholars, such as Foakes-Jackson, find several objections to this story of Peter in connexion with Pentecost, and on them they base their claim that the passage is not historically accurate.[31] But others assert that the rejection of the story simply raises more historical problems than it solves.[32] To be sure, we do not find in Acts a consistent concept of the indissoluble connexion between the receiving of the Spirit and the rite of baptism. In one instance it is reported that the Spirit was given to certain Gentiles prior to their actual baptism,[33] and in another the persons who were baptized knew nothing of the Holy Spirit.[34] It is too strong a generalization, then, to say with A. Richardson that the earliest Christians knew nothing of a baptism which was not of the Spirit.[35] On the other hand, it is undeniably evident that they believed the Spirit to be operative in the act of washing with water, laying on of hands, and invoking the name of Jesus Christ.

This understanding of the nature of baptism helps us to appreciate the reality of the relationship of the Holy Spirit to the *ekklēsia*. The rite of baptism was not then, and still is not, believed to be an act of a narrowly individual relationship between one person and God. It was in the New Testament community, and still is, the rite of admission or initiation into the fellowship of the Church. If it is true that God imparts the Holy Spirit to men and women in baptism, it is consistent to say that the act of becoming a member of the Church involves both the receiving of the Spirit and the empowering by the Spirit to live as new men, men who walk 'not according to the flesh but according to the Spirit'.[36]

For the Apostle Paul the baptizing of believers, being a participation in the very death and resurrection of the Son of God,[37]

---

[30] Acts 2$^{37-8}$; cf. 1 Corinthians 12^{13}.
[31] *The Acts of the Apostles*, pp. 18f.
[32] cf. W. F. Flemington, *The New Testament Doctrine of Baptism*, p. 48; O. Cullmann, *Die Tauflehre des Neuen Testaments*, p. 6f.
[33] Acts 10^{47}.   [34] ibid., 19$^{1-6}$.   [35] In *La Sainte Église Universelle*, p. 139.
[36] Romans 8^4.   [37] ibid., 6$^{3-4}$.

involved the receiving of the power of the Holy Spirit. The reception of this power was manifested not only in the believer's transformation into a new person, growing into the likeness of Christ, but also in the conviction that death has been overcome and resurrection to eternal life in the Kingdom made certain. Thus, the gift of the Spirit was taken to be an eschatological gift.[38] Yet it must be remarked that the first Christians did not regard the gift of the Spirit as a precondition to be fulfilled before one enters the *ekklēsia*. As O. Cullmann points out, the Spirit Himself is active in the baptismal act of incorporation into the community.[39]

Baptism, the gift of the Holy Spirit, and incorporation into the Church—none of these three stands isolated from or opposed to the other two. This close relationship is not an artificial formula, useful for catechetical instruction, but the apprehension in faith of what actually occurs in the experience of a Christian as he responds to the call of God in Christ.

The Holy Spirit is thus a correlate of the Church: this is the teaching of the New Testament, writes J. E. L. Newbigin, and yet it is too often overlooked in modern discussion about the nature of the Church.[40] We have been prone to consider the gift of the Spirit in baptism as a strictly personal matter, whereby the individual believer receives the new birth of which the Fourth Gospel speaks. How much more than this is it, according to the witness of the apostles! As E. Lohmeyer says, Paul considered the Christian community to be so much an expression of God Himself in the world, that the community is in a sense the same as His Spirit (though this interpretation cannot be taken to mean a literal identification, since Paul himself speaks of *having* the Spirit).[41]

Let this emphasis upon the corporate expression of the Spirit be neglected, and the way is clear for a strictly sociological concept of the Church. On the other hand, the emphasis should not be so extreme that the single member becomes excluded from all consideration. The individual is contained within the community, but his value is not less on that account; on the contrary,

---

[38] R. Bultmann, *Theologie des Neuen Testaments*, p. 155f.
[39] *Die Tauflehre des Neuen Testaments*, p. 35.
[40] *The Reunion of the Church*, p. 99f; cf. P.-H. Menoud, *L'Église et les ministères selon le Nouveau Testament*, p. 11.
[41] *Grundlagen paulinischer Theologie*, p. 181.

his whole life is enhanced. As Wedel makes the distinction here, the individual does receive the Spirit, but only as he shares in the life of the community: 'The degree to which an individual (in the New Testament) partook of "spiritual" gifts was commensurate with the degree to which he shared in the corporate disciplines of brotherhood.'[42] A man of faith encounters the Holy Spirit within the *ekklēsia*, which is the 'sphere of the Spirit's working'.[43] The relationship of individual to Spirit and of Church to Spirit is, therefore, not one of 'either-or' but of 'both-and'. In the light of this condition, there are no sharp distinctions to be seen in the primitive Church with regard to the members. 'The Church was not divided into two classes: those who have received the Divine Spirit and those who have not. Not all may be prophets, but all may share in the intimate knowledge of God and His purpose.'[44] There were diversities of gifts and functions, but the same Spirit, imparting to each and all the love of God which is in Jesus Christ.

IV. THE WORK OF THE SPIRIT IN THE CHURCH

What concerns us even more than the giving of the Spirit to persons in the *ekklēsia* is the effective work of the Spirit as it is manifested in the community. The Spirit is generally thought of as effective power, absolute in the sense that God, the Creator, is absolute. This must never mean that he affects us mechanically through the means of grace which we know, 'like the current in an electric motor. He is a Person, and deals with us as persons.'[45] So the effects of His work should not be sought in such impersonal-physical manifestations as tongues of fire or a dove, as primitive imagination saw Him, nor even in the relentless coercion of human beings to do that which in their freedom they do not will to do.

1. The primary work of the Holy Spirit which is to be considered is this: that through Him men are enabled to recognize the presence of Jesus Christ. The mystery of the Trinity is especially pertinent here; for in virtue of the unity of the divine

---

[42] *The Coming Great Church*, p. 61.
[43] J. E. L. Newbigin, *The Reunion of the Church*, p. 99.
[44] R. N. Flew, *Jesus and His Church*, p. 107; cf. J. Moffatt, *The First Epistle of Paul to the Corinthians*, p. 184.
[45] A. G. Hebert, *The Form of the Church*, p. 58.

nature, the presence of the Spirit includes the presence of Christ and of God. This was apparently the belief of the New Testament writers, particularly Paul, who, as we have seen, was seldom careful to use the names of the Three Persons in three distinct and specific ways. But while the Persons are conceived as separate, the divine nature (*ousia*) is not; and in this sense the presence of the Spirit in the community is also the presence of Christ.[46] This belief regards the work of the Spirit as the continuing sequel to the Incarnation. The Word did become flesh at a known time in history, and the Word also ceased to be flesh. It may be assumed, as many do assume, that the possibility of knowing Christ personally was limited to those fortunate few who saw Him and heard Him in the hills of Galilee or the streets of Jerusalem. If this were true, our only knowledge of Him would be the kind of biographical acquaintance we have with great men of the ancient past.

Against this limitation, however, stands the overwhelming testimony of many generations of Christians that Jesus Christ is known in a deeply personal way, in all places and in every year. The knowledge of Christ for the faithful constitutes an actual fellowship with Him, a fellowship between Person and persons, which cannot be disregarded nor explained away as mere pious sentiment. If Jesus Christ were only a figure of the past, we could not today dare even to speak of having communion with Him, for, in H. W. Robinson's words, 'a historical memory is not a fellowship'.[47] But the conviction that this knowledge of Christ today is not just a memory, however well preserved in tradition, but the experience of His actual presence, cannot be shaken without shaking at the same time the foundation of the Christian faith.

This is the view of D. M. Baillie, who appraises the work of the Spirit in making Christ present as follows: 'A new thing had come into the world with Jesus Christ, God manifest in the flesh; and the new thing, while dependent on Him was not confined to the days of His flesh or to those who had known Him in the flesh: it is available in an even fuller form to everybody, everywhere, and in every age, through the Holy Spirit. If we go on to ask whether there is any difference between having God's presence

---

[46] cf. H. Sasse in *Mysterium Christi* (G. K. A. Bell and A. Deissmann, eds.), p. 117.
[47] *The Christian Experience of the Holy Spirit*, p. 146.

with us, having Christ dwell in us, and being filled with the Holy Spirit, we are bound to answer that the New Testament makes no clear distinction. It is not that no distinction is made between the Father, the Son, and the Holy Spirit; but all three come at every point into the full Christian experience of God. It is not a case of three separate experiences: it is all one.'[48]

The Church could hardly hope to apprehend the Gospel and come close to a fulfilment of its calling as the People of God if the Spirit's presence did not thus mean the presence of Christ. In his exposition of the Scottish Confession of 1560, Barth indicates that even such essentials of the Christian life as repentance and thankfulness would be impossible for us if Christ did not come to us daily in the Holy Spirit.[49] Even more emphatically, without this effect of the Spirit, the corporate expression of worship, the proclamation of the Gospel, and the sacramental fellowship of the Holy Communion, would be reduced to empty repetitions of acts of remembrance. As most interpretations of the meaning of the Sacrament, so far as Protestant theologians are concerned, insist, the 'real presence' of Christ is a fact of supreme importance, so long as it is borne in mind that the presence of the Lord is in the hearts of believers rather than in the material elements on the altar. And we experience this divine presence because of the activity of the Holy Spirit among us. Hence, Dodd's emphasis upon the Pauline teaching is ever relevant: 'It was not enough to say that Christ, being exalted to the right hand of God, had 'poured forth' the Spirit. The presence of the Spirit in the Church *is* the presence of the Lord.'[50]

It may be conceded that many humble Christians, taking part in such worship, and aware that therein they are in communion with the Lord, may be ignorant of the Spirit's work in effecting this communion. But their ignorance is neither a negation of the reality of Christ's presence with them, nor is it evidence that the activity of the Spirit is only a theological speculation.

2. There is a second way in which the Spirit works with men, and that is to be recognized in the calling of men to faith and discipleship. This idea is expressed in various ways in the New Testament. It is the meaning of Paul's conviction of being 'led by the Spirit of God' into a filial relationship to God.[51]

---

[48] *God Was in Christ*, p. 153f.   [49] *The Knowledge of God and the Service of God*, p. 122f.
[50] *The Apostolic Preaching and Its Developments*, p. 62.   [51] Romans 8^{14}.

But it must be stressed again that this state of being led by the Spirit is not to be isolated in the case of each person, as though, while being drawn to God, each man were independent of his neighbours. The calling takes place within the bounds of the community: 'You were called in the one Body,' urges Paul.[52] Indeed, as Barth sees it, the Church possesses 'her true nature, unity, and holiness' in this 'electing, calling, directing, and comforting' of the Holy Spirit.[53] To regard the Spirit's work of calling and leading men to God as coinciding with their incorporation into the *ekklēsia* is hardly at variance with the faith of the apostles.

The power of divine calling may also be understood in the sense of 'possession' by the Spirit. Such an idea is not explicitly described in the New Testament, although the correlative idea of being possessed by evil spirits and demons appears very frequently. Hodgson believes that we are justified in thinking of a Christian's being possessed by the Holy Spirit, since the members of the primitive community, and indeed Jesus Himself, considered demonic possession, at least, as being a real condition and not a mere superstition.[54] The doctrine of the Spirit certainly grew up in a *milieu* which believed in possession, writes Hodgson, and whatever distasteful associations the idea may have for us today, it does express an activity of the Spirit which is very real. It is not enough for us to describe the experience of Christians as 'communion with God' in the Spirit, important as this surely is; for communion connotes awareness of intercourse with God, whereas possession carries the connotation of a compulsion, which may be almost unconscious, as, for example, in one's concentration upon the fulfilment of his task or duty. A man whom the Holy Spirit possesses, then, is one who is literally 'inspired' and lives in the power and compulsion of the Spirit.

This is of significance for the Church, because such a view stands in opposition to the secular idea that membership in the community of the Church is purely a matter of one's personal, free decision. Undoubtedly there are great numbers of Christians who also regard their membership in this way, but their numbers do not authenticate their belief. As Lohmeyer declares in his exposition of Pauline theology, individuals do not have full

---

[52] Colossians 3^{15}.   [53] *The Knowledge of God and the Service of God*, p. 157.
[54] *The Doctrine of the Trinity*, p. 38f.

responsibility for deciding to join the *ekklēsia* in faith. It is the power of the Spirit which decides on the individual, calls him and draws him into the one Body of Christ.[55]

3. The third manifestation of the Holy Spirit's work in the Church may be summarized easily in Paul's description of 'the fruit of the Spirit' in Galatians 5^{22}. By this he means that the life of the Spirit-filled man is characterized by 'love, joy, peace, patience, kindness, goodness, faithfulness, gentleness, self-control'. These attributes of the Christian life can and should be the fruit, or 'harvest' (Moffatt), of the Spirit's work for all who are led by Him. The list is not exhaustive, of course. Neither does it take into account the more specialized spiritual gifts, or *charismata*, which are given to certain persons of the Church in varying degrees.[56] Perhaps Paul had a definite purpose in stressing this ethical influence of the Spirit, for, as G. S. Duncan has suggested, there was a tendency for the Christians of that time to think of the Spirit wholly in terms of the extraordinary manifestations of power—prophecy, healing, working miracles, etc.—which were not the common property of all believers.[57] But the life in the Spirit, whereby the life of Jesus Christ is reproduced in the community, should not be considered the peculiar property of a minority, since it is available to all by the Spirit's free action.

The first-named fruit of the Spirit, love, which H. W. Robinson rightly calls the 'supreme gift of the Spirit',[58] and the others which follow in Paul's list, are not in the same category with the ideal virtues of the Greek philosophers. These were thought to be attainable by the striving and discipline of high-minded men, in the same way as the Jews sought to fulfil the moral demands of the *Torah*. But for Paul and the Christians, these virtues are attained less by man's striving than by God's grace, which is made effective in human experience through the Spirit. This belief is the fulcrum on which rests Paul's ethical teaching for the Church, which is the lever which overturns for all time the legalism of the Jews and the striving for virtue of the Greeks. It is nothing other than the divine power at work in the transformation of men according to the pattern of Christ. As D. M. Baillie puts the matter succinctly, 'the God who was incarnate in Christ

---

[55] *Grundlagen paulinischer Theologie*, p. 185.
[56] cf. 1 Corinthians 12^{28}, Ephesians 4^{11}.
[57] *The Epistle of Paul to the Galatians*, p. 173.
[58] *The Christian Experience of the Holy Spirit*, p. 152.

THE CHURCH AND THE HOLY SPIRIT 53

dwells in us through the Holy Spirit; and that is the secret of the Christian life'.[59]

4. The fourth major result of the power of the Holy Spirit is expressed in the Greek word *koinōnia*, which has various shades of meaning in the New Testament. The word is so prominent in the thought of the apostles, and has enjoyed such widespread usage in discussions concerning the Church today, that we must try to understand its full content and implications for faith and living.

In only two places in the New Testament is there a specific reference to the *koinōnia* of the Spirit: 2 Corinthians 13^{14}, where it is part of a benediction, and Philippians 2^1, where it is a ground of appeal to Christian faith. Elsewhere Paul speaks of Christians being 'called into the *koinōnia* of His Son, Jesus Christ'.[60] And in 1 John 1^3 it is asserted that 'our *koinōnia* is with the Father and with His Son Jesus Christ'. Such usage of the word in relation to the Persons of the Trinity obviously means something different from its use in Romans 15^{26} and 2 Corinthians 8^4 and 9^{13}, where almsgiving and distribution of money are meant. Yet another meaning attaches to Paul's use of *koinōnia* in connexion with the cup and the bread of the Lord's Supper in 1 Corinthians 10^{16}. In comparison with these references stands the famous use of *koinōnia* in Acts 2^{42}, a passage which has given occasion for a diversity of interpretations. In considering these representative verses in which the word is used, we can avoid the complexities of thorough-going criticism and still find that they shed much light upon the nature of the Spirit's relationship to the Church.

Most scholars are agreed that the fundamental idea which *koinōnia* conveys is that of 'participation in something in which others also participate'.[61] This definition is sharply distinguished from the generally held, but inaccurate, notion that the word means simply 'fellowship', in the sense of association with other persons. Other English words which come close to being adequate renderings of the Greek, in its primary meaning, are 'sharing', 'joint possession', and 'holding in common'.[62] But in New Testament usage there is nearly always the connotation of participation in something *with* someone else.[63]

[59] *God Was in Christ*, p. 154. [60] 1 Corinthians 1^9.
[61] J. Y. Campbell, '*KOINŌNIA* and Its Cognates in the New Testament,' in *Journal of Biblical Literature*, LI(1932).353; cf. Fr. Hauck, *TWNT*, III.808.
[62] cf. C. H. Dodd, *The Johannine Epistles*, pp. 6f.
[63] J. Y. Campbell, op. cit., p. 356.

General agreement on this basic definition, however, still does not permit the modern scholars to arrive at a consensus on the meaning of the term in the specific passages already cited.

When Paul speaks of 'the *koinōnia* of the Spirit', does he mean (1) the fellowship of the believers as they are united by the work of the Spirit, or (2) personal participation in the Spirit, or (3) common participation in the gift of the Holy Spirit? None of these possibilities is foreign to the faith and experience of the apostles, and yet it is virtually impossible to decide conclusively that Paul meant specifically one or another. Interpreters try to read this phrase, therefore, in the light of other uses of *koinōnia*. Thus, Hopwood finds that the idea of the fellowship of believers is the most consistent with the Christians' conception of their social identity, for they are the one Body in the one Spirit, and their brotherly community, as described in Acts 2, is certainly motivated by the power of the Spirit.[64]

The second interpretation, however, is accepted by L. S. Thornton.[65] He sees that if the first meaning, the simple idea of fellowship, were accepted, the entire benediction, including appeal to the Trinity, would indeed have coherence, so that it could be paraphrased: 'The grace which Christ bestows upon us, the love which God shows to us, and the fellowship which the Holy Spirit imparts.'[66] Nevertheless, Thornton is not satisfied with this first meaning, and considers the strongest reasons to be in favour of the alternate meaning of 'participation in the Holy Spirit'. By this he means that the Spirit is regarded, 'not as the subject who brings us together in fellowship, but rather as the object in which we all share, the focus of our common interest, the fountain of which we all partake, the personal source of grace whom we may be said to possess and to enjoy in common'.[67] And this view, as we shall see, causes him to explain the *koinōnia* of Acts 2[42] in the same way.

To both of these interpretations, H. W. Robinson takes strong exception.[68] To have fellowship *with* the Spirit, or participation *in* Him, as distinguished from the Father and the Son, is unwarranted, he claims. And in order to preserve the parallelism

---

[64] *The Religious Experience of the Primitive Church*, p. 224.
[65] *The Common Life in the Body of Christ*, pp. 69-72.
[66] ibid., p. 70.   [67] ibid., p. 69.
[68] *The Christian Experience of the Holy Spirit*, p. 18; cf. F. C. Grant, *An Introduction to New Testament Thought*, p. 110.

of structure in the benediction, he rejects the idea that *koinōnia* means here 'simply the fellowship with men created by the Spirit, i.e., the Church'. As Robinson reads this verse, it means that we believers enjoy the gift of 'fellowship with God through Christ mediated by or in the Holy Spirit'. And this reading he finds to be in exact agreement with Ephesians 2[18]: 'Through Him (Christ) we both have our access in one Spirit unto the Father.'

Whichever of these explanations is to be preferred, the doctrine of the Person and work of the Spirit is less affected, as Thornton indicates, than the ultimate meaning to be given to *koinōnia* in this and other passages, where the action of the Spirit is described. There is no justification for reading into 1 Corinthians 10[16] or Romans 15[26], where Paul speaks of money gifts, any particular conception of the Spirit's work. However, there is very strong reason for considering *koinōnia* in Acts 2[42] in the light of the Spirit, and to this we now turn our attention.

'And they devoted themselves to the apostles' teaching and *tē koinōnia*, to the breaking of bread and the prayers.' How are we to understand Luke's meaning in this brief summary of the essential activities of the first Christian community in Jerusalem? What was the *koinōnia* and how was it related to the Holy Spirit?

A few recent scholars are content to translate the word by 'fellowship' in its simple sense of group association, inspired by the Spirit, and therefore more closely knit than other social units, but different only by degree from the Aramaic *Habura*, which C. A. A. Scott regards as its prototype.[69] Scott's hypothesis, that *koinōnia* satisfactorily expresses the idea of *Habura* as a designation of the apostolic community, has had cool reception,[70] although his basic assumption, that the idea of fellowship is a sufficient rendering of *koinōnia*, is more widely accepted. For example, H. Seesemann asserts that *Gemeinschaft*, or at the most, *gemeinsames Anteilhaben* can describe the meaning of the word.[71] And such recent translators as James Moffatt and the Committee of the Revised Standard Version of the New Testament have

---

[69] *Christianity according to St. Paul*, p. 160, and *The Fellowship of the Spirit*, pp. 69f. Supported by J. W. Bowman, *The Intention of Jesus*, p. 222.

[70] R. N. Flew calls this suggestion attractive, but sees no evidence for it: *Jesus and His Church*, p. 109. P. G. S. Hopwood gives faint support to Scott's theory: *The Religious Experience of the Primitive Church*, p. 223.

[71] *Der Begriff KOINŌNIA im Neuen Testament*, pp. 87ff.

retained the word 'fellowship', while E. J. Goodspeed uses 'society' of the apostles.

When the basic and widely recognized connotation of *koinōnia* as 'participation' or 'sharing' is understood, there are still several ways in which the word's usage in Acts 2^{42} may be interpreted.

Does *koinōnia* have a special reference here to the Lord's Supper? The idea of participation is certainly implicit in this act of worship, as Paul declares in 1 Corinthians 10^{16}. C. H. Dodd sees fit to write on this point: 'It seems likely that the fellowship of "Communion" of Acts 2^{42} is in fact the primitive Eucharist or Holy Communion, there described as "breaking bread and praying together", an apt enough summary of the minimum essentials of the Liturgy.'[72] He does not develop nor defend this idea in the context, but the mere fact of proximity of *koinōnia* to the two which succeed it in the series is hardly a conclusive argument for such a theory. Indeed, if *koinōnia* means only the Lord's Supper, it would be redundant to be in the series with breaking bread and prayers.

According to the thought of L. S. Thornton, *koinōnia* surely conveys the meaning of 'sharing', and not simply the fellowship of persons. But what do the Christians share? Not goods, he maintains, but *the Spirit*.[73] The interpretation which he gives to 2 Corinthians 13^{14} and Philippians 2^1 is thus attached to Acts 2^{42}. By this he does not mean to exclude the idea of sharing in material goods, which is described specifically in verse 44, but he will keep the wholeness of the concept of *koinōnia* only by emphasizing the participation in the Holy Spirit. This he holds to be the central meaning of the term for Christians, and all other applications of it, such as social fellowship, sharing property, giving alms, and so on, are secondary and derivative. 'We know from the epistles', he writes, 'that the *koinōnia* language covers a great variety of ideas. Yet all of these various ideas can be seen to be closely interrelated in the well-defined pattern of the common life, as that life was shared in fellowship. That life transcended the community because in essence it was a communion with Christ and with the Holy Spirit. On the divine side it was a mystical union with a participation in the life of Christ through receiving the gift of the Spirit. On the human side it consisted

---

[72] *The Johannine Epistles*, p. 7.
[73] *The Common Life in the Body of Christ*, pp. 72-6.

in a fellowship of brethren, whose mutual relations were transformed in quality and significance through the gift which they shared. All the characteristic activities of this fellowship are manifestations of those two fundamental factors, of this one complex yet simple whole with *its two fundamental aspects, the divine and the human*. Such was the *koinōnia* to which the first Christians devoted themselves.'[74]

Thornton's interpretation is perhaps the broadest to have been given to the words as it is used in Acts 2^{42}, and its breadth allows the greatest room for the work and presence of the Holy Spirit. Considering the thoroughly enthusiastic way in which the apostles testified to the effect of the Spirit in their lives, it seems probable that Thornton has come very close to the original intention of the author of Acts.

On the other hand, there are scholars who still insist that an explanation such as Thornton's attempts to draw too broad a religious meaning from *koinōnia* in this context. J. Y. Campbell would agree with Thornton with respect to Philippians 2^1, for example, as meaning 'participation in the Spirit'.[75] But in respect to Acts 2^{42} he must restrict the sense of the participation of the Christians to their sharing in contributions of money to a common cause.[76] Here he is in accord with F. Hauck, whose simple translation for *koinōnia* is *Gütergemeinschaft*, or the fellowship of goods held in common, as described in verse 44. Hauck hastens to add, however, that this conception is not purely material, for it is a spiritual fellowship of brotherly *Zusammenhalten*.[77]

It is apparent, in summary, that the important word *koinōnia* has several meanings, which are all related to the same Christians' experience of community, but which apply to different objects within that experience: the fellowship of persons; the ritual act of breaking bread in Christ's name, participation in the gift of the Holy Spirit or in fellowship with the Son and the Father, or sharing together in common possessions for the welfare of all. Whether the exegetes stress one meaning or another, or choose to combine two or more, there is a fundamental residue of agreement among them as to the *koinōnia* experience of the early Church. The strong brotherly feeling which was so real among

---

[74] *The Common Life in the Body of Christ*, p. 76.
[75] In *Journal of Biblical Literature*, LI(1932).379.
[76] ibid., p. 374. [77] In *TWNT*, III.810.

them was not a solidarity necessitated by their circumstances, by the persecutions they suffered, as A. Schlatter reminds us, but was due to the positive bonds of love which derived from God, who gave the gift in His Spirit.[78] For apart from the *agapē* of God, which Paul declares to have been 'poured into our hearts through the Holy Spirit which has been given to us',[79] the biblical concept of *koinōnia* is completely unintelligible. In short, then, it means 'a oneness in thought, mind, and in the sharing of goods, of sufferings, and of a life which is not their own but Another's'.[80]

So we observe in the New Testament teaching and witness four major contributions of the Holy Spirit to the faith and life of the Church. He makes the presence of the glorified Christ a reality to men in all generations. He calls men to faith and leads them in life as sons of God. He gives them the 'fruit' of Christ-like character. And he binds them together in their sharing of the life of *koinōnia*.

It is a tragic mistake to think that any of the aforementioned works of the Holy Spirit were limited in time to the Church of the first century. To be sure, the reality and significance of the Spirit's work have been less appreciated in some periods than in others. Probably no generation was more fully conscious of the power of the Spirit than was the apostolic one. And it is true that as the Christian faith came to be embraced in Greece and the West, there was a shift of emphasis from the *Pneuma* to the *Logos*, with a consequent loss to the understanding of the Christian life.[81] In succeeding centuries other trends of belief have often done violence to the idea of the presence and power of the Spirit. But today there is a growing consciousness among theologians, and Christians in general, that the Church must discover once more the meaning of the Spirit for its corporate life. 'It is of little use to describe the activities of the Spirit in former ages, if it is impossible to believe that He operates in the same way today.'[82]

By and large, the New Testament description of the work of

---

[78] *Die Geschichte der ersten Christenheit*, p. 28.
[79] Romans 5⁵.
[80] A. M. Ramsey, *The Gospel and the Catholic Church*, p. 30.
[81] cf. R. Bultmann, *Theologie des Neuen Testaments*, p. 151; S. Cave, *The Doctrines of the Christian Faith*, p. 223.
[82] F. W. Dillistone, *The Holy Spirit in the Life of Today*, p. 102.

the Spirit is adequate for the consideration of our own experience in the Church of the present time. Fanatical sects frequently draw attention to themselves by making a spectacle of so-called manifestations of the Spirit, such as babbling in 'tongues' and handling poisonous snakes. Others are wont to believe that to be 'moved by the Spirit' means to have extremely emotional experiences, whether joyous or painful it matters not. But they see no effect of the Holy Spirit in the commonplace ventures of living. These peculiar groups, however, while not excluded from the Christian community, are by no means representative, and their somewhat perverted conception of the faith has little connexion with the normative types of theology, which try to express the Christian faith synoptically and coherently.

The recent study by F. W. Dillistone focuses attention on four results of the Spirit's activity which are as really seen today as they were in the primitive Church. These are: (1) the new life of the believer in Christ; (2) the power to employ the same energy which was operative in Jesus, for overcoming evil, healing, and bearing witness to God; (3) the order for the community of Christians, living as a fellowship; and (4) the glory of the presence of God (the *Shekinah*) which is revealed in the face of Jesus Christ.[83] With certain modifications these four would harmonize with the discussions which has just preceded.

A more ecclesiastical interpretation of the Spirit's work is given by A. G. Hebert from a viewpoint which is not so close to the biblical witness as Dillistone's, but is more in accord with the later theology of the Church. The Spirit 'deals with us through the essential forms of the Church,' he writes, 'and these are the following: (1) He interprets to us the Scripture; (2) He makes the belief formally expressed in the Creed into an act of living faith; (3) He conveys to us the inward and spiritual grace in the outward sign of the Sacraments; and (4) He enables the Minister to speak and act with apostolic power.'[84] In these ways, continues Hebert, the lives of men and women are quickened, and they are empowered to produce such 'secondary forms of the Church' as 'biblical exposition, theology, liturgy, canon law,

[83] F. W. Dillistone, *The Holy Spirit in the Life of Today*, pp. 44, 58, 75, 95.
[84] *The Form of the Church*, p. 58. Here Hebert applies the doctrine of the work of the Spirit to the four essential elements of the Church, as defined in the *Lambeth Quadrilateral* of Holy Scripture, the Nicene Creed, the two Sacraments, and the Historic Episcopate (cf. ibid., p. 13).

music, drama'. It is not clear in this book whether Hebert intends such a summary of the work of the Spirit to be complete, but we may assume that he does not, unless the 'spiritual grace' is meant to include much more than is usually conveyed by the term. Even so, by associating these four forms of the Church, as well as the secondary forms, with the direct activity of the Holy Spirit, Hebert has indicated in a fresh way how the life of the *ekklēsia* is always vitally connected to the Spirit and wholly dependent upon His power.

KOINŌNIA IN THE CHURCH TODAY

Of the several kinds of effects the Spirit has upon men, as they have been presented in the preceding pages, none has received more serious theological attention in recent years than the *koinōnia*. In reality a *renaissance* of the *koinōnia* idea has been taking place in Christian thought and practice. This rebirth has been due in large part to sociological and political influences, as well as theological, for the momentous trends of social history since 1914 have caused a radical change to take place in respect to our attitudes toward an individualism in descendancy and a collectivism in ascendancy. These trends are now too well known to deserve further description here. What is important for this study, however, is the recognition that the perplexities of our present society have driven Christians to search for guidance in the Gospel: and the treasure which their search has uncovered in the *koinōnia*.

It is sometimes thought that the primitive community of Christians enjoyed a degree of fellowship among themselves and in relation to Christ which was so conditioned by their peculiar situation as to be unrepeatable. But theologians who interpret the actual evidence of similar experience of Christians in the Church are convinced that such is not true. Neither our communion with Christ nor our sharing of His love among men need be considered less real because we are long removed temporally from the time of the New Testament. As D. Bonhöffer affirms: 'The first disciples in their bodily fellowship with Jesus could have nothing other or nothing more than we have today; indeed this fellowship of ours is stronger, fuller, and more surely given than theirs. We live in the full presence of the corporal presence of the revealed Lord.'[85] Granted an assurance of *koinōnia* in

[85] *Nachfolge*, p. 160.

relation to Christ today, there should be little question about the possibility of a genuine *koinōnia* among men.

This Christian concept of personal relationship has also received the support of certain philosophy in the past three decades, and primarily that of Martin Buber. In his widely honoured analysis of the problem of human relations, *I and Thou*, he has contributed ideas which go far toward illuminating the essential meaning of *koinōnia*. The following representative paragraph indicates how closely his thought interpenetrates the Christian concept. 'The true community does not arise through people's having feelings for one another (though indeed not without it), but through, first, their taking their stand in living mutual relation with the living Centre, and second, their being in living mutual relation with one another. The second has its source in the first, but is not given when the first alone is given. ... The community is built up out of living mutual relation, but the builder is the living, effective Centre.'[86] Using the language of the New Testament, the Christian might say: A man who has the *koinōnia* with God through the Spirit can also have *koinōnia* with his neighbour, but it is God who gives and sustains both. This, according to 1 John 1³, is the whole purpose of the Gospel, 'that you may have fellowship with us; and our fellowship is with the Father and with His Son Jesus Christ'.

It is well known that this I-Thou concept has had remarkable effect upon the contemporary theology of Germany and Switzerland, and has spread its influence to other lands as well. The very language of Buber is evident in the works of K. Heim,[87] K. Barth,[88] and E. Brunner. Thus Brunner writes: 'A Christian cannot possibly be an isolated individual; to be a Christian is to be a member of the Body of Christ. ... Here not only are the individual and the community not mutually exclusive, but they *are* one and the same thing. Here it becomes evident what a distorted view of individual existence is that which is conceived without a "thou", and how false is every kind of "community" which does not consist of this responsibility toward the *Thou*.'[89]

What is surprising is not that this line of thought should be developed and proclaimed in modern theology, but that it should be acclaimed as something so unusual; for surely the basic concept

---

[86] *I and Thou*, p. 45.
[87] *God Transcendent*, pp. 103-72.
[88] *The Epistle to the Romans*, p. 442.
[89] *The Divine Imperative*, pp. 300f.

of I-Thou is perfectly clear in the New Testament. As E. Lohmeyer shows in his study of Paul, it is not possible to have an I-centred faith in the Christian fellowship; for Paul seldom speaks of *I* in relation to God, but uses instead *We* or the plural *You*.[90] Assuming the accuracy of this generalization about Paul, we may be somewhat startled to read the statement by K. L. Schmidt that, because fellowship with Christ is so decisive, a single man who has such fellowship could and would constitute the *ekklēsia*.[91] This idea has the merit of doing full justice to the importance of the divine relationship in the Church, but is extremely one-sided when expressed to the exclusion of other persons, and it is difficult to reconcile such a unilateral relationship with the several dominant communal teachings of the New Testament. If this were made a definite principle of the Church, and not just a means of emphasizing the importance of fellowship with Christ (as Schmidt uses it), we would have to consider the community of persons in the Church as incidental to the true nature of it. 'But there is a sense in which the phrase "individual Christian" is self-contradictory,' remarks John Knox, 'for the very term "Christian" presupposes a social reality.'[92] This social reality, of course, is the Church, in which the *koinōnia* is manifest in both its human and divine forms. To be sure, it is by the *koinōnia* of the Holy Spirit that we know Christ, and in Him we know God. But this is to be found only in the community (*Gemeinde*), declares Bonhöffer; and because the godly fellowship is found only in the Church, each individualistic concept of the nature of the Church is shattered.[93]

If it can be agreed that the Christian faith cannot be set forth in purely individualistic terms, but that the true *koinōnia* in its divine and human references is to be experienced only in community, we must examine the factors which make this *koinōnia* real for us. In his essay on 'The Church in the Light of the New Testament', G. Aulén uses the word 'Church' and *koinōnia* interchangeably, as though one expresses exactly the same thought as the other.[94] This usage may not be wholly justifiable, but it illustrates how inextricably associated the two concepts are.

Again it must be underscored, however, that the human fellowship or brotherhood in the Church, even in its most profound

[90] *Grundlagen paulinischer Theologie*, p. 183f.   [91] In *TWNT*, III.515.
[92] 'Christianity and the Christian' in *The Christian Answer* (H. P. van Dusen, ed.), p. 239.
[93] *Sanctorum communio*, p. 86.   [94] In *The Universal Church in God's Design*, p. 18.

expression, does not in itself constitute the fullness of the *koinōnia*. No recent theologian has stressed this point with more persistency than L. S. Thornton has. The *koinōnia* language which pertains to this human fellowship 'always points beyond it', he writes: 'As soon as we begin to ask wherein this fellowship consists, it is seen to draw its whole character and significance from its relation to God in and through Christ.'[95] Elsewhere in his book he declares: 'The essence of the *koinōnia* lies in the fact that communion between God and man exists in Christ.'[96] And again: 'The life which we share in common in the Church is not primarily that of human fellowship. Its distinctive character as manifested in human fellowship is wholly drawn from a divine source, and mediated to us in that fellowship through our joint participation in Christ.'[97] What he is opposing is, naturally, the dominating humanistic thought of the present time, which recognizes with genuine appreciation the manifest fellowship within the Church, but lacks the insight, or faith, to know why that kind of fellowship obtains.

More and more it is being understood that the real genius of Christianity can be expressed neither in secular groups and 'brotherhoods' nor in any community—even in the Church—which dissociates human fellowship from communion with God. Members of the Protestant denominations are learning that historic Protestantism, so much as it speaks the minds of the reformers, is not the champion of purely individual religion, but even more community-minded than Roman Catholicism.[98] Not only in theological writing, but in all forms of communication and literature, the principle of *koinōnia* is being interpreted. Even in verse, the eminent poet, T. S. Eliot, asks:

> *What life have you if you have not life together?*
> *There is no life that is not in community,*
> *And no community not lived in praise of God.*

[95] *The Common Life in the Body of Christ*, p. 47. [96] ibid., p. 158.
[97] ibid., p. 327. Karl Barth means much the same thing when he identifies the experiencing of fellowship in the Church with the encountering of God (*Epistle to the Romans*, p. 443): 'It must be Fellowship which is encountered in the community: but this means an encountering of the OTHER in the full existentiality of his utter OTHERNESS. In the *neighbour* it must be the ONE who is disclosed. . . . Fellowship is communion. It is, however, not a communion in which the "otherness" of each particular individual is blurred or limited or dissolved, but that ONENESS which both requires the "otherness" of each individual and makes sense of it.'
[98] cf. F. Kattenbusch, *Die Doppelschichtigkeit in Luthers Kirchenbegriff*, pp. 145f., where he demonstrates that the reality of fellowship (*Gemeinschaft*) of believing members in the Church was an indispensable element in Luther's concept of the Church.

> Even the anchorite who meditates alone . . .
> Prays for the Church, the Body of Christ incarnate.[99]

And to this the preacher responds, the Church's first 'duty is to *be* in living actuality . . . the fellowship of those who have received the power of the Holy Spirit through the revelation of the love of God in Christ'.[100]

It is not the purpose of this study to describe journalistically how the theological rediscovery of *koinōnia* has resulted in renewed fellowship and worship in countless individual churches throughout the world. But Christians *are* finding, by various techniques and to varying degrees of success, forms of group life in which the Holy Spirit's activity is recognized seriously and thankfully, and in which the faith and love of the New Testament Church are being approximated. This contemporary phenomenon ought not to be regarded as the Church's defensive reaction to a modern society which becomes increasingly depersonalized and mechanical, but as a positive demonstration of the basic nature of the Church's existence. 'For the fellowship of faith is the Church,' asserts Brunner, and: 'Where the empirical Church does not exhibit this spirit of fellowship, it merely shows to how slight an extent it is a real Church.'[101] That this judgement applies unconditionally, so that no one can think of any local church which is exempted from its verdict, is strong backing for the claim that the *koinōnia* belongs integrally and indispensably to the very essence of the Church.

To say that the Church cannot exist without *koinōnia* is just another way of saying that it cannot exist without the genuinely divine love, or *agapē*, for there can be no full sharing and fellowship among men, nor communion with God, when love is absent. 'Love is just . . . the vital element of the Church of Christ, that which constitutes it as such,' writes Barth: 'the surrender of the isolated person, by which he ceases to be such; or we might as well say at once: the death which he dies as such, the total annihilation which he experiences as such, and then: his resurrection, now no longer as an isolated person, but as One in the service of his Lord, or, what comes to the same thing: as One in the Whole, who also

---
[99] 'Choruses from "The Rock" ' in *Collected Poems, 1909-35*.
[100] William Temple, *Christian Unity and Church Reunion*, p. 13.
[101] *The Mediator*, p. 615.

is the Whole in him, the One.'[102] It is just this divine *agapē*, revealed in Jesus Christ, and 'poured into our hearts through the Holy Spirit', which informs and sustains every experience of *koinōnia*, whether in the first or the twentieth century, and which distinguishes the fellowship of Christians in the Church from the fellowship of other persons.

The relationship of *koinōnia* may be manifesting itself in all of the personal associations of members of a local church, for wherever two or three are gathered in the name and presence of Christ, they participate in the life of the Spirit. This is true in all aspects of their communal life, but supremely in the practice of common worship and in their participation in the Sacrament of the Lord's Supper. Here are focused all the primary elements of *koinōnia*: the *agapē* for God and other persons, the devout awareness of the gifts of the Spirit, the true faith in God through Jesus Christ and the assurance of His presence. None of these is absent in sacramental worship, for they virtually constitute it. As Y. Brilioth has concluded, after studying many beliefs and attitudes toward the Lord's Supper: 'It is of the essence of the eucharist that union with the Lord and union with the brethren are inseparable from one another. It is only for theoretical purposes that the two aspects can be separated.'[103] It is not an inviolable rule, of course, that all Christians must seek the *koinōnia* experience in eucharistic worship, for some minority groups, such as the Quakers, have dispensed with this sacramental practice without any apparent loss of the human and divine, the horizontal and vertical, relations of love. But in the experience of the great majority of Christians, as Brilioth demonstrates, it is at the Lord's Table that the *koinōnia* is most vividly realized.

But can this *koinōnia* not be known outside the Church? Is it not a narrow dogmatism to insist that the Spirit, who gives life and reality to the *koinōnia*, must be limited in His activity by the form and structure of the Church? This question is part of a much larger problem, involving the whole Christian claim to uniqueness and the definition of the dimensions of the Church, so no single and facile answer can be given. However, many theologians of dissimilar tradition and persuasion, without daring to suggest that the work of the Spirit can be circumscribed or

---

[102] *The Resurrection of the Dead*, p. 90.
[103] *Eucharistic Faith and Practice, Evangelical and Catholic*, p. 27.

bounded by humanly conceived definitions, still testify to the inseparability of the Spirit and the Church. Thus Eric Hayman writes: 'We do not assume any perfection in the present and visible structure of the Church. We simply assert . . . that within its supernatural fellowship and its communion life men are able to realize powers and energies which they are not otherwise able to imagine, let alone to achieve.'[104] So the question is most readily answered by testimony rather than rational argument.

Speaking from the Reformed tradition, and in terms which deal more explicitly with the action of the Spirit, Philippe-H. Menoud[105] asserts: 'The Church without the Spirit would be a body without the principle of life. . . . The Spirit without the Church would be a power without the means of permanent action. . . . The Church is the place where the Spirit acts. The Spirit of the glorified Christ is not a force which goes at random. It is a power which works in the frame of what is believed.' This statement of faith is by no means to be construed as meaning a conscious stricture upon the sphere of the Holy Spirit's work. It does mean that persons standing within the fellowship of the Church are, by the aid of the Spirit, constantly expanding the fellowship to include those who are outside it and enlarging the sphere of influence of the Spirit. A similar interpretation may be made of the dictum of Paul, which at first seemed very exclusive, that 'anyone who does not have the Spirit of Christ does not belong to Him'.[106]

To be the object of the transforming work of the Holy Spirit, to be called by Him into the relationship of faith in Christ, to receive power from Him and to enjoy the fruit of His benefaction, and so to be drawn into true community with other persons— all this means to participate in the *koinōnia* of the Church. This is not an abstract principle nor a poetic speculation about human relations, but the fact of experience which is attested to by multitudes of Christians from the apostolic generation onward. It can be well appreciated within the discussion about the work of the Spirit in the Church; but probably we may find the meaning of *koinōnia* to be more apprehensible when we have investigated the organic nature of the Church, as expressed in the idea of the Body of Christ.

---

[104] *Worship and the Common Life*, p. 83. The extraordinary dependence of Quakerism upon the presence and direction of the Spirit is indicative of a high degree of *koinōnia*-consciousness.

[105] *L'Église et les ministères selon le Nouveau Testament*, pp. 11-13.   [106] Romans 8⁹.

CHAPTER THREE

THE CHURCH'S RELATION TO CHRIST

I. THE 'BODY OF CHRIST' IN NEW TESTAMENT THOUGHT

IT IS OFTEN observed that certain words and phrases of the Bible are so ambiguous or enigmatic that they defy any interpretation which can satisfy all Christians. But there are few words so puzzling as the phrase, 'Body of Christ', as it is applied to the Church.[1] Unfortunately there are many theologians and preachers who use the words glibly and without discrimination, very often having no definite concept of their meaning. Is the term 'body' merely a metaphor, illustrating how Christians live in organic unity, co-operation, interdependence, and harmony? Is it a personification of the whole Church, which is convenient for rhetorical purposes? Or is the 'Body of Christ' intended to mean such a reality that the Church can be conceived as a living organism of mystical nature, which is somehow identical with the transcendent Christ? The implications of these different interpretations are of such far-reaching importance to our total concept of the Church, that the phrase ought to be employed only with the greatest caution, if one is uncertain as to the meaning he attaches to it.

Aware of the confusion which is so apparent in the minds of many persons who speak of 'the Body of Christ' indiscriminately, modern biblical scholars and theologians have devoted much study to the two-fold problem of the actual meaning of the phrase in the New Testament and the meaning of it for our contemporary thought about the nature of the Church. This study involves not only the exegesis of those passages which include *sōma Christou*, or its equivalent, but also the clarification of thought and belief which pertain to the relationship existing between Christ the Lord and the Church bearing His name. A review of the results of the inquiry into both aspects of the problem, therefore, ought to

[1] For example: 'Now you are the body of Christ,' 1 Corinthians 12^{27}; 'so we, though many, are one body in Christ,' Romans 12^5; 'He is the head of the body, the church,' Colossians 1^8; 'for building up the body of Christ,' Ephesians 4^{12}.

dispel some of the darkness of imprecision of thought concerning the Body of Christ.

The idea is primarily Pauline, of course, so it is worthwhile to ask how Paul came to use such an epithet in reference to the *ekklēsia*.

The word for 'body' (*sōma*) was common enough in secular Greek writing, but it could be interpreted in several ways. Basically it meant the human body, but it could also mean a 'living person', or a 'corpse', or even a 'slave'.[2] In opposition to 'shadow' (*skia*) it denoted the 'reality'. Very often it simply stood for 'mass' or 'bulk'. But so far as A. M. Ramsey and A. E. J. Rawlinson can determine, the word *sōma* in pre-Christian usage did not refer to a 'corporate society' or a 'body of people' at all.[3] Even so, the concept of corporeity, if not the word, was not strange to the Greeks, as O. Michel points out; for in mythology and the fables of Aesop, the body and its members was a common illustration of the organic principle.[4] And in Plato's *Republic* (Book V, 462) the state is described as a body, which suffers because of the evil of its individual members: and this, according to the view of C. Chavasse, was really the source of Paul's concept of *sōma Christou*.[5]

Furthermore, the Greek world was familiar with the use of the body-concept in both Stoicism and Gnosticism. 'For the Stoics the whole universe was a living thing, a Body, the life or spirit of which was God—God exclusively immanent, without any transcendence.'[6] Likewise the Gnostics had borrowed the terminology of ancient Indian myths, which depicted the world as a living organism.[7] It is at least plausible that Paul was no stranger to this kind of philosophy and occult speculation, but

---

[2] cf. G. Gloege, *Reich Gottes und Kirche im Neuen Testament*, pp. 297f., wherein he says that Paul carried over the meaning of *sōma* as 'slave' into thought on the Church: 'The Church is the slave of Christ, subordinate to Him in the obedience of faith and at the same time bound to Him in just this obedience of faith.' Few commentators have pursued this line of thought, however.

[3] Ramsey, *The Gospel and the Catholic Church*, p. 35; Rawlinson, 'Corpus Christi' in *Mysterium Christi*, pp. 225f.; cf. J. Moffatt, *The First Epistle of Paul to the Corinthians*, p. 186.

[4] *Das Zeugnis des Neuen Testaments von der Gemeinde*, pp. 44f.

[5] *The Bride of Christ*, p. 75: a very singular opinion! For extensive philological study of *sōma*, cf. T. Schmidt, *Der Leib Christi*; E. Käsemann, *Leib und Leib Christi*; E. Percy, *Der Leib Christi (Sōma Christou) in den paulinischen Homologumena und Antilogumena*.

[6] T. A. Lacey, *The One Body and the One Spirit*, p. 56; cf. W. L. Knox, *St. Paul and the Church of the Gentiles*, p. 161.

[7] Michel, *loc. cit.* (Note [4]).

the extent to which he depended upon such ideas for his thought of the 'Body of Christ' is an open question. Both H. Schlier and E. Käsemann have stressed the influence of Gnosticism upon Paul's thinking, and Michel and Bultmann point out the Gnostic ideas in Paul's mind.[8] That the Pauline concept of the Body of Christ was pure Gnosis and 'nonsensical farrago' is pronounced by Loisy without qualification, and he applies this harsh judgement to the other figures of 'bride' and 'building' as they are applied to the Church.[9] The aforementioned scholars, however, have not regarded these Gnostic ideas in the epistles as nonsense; rather, they have tried to reach a clearer understanding of the original meaning of the Body of Christ, and if it was a Gnostic concept, it must be understood as such.

Two factors have contributed to this interpretation of the Body of Christ in terms of the Gnostic mythology. One was the research in the field of Hellenistic and Oriental mystery religions, carried on by R. Reitzenstein[10] and his colleagues, which brought to light the esoteric religious beliefs and cosmologies that prevailed in New Testament times. The other was the rather recent way of explaining the anthropological view of Paul according to Hebrew rather than Greek thought; i.e., rejecting the Greek dualistic idea that man is a combination of soul and body, the body being infused by the soul, and embracing the Hebrew idea that the body and soul are indissoluble.[11] If *sōma* should be understood in the Greek sense, the *sōma Christou* means that the Church is infused by Christ as the body is by the soul.[12] But if the Hebrew interpretation is correct, the *sōma*, the Church with all its members, must represent the person of Christ. How could one conceive of something so fantastic though—that the Church is the body, which means the person, of Christ? The answer is found in the Anthropos-myth of Gnosticism, a complex cosmological scheme in which the divine Redeemer descends to earth in order to save mankind by assimilating the race into his body and bearing it to heaven. Such a scheme, it is held, was in the mind of the author of Ephesians when he described the Church as the

[8] Schlier, *Christus und die Kirche im Epheserbrief*, p. 39, and Article *Kephalē* in *TWNT*, III.679; Käsemann, *Leib und Leib Christi*, pp. 163ff.; Michel, *Das Zeugnis des Neuen Testaments von der Gemeinde*, pp. 46ff.; Bultmann, *Theologie des Neuen Testaments*, p. 178.
[9] *The Birth of the Christian Religion*, pp. 289, 296.
[10] *Die hellenistischen Mysterienreligionen nach ihren Grundgedanken und Wirkungen.*
[11] W. Gutbrod, *Die paulinische Anthropologie*; Bultmann, op. cit., p. 189.
[12] Thus understood by T. Schmidt, *Der Leib Christi*, pp. 142ff.

Body of Christ, and it informed to a somewhat moderate degree the thought of Paul on the problem.[13] If Christ is substituted for the mythical Anthropos, or Primal Man, it is conceivable that Gnosticism can provide illumination for the meaning of the Church as His Body.

This novel basis for exegesis of the *sōma Christou* passages has not been widely accepted, and by some scholars has been vigorously attacked,[14] for they believe that the Body of Christ can have a distinctly Christian meaning which is not lifted out of historical reality by mythical speculation. While it is an exaggeration to interpret the Body of Christ as nothing but Gnosticism, however, it remains to be demonstrated conclusively that such an influence upon the biblical concept was negligible.

If one cannot be satisfied that the source of the Body-concept lay in Gnostic myth, where else might he look for it? According to the theory of A. E. J. Rawlinson, that source may be found in the meaning of the Eucharist.[15] The crucial passage on which this theory rests is 1 Corinthians 10[16-17]: 'The bread which we break, is it not a participation in the body of Christ? Because there is one loaf, we who are many are one body, for we all partake of the same loaf.' The connexion between these sacramental words and Paul's specific references to the Church as the Body of Christ is not coincidental nor insignificant, Rawlinson believes. 'Between the use of the phrase "Body of Christ" as a description of the Church and the use of the same phrase as a description of the sacramental "loaf" of the Eucharist it is permissible to suspect a connexion, and the rite, surely, precedes the doctrine.' If the language of the early Christians' practice of the Eucharist already included a concept of the 'body' as being a reality which every believer could understand and in which he could participate, Paul could use the word in his advice to the Corinthians as an exhortation which needed neither elaboration nor explanation, and they would readily perceive how the 'one loaf' and the 'one body' signified their unity in Christ. Moreover, Paul's statement that 'by one Spirit we were all baptized into one

---

[13] cf. Schlier, *Christus und die Kirche im Epheserbrief*, pp. 41ff.

[14] cf. the refutations set forth by H. Köhnlein, *Revue d'histoire et de philosophie religieuses*, XVII(1937).364-6; E. Percy, *Der Leib Christi, usw.*, p. 39; S. Hanson, *The Unity of the Church in the New Testament*, pp. 114f.

[15] 'Corpus Christi' in *Mysterium Christi* (G. K. A. Bell and A. Deissmann, eds.), pp. 227ff.

body . . . and all were made to drink of one Spirit' (1 Corinthians 12¹³) adds weight to the argument that the Christian use of the 'body' derived from sacramental practice and belief.

This interpretation by Rawlinson has been received with enthusiasm as a most likely analysis of the origin of Paul's idea, against the strictly Gnostic influence. Both C. H. Dodd[16] and L. S. Thornton[17] admit no better supposition, and O. Michel[18] is favourably disposed toward the theory.[19] Likewise, the whole content of this hypothesis is concretely restated by C. C. Morrison as follows: 'Paul is struggling to bring together the two concepts of the physical body of Christ broken in death and the body of Christ which is the church, and to identify them in the Eucharistic act. His mind is prepossessed with the organic conception of the church as Christ's body—"we who are many are one bread, one body".'[20] It is impossible to say with certainty that the idea of the Church as the Body of Christ originated in Paul's understanding of the Eucharist, but it is apparent that a clue to the meaning of the term is provided by this reference to the 'one loaf'.

Another factor to be recognized before we can appreciate the Pauline meaning of the Body of Christ is to be found in the characteristic Hebrew idea of personification. How can the countless individual Christians who constitute the Church be considered as the body of the one Christ? The notion seems unintelligible to our modern manner of thinking. Yet, the Hebrew thought-forms, which Paul had inherited, had no difficulty in expressing the idea that one man represents, or even embodies, a whole people. For example, Adam, Abraham, Moses and Elijah were never merely human figures for the Jews, but 'living manifestations of divine will, revealing the present demands of a living God. Each of them is at once himself and the race'.[21] The same could be said of David's imploring God in Psalm 69 to confound his enemies, which are really the enemies of the whole people. Another familiar example, generally interpreted as meaning not one person by Himself but the whole

[16] *The Epistle of Paul to the Romans*, p. 195.
[17] *The Common Life in the Body of Christ*, pp. 291, 330.
[18] *Das Zeugnis des Neuen Testaments von der Germeinde*, p. 44.
[19] For a recent discussion of this theory, cf. E. Käsemann, '*Anliegen und Eigenart der paulinischen Abendmahlslehre*,' *Evangelische Theologie* (1947-8), pp. 263ff.
[20] *What Is Christianity?* p. 160.
[21] P. S. Minear, *Eyes of Faith*, p. 87.

people of Israel, is the figure of the Suffering Servant in Isaiah 53.[22] If these personifications were then taken for granted by the first Christians in their reading of the Old Testament, it was surely no trouble for them to understand how Jesus Christ embodies His people, the *ekklēsia*—and yet in a way which surpasses the degree of unity of the patriarchs and their people.

There are some scholars who see the personifications of the Old Testament not only as a clue to the understanding of the Body of Christ, but as the most important basis for such an understanding. Particularly do they recognize in Romans 5^{12-21}, where Paul contrasts Adam and Christ, the key to the mystery of the Body. According to S. Hanson, the old, sinful mankind is personified by the body of Adam, who was a type of the Christ to come. And Christ is the Head of the new, redeemed mankind. 'Consequently, in the conception of the second Adam, Christ reveals Himself not as an individual but as the representative and incarnation of the New People of God, a New Humanity.'[23] This contrast between Adam and Christ was so significant and influential, declares Hanson, that the figure of the Body of Christ can be interpreted most satisfactorily in terms of it. It is a type of speculative thinking which has much in common with Gnostic thought, except that it remains within the framework of a peculiarly Jewish kind of Gnosticism. Hanson believes that there is greater plausibility in regarding Paul's own idea of the Body of Christ as an expression of Jewish thought than of Greek or Iranian.

Against such a background, Paul's frequent employment of the figure of the Body of Christ takes on far richer meaning than when it is read only from our modern point of view, as an analogy of an organism and nothing more. To illuminate our understanding of the figure still more, however, we must survey briefly the various passages of the New Testament in which the concept of *sōma Christou* is developed, with special attention being given to the views of various biblical scholars of the present time.

---

[22] cf. C. A. A. Scott, *The Fellowship of the Spirit*, p. 222; A. M. Ramsey, *The Gospel and the Catholic Church*, p. 19f.

[23] *The Unity of the Church in the New Testament*, pp. 68-70, 116. Hanson names four others whom he follows in this emphasis upon the representative meaning of Adam and of Christ: A. Nygren, 'Corpus Christi' in *En bok om kyrkan av svenska teologer*, pp. 16f.; A. Wikenhauser, *Die Kirche als der mystische Leib Christi nach dem Apostel Paulus*, pp. 125f.; E. Percy, *Der Leib Christi*, pp. 41f.; and N. Johansson, *Det urkristna nattvardsfirandet*, p. 220. cf. John Knox, *Christ the Lord*, pp. 120-2.

THE CHURCH'S RELATION TO CHRIST

The phrase 'Body of Christ' and its synonyms appear most frequently in 1 Corinthians, noticeably in 6^{15}, 10^{16-17}, 11^{29}, and $12^{12, 27}$. In each case the context differs from the others', so that none may be extracted from its special position. For example, in 6^{15} Paul's primary concern is to forbid the Christians from committing sin with prostitutes. 'Do you not know that your bodies are members of Christ? Shall I therefore take the members of Christ and make them members of a prostitute? Never!' The association of the 'body' in this passage with the Church is extremely vague, of course, and many would agree with M. Goguel in denying any connexion at all.[24] However, two aspects of the saying are worth remarking. Rawlinson emphasizes the words 'Do you not know...' as a clear indication that the readers and hearers of his letter were already familiar with the idea that the bodily 'members' of Christ's Body were themselves.[25] Thus Paul could assume that the Corinthians would connect his moral exhortation to their participation in the Body of Christ, and that they would be prepared to understand completely his remarks about the Church as the Body of Christ in the remainder of the letter.

The second allusion is drawn by Moffatt from the idea that by *physical* intercourse a man becomes *fully* joined to a harlot, not only in his natural body but in soul as well.[26] In Paul's thought, the *sōma* of a man denotes more than his body: it is his whole person, flesh and spirit. Upon this understanding of the word, it thus becomes more intelligible to us how men and women can be actual members of and participants in the larger Body of Christ.

The next passage, 10^{16-17}, which concerns *koinōnia* in the Body of Christ in the Holy Communion, has already been discussed.[27]

While treating the problems of the Lord's Supper a second time, 11^{27-9}, Paul uses a provocative phrase which suggests a deeper meaning than appears on the surface: 'For any one who eats and drinks without discerning the body, eats and drinks judgement upon himself.' In what way can the idea of 'discerning (*diakrinōn*) the body' refer to the Church as Christ's Body?

As G. Johnston has found, many commentators simply fail to

[24] *L'Église Primitive*, p. 44.
[25] In *Mysterium Christi* (G. K. A. Bell and A. Deissmann, eds.), p. 226.
[26] *The First Epistle of Paul to the Corinthians*, p. 72.
[27] pp. 53f. *supra*.

see in their studies any connexion between the two senses of the 'body', while a few explicitly reject the idea of connexion of meaning.[28] On the other hand, certain men have recently been disposed to find an intentional association of the two ideas in Paul's mind and to lay much stress upon such an interpretation. In fact, Thornton goes so far as to say: 'In these words about "discerning the body" we see one of St. Paul's greatest contributions to religion.'[29] According to Thornton's exegesis, 'discerning the body' means 'to discern also the common life in the Body of Christ, that is to say, nothing less than the significance of the Gospel in and for the Church'. The purpose of the Lord's Supper, according to Paul, is two-fold: attention is centred upon the sacrificial suffering and death of Jesus, but also on the fellowship of the faithful brethren who are united in Christ. When the Corinthians turned the Supper into an occasion for gluttony and revelry, the wealthier ones ignoring the hunger of the poorer, they saw neither the sacrificed body of the Lord nor the loving fellowship of the *ekklēsia*. As Paul demanded of them in verse 22: 'Do you despise the Church of God?' So Moffatt explains: 'The Lord's Body was really represented in what they ate and drank, but not less really in their fellow-Christians, in whom, as well as for whom, the Lord lived.'[30] That is why their failure to perceive the meaning of the rite, in both of its aspects, brought 'judgement' upon them, which was so severe that many became ill and died (verse 30)!

Continuing the discussion of the Christians' life together in the *ekklēsia*, Paul takes up the problem of the meaning and value of the various gifts of the Spirit to individuals, and in this connexion he develops the meaning of the Body of Christ in detail. The human body has many separate parts, and yet all are one organic body—'so also is Christ' (12[12]). Paul then describes the essential interdependence of the parts of the Body, and concludes by reminding the Corinthians: 'Now you are the body of Christ and individually members of it.' The figure is graphic and illustrative, so that only the most uncomprehending could fail to understand the plea for social harmony and sympathetic co-operation.

---

[28] *The Doctrine of the Church in the New Testament*, p. 90.
[29] *The Common Life in the Body of Christ*, p. 342.
[30] *The First Epistle of Paul to the Corinthians*, p. 173.

But is this use of the metaphor only figurative? Is it no more than an illustration of what the life of the community ought to be? H. W. Robinson insists that 'we must constantly remember that it *is* a metaphor' and nothing more, or else we fall into the danger of materializing its application.[31] He admits that the body which is referred to here is a 'supra-sensible reality of fellowship into which believers are baptized in the Spirit', but he cautiously avoids too closely a connexion between this body and Christ.

Robinson's view is representative of one school of thought on the exact meaning of 'body' here, but there are many who do not share it. Moffatt would point out, for example, that Robinson fails to comprehend the strength of the phrase, 'so also is Christ,' in verse 12.[32] If this were only an analogy concerning the community, Paul would have done better to say, 'so also are *you*, the church.' Furthermore, the emphatic 'you' of verse 27 shows specifically how Paul means that the Church, including its members at Corinth, because bound to Christ, constitutes the Body of Christ, which is the subject of this whole section. So Thornton, comparing this verse with the next one, in which Paul speaks of the ministries of the Church, remarks: 'The Body is not thought of as a collection of individuals. For as soon as metaphor is dropped the Church appears in place of the aggregation of members.'[33] The community is, therefore, not *like* the Body of Christ, but it *is* the Body of Christ on earth. This distinction is underscored by Eduard Schweizer as being both valid and crucial for the Church. 'Paul therefore knows and takes earnestly the fact that the Body of Christ is at the last nothing else but Christ Himself, living in the community. The community is the secondary, special form of existence of Christ.'[34] Stated differently and with much emphasis by Bultmann, Paul did not think here of the Body as being constituted by differing but united individual members; in reality, the differences of individuals become meaningless in the Body because they belong to Christ, and the Body is constituted through Christ rather than through them.[35] Thus we are confronted in this passage by the idea which is

---

[31] *The Christian Experience of the Holy Spirit*, p. 149. E. F. Scott agrees that the 'body' is no more than a metaphor, *The Epistles of Paul to the Colossians etc.*, p. 24.
[32] *The First Epistle of Paul to the Corinthians*, pp. 185f.
[33] *The Common Life in the Body of Christ*, p. 256.
[34] *Das Leben des Herrn in der Gemeinde und ihren Diensten*, p. 51.
[35] *Theologie des Neuen Testaments*, p. 306.

expressed even more forcefully in Colossians, and which receives its most far-reaching exposition in Ephesians—that the Church is in a very real sense, not a figurative sense, the Body of Christ.[36]

Paul makes references to the 'Body' in Romans, adding in a certain measure to the implications of the concept for the Christian faith. In 7[4] he writes: '. . . you have died to the law through the body of Christ, so that you may belong to another, to him who has been raised from the dead in order that we may bear fruit for God.' Embedded in a discussion of the law, rather than of the Church, though it is, this verse may still be taken to mean that Paul 'saw the death of the whole people of God to sin, law, and the flesh' in the death of the Lord on the cross.[37] This belief is closely related to 6[6-8], in which Paul depicts the believers as dying and rising with Christ in virtue of baptism. Both Dodd and Thornton favour this meaning of the Body of Christ[38] in 7[4], although other scholars either fail to see the relation to the Church or else they prefer not to.

We meet the figure of the Body and its members again in Romans 12[4-5]. However, this passage contributes to the idea nothing which may not be found in 1 Corinthians. In fact, as Dodd remarks, the mystical and sacramental background of the saying, so prominent in 1 Corinthians, is altogether lacking here.[39] So this reference must be read in the light of the other developments in Paul's theology. But by itself it would hardly be an adequate expression of his idea, for, as M. Goguel observes, a body 'in Christ' is not the same as the Body 'of Christ'.[40]

From these two earlier epistles has been adduced a Pauline concept of the Church as the Body of Christ which is kerygmatic rather than didactic or doctrinal. Because the exposition of the idea has been at times indistinct, ambiguous, and unsystematic,

---

[36] cf. A. E. J. Rawlinson in *Mysterium Christi* (G. K. A. Bell and A. Deissmann, eds.), p. 235: 'We are expressing St. Paul's thought with complete accuracy when we say, with a conscious realization of what the words literally mean, that we are *incorporated* by Baptism into Christ.'

[37] C. H. Dodd, *The Epistle of Paul to the Romans*, p. 102.

[38] cf. Thornton, *The Common Life in the Body of Christ*, p. 148.

[39] *The Epistle of Paul to the Romans*, p. 195. It is interesting that Karl Barth reverses his decision on the interpretation of this passage which he held in the first edition of *Der Römerbrief*. In the sixth edition, from which Hoskyns's translation is made, he refutes the 'romantic, conservative . . . Catholic' idea that the 'body' of Christ is organically the Church. Men encounter God in their own particular, individual tribulation and hope, and not through some notion of the 'whole': *The Epistle to the Romans*, p. 441.

[40] *L'Église Primitive*, p. 45.

without a clear relation to Paul's christology, there is justification for sharply diverse interpretations.

In Colossians and Ephesians, however, most doubts concerning the intended meaning of the Body of Christ are dispelled. Christ is called the 'Head' of the Body: He is the very centre of its organic life and growth. And the whole concept of the Church, of its life and ministry, membership and destiny, is linked indissolubly to the Person of Christ. In these two letters we encounter a high developed theology of the Church, and this accounts for their popularity among theologians in the present time, when the problem of the Church is so often in the foreground of Christian thought and discussion. There is abundant evidence to support the assertion of Metzger, that Ephesians may be the centre of the modern reformation of the Church, just as Romans and Galatians were central for Luther's time.[41]

It has been objected by some scholars of the past two generations that one does violence to the text to treat Ephesians as either an authentic letter of Paul or a true statement of Pauline thought on the Church. Both Käsemann and Schlier distinguish between what they believe to be the truly Pauline meaning of the Body of Christ in Romans and 1 Corinthians, and that which appears in Ephesians.[42] (These men, with Bultmann, also reject the Pauline authorship of Colossians.) The matter of authenticity is a debatable one, with representative scholars taking one side and the other.[43] However, the technical aspects of the problem need not detain us here. Most theologians who are not definitely convinced that Ephesians is not the work of Paul, and even some who are so convinced, treat the content of the letter as though it were from Paul's own hand. 'It may confidently be said that there is nothing in Ephesians which Paul might not have written,' concludes E. F. Scott.[44] And K. L. Schmidt, without attributing the letter to Paul, can still declare that, whoever the author was,

---

[41] 'Paul's Vision of the Church' in *Theology Today*, April (1949), p. 61.

[42] Käsemann, *Leib und Leib Christi*, p. 160; Schlier, *Christus und die Kirche im Epheserbrief*, p. 40.

[43] Among those who deny the authorship of Paul are A. Schweitzer, *The Mysticism of Paul the Apostle*, p. 120; W. L. Knox, *St. Paul and the Church of the Gentiles*, pp. 182-4; G. Johnston, *The Doctrine of the Church in the New Testament*, pp. 136-8. Supporting the Pauline authenticity are C. A. A. Scott, *The Fellowship of the Spirit*, p. 73; W. J. Phythian-Adams, *The People and the Presence*, p. 195; E. F. Scott, *The Epistles of Paul to the Colossians etc.*, pp. 119-21. An excellent, exhaustive and up-to-date discussion of the problem is found in E. Percy's *Die Probleme der Kolosser- und Epheserbriefe*.

[44] op. cit., p. 121.

the ideas of the letters are '*durchaus paulinisch*' and in full accord with the other letters of Paul.[45] In examining the concept of the Body of Christ in Ephesians, then, and bearing in mind that some scholars would still object, we may provisionally regard it as essentially in harmony with the thought of Paul.

The important thing to remember in reading both Colossians and Ephesians is that we cannot reach an understanding of the mind of Paul until we discard temporarily some of the presuppositions about the Church which we hold in the present time. This is no easy thing to do. And yet it is apparent that for most Protestants the ideas and terminology of these letters seem quite foreign. They express a belief about Christ's nature, His work on earth, and His continuing relationship to the Church, which strikes the Protestant mind as being—depending upon one's viewpoint—imaginary, mystical, occult, or unfathomable. For in these letters, Paul (or his unknown imitator) speaks of the pre-existence of Christ and the fore-election of those to be saved.[46] In baptism the believers have been buried and raised with Christ to new life in Him;[47] and so they come to share in the revelation of the divine 'mystery' of God.[48] There is strange talk of 'elemental spirits of the universe' and demonic 'powers' of the air, against which Christ contended and over which He triumphed.[49] Here there is no hesitation about asserting that the Church is the Body of Christ,[50] whether it be literally or figuratively intended; but Christ is now designated as the 'Head' of the Body, which is a new idea, not found in the earlier letters of Paul.[51] Furthermore, in Ephesians we meet the enigmatic concept of the 'fullness' of Christ in connexion with the Church, His Body.[52] Then there are other metaphors applied to the Church: it is a 'building' which 'grows into a holy temple',[53] or it is the 'bride' which is loved and consecrated by Christ, the husband.[54]

How are all these curious concepts and expressions to be interpreted according to our contemporary Western patterns

---

[45] In *TWNT*, III.514; cf. M. Goguel, in *The Ministry and the Sacraments* (R. Dunkerley, ed.), p. 309n; G. Johnston, *The Doctrine of the Church in the New Testament*, p. 92, and especially his tabulated comparison of Ephesians with Colossians, pp. 137f.
[46] Colossians 1^{15-18}, Ephesians 1^4.
[47] Colossians 2^{12}, 3^{13}.
[48] ibid., 1^{16}, 2^8, $^{15, 20}$, Ephesians 2^2, 3^{10}, 6^{12}.
[49] Colossians 1^{16}, $2^{8, 15, 20}$, Ephesians 2^2, 3^{10}, 6^{12}.
[50] Colossians $1^{18, 24}$, 2^9, ^{19}, 3^{15}, Ephesians 1^{23}, 2^{16}, 3^6, $4^{4, 12}$.
[51] Colossians 1^{18}, 2^{19}, Ephesians 1^{22}, 4^{15}, 5^{23}.
[52] Ephesians 1^{23}, 4^{13}.   [53] ibid., $2^{20, 21}$.   [54] ibid., 5^{25-32}.

THE CHURCH'S RELATION TO CHRIST 79

of thought? How can the empirical Church, as we know it in our society, be compared to the exalted, divinely-constituted entity which is called the Body of Christ? With these elusive and complex problems of biblical interpretation Christian theologians have been wrestling vigorously during the past three decades. And some of the results of their labours thus far are now to be reviewed.

In order to devote full attention to the problem of the Body of Christ, we can first consider briefly the related figures of the 'building' and the 'bride' as they are treated in Ephesians. When the writer describes the Church as the 'household of God, built upon the foundation of the apostles and prophets, Christ Jesus himself being the chief corner-stone, in whom the whole structure is joined together and grows into a holy temple of the Lord,' there can surely be little doubt about the intended meaning of the metaphor. As the many parallels to this language in the New Testament show, the figures stimulated rich and graphic associations in the minds of the early Christians. According to the Markan tradition, Jesus had applied the figure of the rejected corner-stone, taken from Psalm 118, to His own destiny;[55] and the use of this reference must have been very extensive during the first century. Moreover, the tradition was being preserved that the charge made against Jesus at His trial before the high priest was that He had threatened to destroy the temple and rebuild it in three days,[56] a saying which the Fourth Evangelist specifically interprets as a reference to the resurrected body of Jesus,[57] and which subsequent Christians readily understood to mean the temple or sanctuary (*naos*) which is the Church. And the words of Paul in 1 Corinthians 3^{17}—'Do you not know that you are God's temple?'—come immediately to mind in connexion with this use of the metaphor in Ephesians 2^{21}. Both here and in the other passages in the New Testament, the imagery of the figure conveys an idea which was revolutionary in the Jewish society, with its reverence for the great temple at Jerusalem. Because of Christ, the 'inner sanctuary' of God was no longer the place where the priests alone might be confronted by the divine presence. Such a concept was destroyed by Christ, and the new Temple, the Church, took its place, admitting all faithful persons, whether Jew or Gentile.

[55] Mark 12^{10-11}; cf. Matthew 21^{42}, Luke 20^{17}, Acts 4^{11}, 1 Peter 2^7.
[56] Mark 14^{58}, Matthew 26^{61}.   [57] John 2^{21}; cf. E. C. Hoskyns, *The Fourth Gospel*, p. 195.

What is more important, however, is the way in which the passage in Ephesians uses the figure to show the *organic* relationship existing between Christ and the Church. The 'building' is not to be conceived as a static structure, once and for all constructed, nor even as one to which addition may be made. The apostles and prophets constitute the foundation, and the cornerstone is Christ. However, 'Christ is not only the beginning of the Church but continues to be the power that holds it together and shapes it'.[58] The building is, therefore, not only a 'dwelling-place of God' but God Himself is the builder in Christ.[59] Ever being built, it is never complete on earth until the final purpose of God is to be consummated.[60]

Very seldom in writing about the nature of the Church do theologians give much attention to the idea of the Church's being the 'Bride of Christ'. For some, the metaphor seems too fanciful to merit conscientious exposition, while others have seen in it no more than a practical exhortation to married couples that they remain constant in their relationship of love. Nevertheless, at least one theologian has recognized this figure of speech as the most important clue to the understanding of the Church's relation to Christ. Drawing upon Jewish marriage lore for the elucidation of the figure, Claude Chavasse has contended that the concept of the Church as the Bride is far richer in meaning and nearer the truth than that of the Body of Christ. Of the latter he writes: 'It cannot express the fundamental and original apartness of Man and the Word of God, nor the astounding love which impelled the Bridegroom to come down from heaven, to humble himself to the level of his creation, that, in uniting himself to humanity, he might raise humanity to the heaven from which he came. A Body is a unity which was always one. A Marriage is the union of two which grows into perfect unity through love.'[61] Even the metaphor of the Vine and the branches[62] is preferable to that of the Body, declares Chavasse,[63] but no figure can conceivably surpass the Bride-Bridegroom, which so adequately

---

[58] E. F. Scott, *The Epistles of Paul to the Colossians etc.*, p. 178.
[59] cf. Eric Wahlstrom, Files of Commission I, W.C.C., Geneva.
[60] An illustrative parallel is given by Karl Heim, *Der evangelische Glaube und das Denken der Gegenwart*, III.232: 'The community is a house which is built completely on the invisible foundation of an event which is still wholly future.'
[61] *The Bride of Christ*, p. 17.
[62] John 15[1-6].
[63] p. 61. So also T. A. Lacey, *The One Body and the One Spirit*, p. 44.

illustrates the actual relationship between Christ and the *ekklēsia*, in Ephesians 5²¹⁻³³.⁶⁴

A usual manner of interpreting the figure is to emphasize only the attributes of obedience and purity which the Church ought to possess. Just as the wife is subject to her husband, in the strict sense of Oriental custom, so the Church must be unconditionally subject to her Lord. Also, according to this interpretation, the Church must be washed clean and become pure, even as the bride submitted to the ceremonial bath before being arrayed in her marriage dress.⁶⁵ Such simple analogy, useful though it may be, is not true to the words of the text, however. For it says specifically that wives are to obey their husbands *because* the Church is subject to Christ, not vice versa. Husbands are to love their wives *because* Christ loved the Church. In other words, the established fact which the writer has in mind is the existing marriage between Christ and the Church; and this is the true prototype of human marriage.⁶⁶ In addition, there is more intended here than a reference to a simple ceremonial bath. As J. Moffatt translates the text: '. . . by cleansing her in the bath of baptism as she utters her confession' (verse 26). Thornton believes that what is meant is an actual baptism of the Church at the hand of Christ, an act which occurred historically in the period beginning with Jesus' own baptism and climaxing in the consecrating event of Pentecost.⁶⁷ It was thus the Lord's doing, that the Church was made 'holy and without blemish' in order to become the Bride.

This line of thought takes seriously the ancient belief that Israel was the Bride of Yahweh,⁶⁸ a concept which must have still been very strongly held in the first century, for Jesus is said to have referred to Himself as the 'bridegroom' in Mark 2²⁰, and Paul speaks of his having 'betrothed' the Corinthians to Christ as a bride to her husband in 1 Corinthians 11².⁶⁹ It avoids the error of trying to understand the metaphor in terms of our modern view toward the nuptial idea of God and His people, a view which is either condescending to the idea or scornful of it.

---

[64] While H. Schlier considers the Bride to be another figure borrowed from Gnosticism, E. Percy asserts that only the primitive Christian conception of the community of believers is meant by it; cf. *Die Probleme der Kolosser- und Epheserbriefe*, p. 328.
[65] Described but not accepted by E. F. Scott, *The Epistle of Paul to the Colossians etc.*, p. 240.
[66] C. Chavasse, *The Bride of Christ*, p. 77.
[67] *The Common Life in the Body of Christ*, p. 227.
[68] cf. Isaiah 62⁵, Hosea 3¹.   [69] cf. Revelation 19⁷⁻⁹, 21⁹.

It should be noted, moreover, that the Church's obedience and purity do not constitute the complete meaning of this passage. Of at least equal importance are the implications of the love of Christ for the Church: He gave Himself up in sacrifice for the sake of the Church, and so the Church became 'one flesh' with Him. The joining of man and woman so that 'the two shall become one' is called a great 'mystery', and it means Christ and the Church. But it is not, as G. Gloege remarks, the quality of this union which is called a *musterion*, but the bare fact that Christ has so much love that He came to earth in order to build the community and sustain it by His love.[70] This is the whole point of the figure of the marriage of Christ and the Church.

'Man is made for fellowship of the most intimate kind,' writes Thornton: 'The highest earthly example of this fact is human marriage. For this is the "natural sacrament" of the common life. Man, however, was made for a higher and more intimate fellowship still. He was made for communion with God; and this end has been finally secured through the gracious condescension of God's Son.'[71] The divine *koinōnia*, expressed both in the love of Christ toward the Church and the responding love of Christians toward Him and one another, is experienced also in the marital love of husband and wife. And although the author of the letter intends to draw the analogy from the Christ-Church marriage and apply it to human marriage, the figure is so suggestive that it works both ways, and we can find deeper appreciation of either one in comparison to the other.[72]

There are few authorities who follow the thought of Chavasse, that the figure of the Bride of Christ is more fruitful for the understanding of the Church's nature than that of the Body of Christ. Nevertheless, Chavasse and Thornton have demonstrated that, with respect to the subjection of the Church to God's will, the purity of its members, the sacrifices of Christ for their salvation, the love and *koinōnia* of Christ and the Church, and the essential unity of the Bridegroom and the Bride, this paragraph of Ephesians possesses an abiding value which must not be ignored.

Significant and illustrative as the Bride and the Building may

---

[70] *Reich Gottes und Kirche im Neuen Testament*, p. 303.
[71] *The Common Life in the Body of Christ*, p. 225.
[72] cf. K. L. Schmidt in *TWNT*, III.512.

be as figures of the Church, the Body still plays a far more important rôle in the thought of Ephesians and Colossians and in contemporary theology. Both letters speak of the Church and the Body in such a way as to present them, at least grammatically, as identical entities.[73] They also declare that there is a specific relationship of Christ to the Body: He is the Head of it, the source of its nourishment, growth, direction, and life.[74] No division or schism in the Body is to be admitted, since it is the 'one Body'[75] of which all believers are members.[76] So much is quite clear in the text; but the implications of these ideas are so extensive for our thought about the Church that some very diverse interpretations have been given to them.

We have noted already that in the letters which are concerned with the Church and the Body of Christ, there is no final guarantee that the figure is meant to be understood literally, on the one hand, or metaphorically, on the other. The question has admitted no final answer with respect to 1 Corinthians. However, the argument of those favouring the literal reading becomes increasingly strong as Colossians and Ephesians are studied. There is still no consensus, to be sure. The language of Ephesians is mystical and poetic, rather than prosaic, observes G. Johnston, and he warns that 'there is no need to look for literal realities in the presentation of the doctrine'.[77] Likewise, Brunner says of the Body of Christ, though not in respect to scriptural exposition, that it 'is only a simile, it is not an organic principle'.[78] But the majority of New Testament scholars concur in regarding the Body in Ephesians and probably in Colossians, as the literal Body of Jesus Christ.

Holding in abeyance for a time the problem of *how* the Church is Christ's Body, we observe the following contemporaries agreeing on the literalness of the figure. K. L. Schmidt asserts that in Ephesians 'Christ is the *ekklēsia* Himself, since this is the *sōma Christou*. But then Christ also stands over against the Church, of which He is the *kephalē*. . . . In any case, christology is the same as ecclesiology, and conversely.'[79]

In the same way, S. M. Gilmour states that, although the New Testament use of the 'Body of Christ' wavers between

---

[73] Colossians $1^{18, 24}$, Ephesians $1^{22, 23}$, 5^{23}.
[74] Colossians 1^{18}, 2^{19}, Ephesians 1^{22}, $4^{15, 16}$, 5^{23}.
[75] Colossians 3^{15}, Ephesians 2^{16}, 3^{6}, 4^{4}.   [76] Ephesians 2^{19}, 3^{6}, 5^{30}.
[77] *The Doctrine of the Church in the New Testament*, p. 93.
[78] *The Divine Imperative*, p. 300.   [79] In *TWNT*, III.512.

metaphorical and mystical meaning, in Ephesians 'the Church is the actual Body of the risen Christ, conceived in realistic terms'.[80]

Even though Schlier regards much of this thought as borrowed Gnosticism, he treats the material according to the view that the author of Ephesians meant his words literally, and concludes that 'the Church is the earthly-present Body of the heavenly-present Head'.[81] This all may sound 'fanciful and unreal' to us, observes C. A. A. Scott, and yet 'it represents, so far as a concrete and visible thing can represent an abstract and invisible, the relations and the functions of the community, alike within itself and in relation to its visible Head'.[82] If this is not forthright enough, we may find in the words of B. S. Easton a definitive summary of this view, which considers the Church to be truly the Body of Christ, 'not in the sense of a corporate group but in the wholly realistic sense of an organism filled with life from a single source. The "Body", therefore, is nothing less than the veritable Body of Christ, in which He lives and through which He acts on this earth.'[83]

II. THE 'BODY OF CHRIST' IN CONTEMPORARY THEOLOGY

So may the witnesses be summoned to testify to the realistic interpretation of the Body of Christ. There seems to be little room for doubt that, in the context of the epistles, this was the intended meaning. It was a doctrine of the nature of the Church which fit the religious understanding of Hellenistic Christians especially well. One of the major accomplishments of recent scholarship has been the rediscovery of the nature of the pagan soil on which Christianity had to grow. Much of the thought behind the word 'mystery' in Ephesians can be appreciated in the light of this paganism. For the concept of the Church as the actual Body of the Lord was a mystery indeed; and the author of Ephesians, as W. L. Knox demonstrates, 'established Christianity as a "mystery" as against other "mysteries" which threatened to prove more attractive,' thus being able 'to provide the Church with a more adequate counter-attraction to the mysteries of

[80] In *Christendom*, VI.3(1941).393; cf. W. N. Pittenger, in *Christendom*, IX.2(1944). 209; T. A. Lacey, *The One Body and the One Spirit*, p. 39; O. Cullmann, *Königsherrschaft Christi und Kirche im Neuen Testament*, p. 29; and E. F. Scott, *The Epistles of Paul to the Colossians etc.*, p. 24.
[81] Article *Kephalē* in *TWNT*, III.679. [82] *The Fellowship of the Spirit*, pp. 73, 222.
[83] In *Anglican Theological Review* XXII(1940).166.

Gnosticism'.[84] This judgement is a strictly historical one, and it is well substantiated. However, it would be a distortion of the facts to claim that the Body of Christ can have meaning only in association with the esoteric ideas of the pagan mysteries, as Käsemann and Schlier imply.[85] Apart from these religions, and in terms of biblical thought, the figure of the Body is a comprehensible and thoroughgoing concept of the Church, whether interpreted against the background of paganism or according to modern theology.[86] If this were not so, we would have to discredit all current use of the Body of Christ, so far as it is really serious use, as anachronistic and irrelevant. But this usage of the phrase in present theological discussion about the Church is most frequent, and it raises some critical problems for biblical theology and the Christian faith.

When, for example, the many delegates to the World Conference on Faith and Order, held in Edinburgh in 1937, coming from diverse denominational and theological backgrounds, could proclaim: 'We are at one in confessing belief in the Holy Catholic Church. . . . It is the body of Christ, whose members derive their life and oneness from their one living Head,'[87] it is clear that the concept of the Body is not confined to the time or context of the New Testament. Furthermore, when the spokesmen for the Church of Scotland went farther than the Edinburgh Report, stating their belief more specifically by saying, 'The Church is essentially a Body: it is the Body of Christ, the earthly instrument and vehicle of His Spirit,'[88] they indicated their intention of taking the idea as seriously as did the original readers of Colossians and Ephesians.

But what is specifically involved in taking the Body of Christ 'seriously' in the present time? The problems which come to the fore may be clarified in the course of the discussion of the following subjects: (1) The meaning of being 'in Christ' as related to being 'in the Church'; (2) the relation of Jesus Christ, the Head, to the Body; (3) the idea of the Church as the 'extension of the

---

[84] *St. Paul and the Church of the Gentiles*, pp. 190f.
[85] Käsemann, *Leib und Leib Christi*, pp. 163f.; Schlier, *Christus und die Kirche im Epheserbrief*, pp. 37-48.
[86] A. Schweitzer, *The Mysticism of Paul the Apostle*, p. 121, points out that the author of Ephesians, in placing speculation about the Church alongside the idea of the Body of Christ, failed to see that the Body exhaustively expresses all that can be said about the Church.
[87] *Faith and Order, Edinburgh 1937* (edited by L. Hodgson), p. 230.
[88] From the *Report of the Commission for the Interpretation of God's Will in the Present Crisis*, quoted by F. W. Dillistone, *Theology Today* (1945), p. 57.

Incarnation'; and (4) the consequences of conceiving of the Church as a true organism.

(1) The numerous occurrences of the phrase 'in Christ' in the letters of Paul indicate that this idea occupied a primary position in his thought, but it has long been a point of controversy for modern interpreters of Paul. To a wide extent, this phrase, which has been termed the expression of Paul's 'Christ-mysticism', has been understood as a mystical experience of union between the individual person and the ever-present Christ. Support for such an interpretation is not difficult to find. Paul writes that he was crucified with Christ,[89] baptized into His death, and brought to newness of life in His resurrection.[90] Everyone who is 'in Christ' escapes the sentence of eternal death;[91] he is a 'new creation' (or at least lives in a new creation).[92]

It can hardly be questioned that Paul felt this deep sense of identification with Christ, particularly with regard to both his sufferings and his new-found joy in the life of faith. Neither can it be denied that this feeling, as well as the language describing it, are mystical. Still, many theologians are dissatisfied with the purely individualistic interpretation of being 'in Christ'. They maintain that this idea must be considered together with the strong communal element in Paul's teaching, his emphasis upon the meaning of baptism, and his conception of the *ekklēsia* as the Body of Christ. When these factors are included in the whole context of Paul's thought, the meaning of being 'in Christ' must be altered considerably. Instead of a union between the individual and Christ, we now see the individual in relation to the community, which is the Body of Christ. In short, Paul's phrase, 'in Christ', is said by many to be the equivalent of 'in the Church'.[93]

This is the way in which R. Bultmann reads Paul's thought. 'Far from being a formula for mystical alliance, *en Christō* is primarily an ecclesiological formula and designates the being inducted in the Body of Christ through baptism,' he writes; and 'since the community into which baptism incorporates is the

---

[89] Romans 6³, ⁵, Galatians 2²⁰, Colossians 2¹², 3³. [90] Romans 6⁴, Colossians 2¹², 3¹.
[91] Romans 8¹. This is basic meaning of 'in Christ' for Barth; cf. *The Epistle to the Romans*, p. 272.
[92] 2 Corinthians 5¹⁷, which Goodspeed translates, 'So if any one is in union with Christ, he is a new being,' but which Moffatt renders: 'There is a new creation whenever a man comes to be in Christ.' The latter has an eschatological reference.
[93] After his study of the phrase, A. Oepke finds this to be just one of five possible meanings of *en Christō*: Article *en* in *TWNT*, II.573f.

eschatological community, the formula has at once an ecclesiological and eschatological sense'.[94]

The same line of thought is developed by A. Schweitzer in the following way: The transition in Paul's thought from the state of faith-in-Christ to that of being-in-Christ occurs automatically in baptism, and only then.[95] 'The mystical body of Christ remains an enigma so long as it is not understood in the light of the fundamental concept of the community of God. . . . The being-in-Christ is in fact inexplicable until it is made intelligible by the concept of the mystical body of Christ.'[96] This ecclesiological interpretation of the phrase is a radical departure from the individualistic one, and it has lately been championed by leading scholars.

C. H. Dodd makes this view the principle for understanding 'in Christ' in the epistles. 'Paul's sense of union with Christ is conditioned by the experience of life in a society controlled by His Spirit, as well as constituted historically by His act. It is a sense of being included in the "corporate personality" of Christ which is manifest in the Church. . . . To be "in Christ" does not depend on states of abstraction or ecstasy—though Paul knew such states. It depends on active fellowship with others who are also "members of Christ" '.[97] If such is the accepted meaning of being 'in Christ' in Paul's undisputed letters, it is true also in Ephesians, where Christ and the Church are brought so closely together.[98]

Following the lead of these biblical scholars is not to the liking of G. Johnston, however. He finds fault in particular with the view of Schweitzer. '*En Christō* cannot always mean in the Body of Christ,' he asserts, 'nor is it certain that the corporate idea is the original of the personal'.[99] Christ is not to be so nearly identified with the community, he continues, nor is baptism the act by which, for Paul, a man becomes 'in Christ', since faith working through love in the heart of a man is the prerequisite for baptism, and the rite simply seals what has already happened. In addition, Johnston criticizes Schweitzer's failure to perceive that Christ, while being integrally connected with the Church, is also standing separately and over against the community as its Lord and Redeemer.[100] Here he makes a valid distinction, contradicting those

---
[94] *Theologie des Neuen Testaments*, p. 307.
[95] *The Mysticism of Paul the Apostle*, p. 116. [96] ibid., p. 117.
[97] *The Epistle of Paul to the Romans*, p. 88; cf. R. N. Flew, *Jesus and His Church*, p. 153.
[98] cf. E. Käsemann, *Leib und Leib Christi*, p. 156.
[99] *The Doctrine of the Church in the New Testament*, p. 88. [100] ibid., p. 89.

who would see in Pauline theology and modern faith the necessity for regarding Christ and the Church as virtually and exhaustively identical.

Such complete identification is admitted and defended by certain theologians, for whom the concept of being 'in Christ' is equivalent to being 'in the Church'. Such was the contention of the Congregationalist, P. T. Forsyth, when he wrote: 'To be in Christ is in the same act to be in the Church. Anything we do in the way of joining the Church by a confession of faith is only making explicit in the statement what is already implicit in the fact.'[101] This may sound extremely 'Catholic' to others of the evangelical tradition, but it is not uncommon to find the same point of view among theologians of the 'low church' wing of Protestantism. The ecclesiology of C. C. Morrison is a fair example. Developing his thought on the basis of what he considers to be the truly Pauline position, he stresses the complete identification of the Church with Christ, and conversely, so that to be 'in' either Christ or the Church amounts to exactly the same thing.[102]

Now this doctrine is very uncongenial to the faith of many Protestants, of course, for ostensibly it would make the names 'Christ' and 'Church' interchangeable, thereby depriving Christ of the uniqueness He possesses as Son of the Father, and exalting the Church in a way which seems to them unwarranted, or even undesirable. Perhaps, however, the idea of identification is not held in such a thoroughgoing manner as the casual reader might think. It is hardly conceivable that any Christian would believe in the Church as the Messiah, Redeemer, and Second Person of the Trinity, though imprecise usage of language about the Body of Christ may actually imply such a belief. This is no more justifiable in the light of Paul's teaching than the opposite belief, which considers the relationship between the believer and Christ as an exclusively individualistic one. Neither pole of thought, if held in the absolute sense, would take into account the paradoxical connexion between Christ and the Church. For while there is certainly unity of the believers in and with Christ, there is also a fundamental distinction between the Lord and the people. The Christian is a participant in the life of Christ, both in His

---

[101] *The Church and the Sacraments*, p. 57.
[102] *What is Christianity?* p. 156; cf. the identical idea in F. Kattenbusch, *Festgabe für Harnack*, p. 158: 'So is it for Paul the same, whether one lives *en Christō* or *en ekklēsia*.'

suffering and crucifixion, and in baptism into newness of life.[103] Thus the many are included in the one Man, Christ, without the loss of individual identity. The Body is Christ and yet He is the Head of the Body: the Body is inseparable from the Head and yet distinct from Him. For practical purposes of faith and experience, therefore, it can well be said that the man who is 'in Christ' is in the Body of Christ, the Church; and he who is in the Body as a truly faithful person is 'in Christ'. But the Body and its members have not yet attained the completeness of Christ, the Head.[104] 'Which things are a paradox,' comments Dillistone, 'but only within the paradox can the Church continue to live.'[105]

(2) The tension existing between these two strains of thought on Christ and the Church may appear even more obvious when we consider more carefully the meaning of the term 'Head', as it is applied to Christ in both Colossians and Ephesians. Even in its scriptural use, the word's meaning is contestable and uncertain, so that today there is no unanimity in either its textual interpretation nor in its application to the doctrine of the Church.

To be sure, there exists between the Head and the Body of the Church an inseparable connexion, as in a living organism. To varying degrees of emphasis, most theologians agree upon this point. 'The Lord and the *Ecclesia* belong to each other in such a way that it is impossible to think of one without at the same time thinking of the other,' declares Sasse.[106] There is such an interrelationship between them, observes R. Will, that we may say, Christ lives in the Church and the Church lives in Christ.[107] F. J. Taylor puts the belief in the historical context when he writes: 'Apart from Christ the Church has no meaning and no life, and apart from the Church, Christ is not known in the world. If the Church is spoken of in such a way that it appears to possess a life of its own, aims of its own, and authority of its own, then the facts of its origin and meaning are subjected to a violent treatment they will not bear.'[108] Defined in christological terms, the Church, according to F. Ménégoz, 'is in principle no more separable from Christ than Christ is separable from God'.[109]

---

[103] 2 Corinthians 5$^{14, 15}$, Galatians 3^{27}. These two points of participation are called by L. S. Thornton the 'double polarity' of Paul's thought: *The Common Life in the Body of Christ*, p. 57.
[104] Ephesians 4^{13}.   [105] In *Theology Today* II.1(1945).68.
[106] In *Mysterium Christi*, p. 112.   [107] In *Le Problème de l'Église*, p. 75.
[108] *The Church of God*, p. 71.   [109] *Convictions* (edited by L. Hodgson), p. 12.

What these men declare dogmatically is well illustrated by the analogy of the Head and the Body.

But does this *inseparability* imply an actual *identity*? Again this problem arises, which confronted us in connexion with the meaning of being 'in Christ'. And again there are those who are persuaded that full identity is the scriptural meaning. So A. Nygren asserts: 'Christ is not the Head merely, but the Head of the Church; the Church is not merely the Body, but the Body of Christ. The Body of Christ is Christ Himself. The Church is Christ as He after the resurrection is present among us and meets us here on earth.'[110] Almost the same words are employed by his Swedish colleague, G. Aulén, who writes: 'The Church is not the Body isolated from the Head, but the Body of Christ. The Body of Christ is Christ Himself, the Risen Christ, alive and active on earth.'[111] There is nothing conditional about such statements, and a more positive expression of identity can hardly be imagined. Not even a subordination of the Church to Christ is admitted, since the two are fully one. Most theologians will subscribe to the ancient Ignatian formula, '*ubi Christus, ibi ecclesia*,' but only a few will invert the phrases, as Aulén does,[112] and say, '*ubi ecclesia, ibi Christus*,' thereby exceeding even the New Testament teaching, which, as we have seen, goes very far in the direction of identification but not all the way.

And we are reminded of the importance of the fact that the New Testament does not go all the way to complete identification. Great caution is used, therefore, in the use of these terms by some of the very men who have most earnestly championed the literal interpretation of the Body of Christ. For example, D. Bonhöffer writes in one place: 'The Church is the present Christ Himself. Therewith we gain back an idea about the Church which is often forgotten. We are accustomed to think of the Church as an institution. But the Church should be thought of as a Person.'[113] However, before allowing this idea to be taken in an absolute and unqualified sense, he adds that the lordship of Christ over the Church is the complementary truth, clearly taught in the distinction between the Head and the Body, since Christ has ascended and will come again. Thus, while embracing a realistic

---

[110] In *En bok om kyrkan av svenska teologer*, p. 20; cited by E. Wahlstrom, *Christendom*, XIII.2(1948).232.
[111] In *The Universal Church in God's Design* (W.C.C.), p. 20.
[112] ibid., p. 19.   [113] *Nachfolge*, p. 164.

concept of the Body of Christ, Bonhöffer rejects the extreme view in which Christ and the Church are seen, as it were, to coincide perfectly. Against such a view, T. A. Lacey warns: 'To say that the Church is the body of Christ is not the same as to say that the Church is Christ.'[114]

This warning is intended to keep men from overstepping the limits of what may be understood by the New Testament figure of the Body and the Head. When Aulén asserts that the Body of Christ is Christ Himself, he is promptly accused of pronouncing an outright heresy by I. Wennfors, who points out that in the New Testament, in particular Ephesians 5^{23}, Christ is called the Saviour of the Body, but not of Himself.[115]

As K. Barth expresses this relationship, Jesus Christ is the heavenly Head of the Church; but the Church is, 'as His earthly body, bound to Him as such, and yet as such distinct from Him, who possesses the Church in Himself, but not the Church Him in herself, between whom and her there is no reversible, interchangeable relationship, as certainly as the relationship of master and servant is not reversible.'[116] High as we may exalt the nature of the Church and see in it an expression of the presence of Christ, we are under restraint to keep from reaching the degree of exaltation where the Church and Christ are no longer distinguished from each other.

A similar appeal for restraint and accurate exegesis is made by T. F. Torrance to the writers of the pamphlet, *Catholicity*, written by several Anglican theologians. He criticizes them for regarding the body of the risen Lord as being in no way at all different from the Body of Christ, mystically considered as the Church. But the very purpose of the designation of Christ as Head of the Body is to keep this identification from being made, he declares.[117] While the Body is indeed Christ's, it is not Christ Himself, for He is the Head, 'the inner principle of growth', as Craig remarks.[118] Then how is this riddle of distinction within unity to be understood? If Christ be not identical with the Church, what is the exact relationship He has to it?

One conventional idea is that the Church possesses two natures,

---

[114] *The One Body and the One Spirit*, p. 58.
[115] Files of Commission I, W.C.C., Geneva.
[116] *The Doctrine of the Word of God*, p. 113.
[117] In *Scottish Journal of Theology* II.1(1949).88.
[118] In *The Universal Church in God's Design* (W.C.C.), p. 41.

the divine and the human, even as Christ, and that the divine Head and the human Body can be illustrated by analogy to the dual nature of Christ Himself. Within the framework of this notion could be placed an older interpretation of Ephesians, in which Christ was called the Head of the Body but the Church only its torso, or *Rumpf*, on earth. This was H. J. Holtzmann's way of carrying the figures of Ephesians to their literal conclusion, giving the Church a heavenly direction for its earthly form. Although K. L. Schmidt[119] and H. Schlier [120] have both adopted this idea in recent years, it has been rejected as untrue to the text by Johnston[121] and as oblivious to the ancient understanding of the figure itself by A. V. Ström.[122] According to Ström, this enigmatic figure of the Head must be read in the light of the then contemporary ideas of how one person represents a whole group. The head of the Jewish family, for example, was also considered identical with the whole family. Therefore, when Christ is at one time designated as Head of the Body, and at other times as identical with the Church, it is simply two ways of expressing the same idea. 'Head' and 'torso' did not have to be taken so literally in terms of the human body in the time of the writing of Ephesians, nor was the distinction between the divine and the human in the Church intended to be so exacting and well delineated.

Equally misleading from this point of view is the theory that Christ is to the Church as the soul of a man is to his body. This is an attractive equation and can easily be grasped, and the reasoning seems to proceed as follows: (*a*) man is a unity of soul and body; (*b*) in the same way, the Church is a unity of an invisible nature and visible form; (*c*) in the same way, Christ is the unity of the divine nature and human nature; therefore, (*d*) the Church is a unity of Christ (the soul) and His people (the body). This process moves more by intuition and analogy than by logic, and it breaks down in the comparison of statement (*c*) with (*d*). For so far as we can speak of the mystery of the Incarnation and the Person of Jesus Christ, we must refrain from thinking that His divine nature is merely the *soul* of His human nature. By no analogy can it be shown that the two natures of Christ may be equated with the soul-body relationship in human nature. This dual nature of

[119] In *TWNT*, III.513. [120] *Christus und die Kirche im Epheserbrief*, p. 38.
[121] *The Doctrine of the Church in the New Testament*, p. 92.
[122] In *Svensk Exegetisk Årsbok*, VIII(1943).123.

Christ must always be regarded as the unique and unrepeatable miracle, to which not even the divinely-constituted Church may be compared.

As Torrance distinguishes the ways of thinking about the divine and human elements of the Church, the analogy does not run, 'as God and Man are related in Christ, so the divine and human are related in the Church,' but rather, 'as God and Man are related in Christ, so Christ and the Church are related'.[123] By this he implies that the Church, without losing its character as the true Body of Christ, should not be conceived as having the same relationship to God as Christ has to God, and therefore not be completely identified with Christ. 'If we are really in earnest about thinking of the Church in this fallen world as the Body of Christ (and surely we ought to be), must we not think of her in the form of Christ's humiliation?' he asks.[124] In this question he guards against the unrestrained enthusiasm for the literal interpretation of the Body of Christ, which leads some theologians to ignore the mundane and sinful elements of the Church and regard it as already perfect, in unqualified unity with Christ. Exactly the same caution evidently informs the study with which J. E. L. Newbigin makes his contribution to an understanding of this problem. He concludes that the reason why it is out of the question to regard Christ as the 'soul' of the Church is that there is within the Church another spirit, 'the collective and separate prides and egotisms . . . the unruly wills and affections of sinful men,' which cannot be reconciled to the perfect goodness and sinlessness of Christ.[125] Thus, also, H.-D. Wendland declares that the Church, while being in the form of spirit-body (*geistleibliche Gestalt*), is not the same as the spirit-body of Jesus Christ, because He knew no sin and is not subject to earthly bonds.[126]

As Head of the Body, then, Christ is considered both distinct from the Body and inseparable from it. He unites the Body in Himself, and is yet not to be identified with it. His Spirit gives the Church life and direction, but He is not just the soul of the Church. Again the paradoxical relationship of Christ to the Church, the Head to the Body, becomes manifest.

In connexion with the exegesis of 'Head' (*kephalē*) in Colossians

---

[123] In *Scottish Journal of Theology* II.3(1949).248.
[124] In *Scottish Journal of Theology* II.3(1949).248.
[125] *The Reunion of the Church*, p. 65. [126] In *Luthertum* (1939), p. 234.

and Ephesians, another significant word, equally ambiguous, must be dealt with. This is *plērōma*, the 'fullness' of Christ, of the Church, or of God, depending upon interpretation. Here again the language, though not necessarily the thought, has close parallels in the mystic ideas of Gnosticism, which threatened to adulterate the Christian faith among the people of Asia Minor.[127] However, we may disregard those passages in which the word is used with respect to the fullness of deity in Christ, and examine briefly those in which the Body, or Church, is concerned: Ephesians 1[23] and 4[13].

In speaking of God's action through Christ, the writer of Ephesians declares that God 'has made him the head over all things for the church, which is his body, the fullness of him who fills all in all'. Does *plērōma* here connote an active sense—the Body filling the Head—or a passive sense—the Body is filled by the life of Christ? According to older commentaries, such as W. Lock's, the active sense is probably intended: the Body is 'that which "fills", "completes" Him, makes His revelation and action complete before the world's eyes'.[128] If such be the true meaning, the Church must be indispensable for Christ, for without it He would be incomplete and His revelation imperfect, needing the complementary life of the *ekklēsia* in the world to bring Him to fullness. This interpretation lifts the Church to an exalted position in the divine purpose, but it does so at the expense of the autonomy and lordship of Christ.

The greater number of scholars, therefore, prefer the alternative meaning of *plērōma*, that is, the passive sense. This is expressed with certainty by E. J. Goodspeed's translation: '. . . the indisputable head of the church, which is his body, filled by him who fills everything everywhere.'[129] And it is aptly paraphrased by W. L. Knox in the following way: 'This supremacy of Jesus in the cosmos carries with it supremacy in the Church, the body which He continually fills with Himself just as He is Himself continually being filled with God.'[130] With this exposition, Thornton, E. F. Scott, and Hanson, are in accord.[131] They feel

---

[127] cf. W. L. Knox, *St. Paul and the Church of the Gentiles*, pp. 163f.; L. S. Thornton, *The Common Life in the Body of Christ*, p. 289.
[128] *The Epistle to the Ephesians*, p. 27.
[129] *The New Testament, an American Translation*.
[130] *St. Paul and the Church of the Gentiles*, p. 168.
[131] Thornton, *The Common Life in the Body of Christ*, p. 306; Scott, *The Epistles of Paul to the Colossians etc.*, p. 159; Hanson, *The Unity of the Church in the New Testament*, p. 129.

that a more suitable kind of New Testament christology is manifest in this reading of the text. Christ is still, in a sense, 'dependent' upon the Church for completing His work, but the dependence is not carried to so great a degree as under the former exegesis.

As Thornton develops the fundamental idea of this passage: 'The Church, therefore, is not filled directly with the Godhead . . . Between pure deity and redeemed humanity stands the "one mediator". . . . As Christ is the indispensable mediator of God's fullness, so the Church is the indispensable containers of Christ's fullness. On the first view the Church is empty apart from Christ; on the second view Christ is inaccessible without the Church. The Church apart from Christ would be like an empty wine-cup. Christ without the Church would be like wine which, for lack of a wine-cup, no one could drink.'[132]

However much Christ may need the Church as the instrument of His redemptive work in the world, therefore, it remains subordinate to Him in nature, drawing whatever meaning and value it has from its relation to Him. The Body lives only because it draws power from the Head, but it is not identical with the Head.

The same meaning is inherent in Ephesians 4[13], although here the writer has extended the idea in a cosmological direction, so that he regards Christ as filling the whole universe and not just the Church.

(3) In the foregoing discussion of the relationship between Christ and the Church, as revealed in the biblical concept of the Body of Christ, we have been continually aware of the fact that theologians are tempted to make very extreme statements regarding the identity of Christ and His Church—statements which we suspect in many cases of being unintentional. But perhaps no phrase within this general context has been, and still is, so loosely employed as the one which describes the Church as 'the extension of the Incarnation'.

It cannot be charged, of course, that *all* theologians who use this phrase do so without full understanding of its great implications. Any who adhere to the 'Catholic' ecclesiology, in which there is little reluctance to equate the Church with Christ, can speak of the 'extension of the Incarnation' with no breach of consistency. Thus J. A. F. Gregg begins his essay on the Church

[132] op. cit., p. 310.

by saying: 'The Church is the extension in time and space of the Incarnate Word of God, crucified, ascended, glorified. . . .'[133] While developing the doctrine of the Bride of Christ, Chavasse declares that, just as Eve was the continuation of Adam's body, 'so the Church, her antitype, is the continuation of Christ's Incarnation'.[134] In slightly altered wording we find the same concept in the writings of O. C. Quick,[135] L. S. Thornton,[136] and W. J. Phythian-Adams,[137] all of the Anglican Communion. When pronounced by these men, the idea is quite in harmony with their theological standpoint.

The reader is justifiably astonished, however, to find the same words used by theologians who otherwise have little inclination to make the identification between Christ and the Church in so thoroughgoing a way. When R. Will, for example, discusses the nature of the Church, he explains that because the origins of the Church are divine, 'it is *the incarnation of Christ par excellence*'.[138] In an equally positive mood, J. S. Whale asserts that the 'Church is rightly known by all Christians as "an extension of the Incarnation" ' since it is 'the supreme agency of mediation following upon that of the Incarnate Son of God Himself'.[139] Other theologians, known to be of either Reformed or Evangelical tradition, who have committed themselves to this idea, and generally without attempt to explain what they mean by the words, are W. M. Horton,[140] H. W. Robinson,[141] J. Knox,[142] and William Robinson.[143] Even E. Hayman, writing then as a Quaker, describes the Christian community as 'a new and continuing incarnation'.[144] Somewhat more cautious is E. Lewis, who does claim that the Church is the extension of the Incarnation but only when the 'inner being' of the Church is meant—'inner being' allowing no satisfactory description, he admits![145]

[133] In *The Universal Church in God's Design* (W.C.C.), p. 59.
[134] *The Bride of Christ*, p. 70.
[135] *The Christian Sacraments*, p. 123.
[136] *The Common Life in the Body of Christ*, p. 315.
[137] Files of Commission I, W.C.C., Geneva.
[138] In *Revue d'histoire et de philosophie religieuses*, XII(1932),482.
[139] *Christian Doctrine*, p. 140.
[140] In *The Nature of the Church*, American Theological Committee, p. 51.
[141] *The Christian Experience of the Holy Spirit*, p. 151.
[142] In *The Christian Answer* (H. P. van Dusen, ed.), p. 243.
[143] *Essays on Christian Unity*, pp. 25, 173.
[144] *Worship and the Common Life*, p. 98.
[145] *A Philosophy of the Christian Revelation*, p. 77; and in *The Ministry and the Sacraments* (R. Dunkerley, ed.), pp. 478f.

What does this catalogue of names indicate? It would seem that the very number of theologians agreeing upon this idea is ample testimony to its validity as a theological concept. However, arrayed against them is a considerable number of theologians, who are generally of the same or similar tradition and viewpoint held by the eight men named above; but they are very suspicious, or very critical, of the idea that the Incarnation is extended in the Church.

Some simply propose moderation or restraint in the use of the phrase. 'We may say, if we will, that the Church is the continuation of the Incarnation,' writes T. W. Manson, 'but this, though true, is more awe-inspiring than illuminating. . . . It is, I venture to think, more profitable to begin more modestly and say that the life of the Church is the continuation of the Messianic Ministry.'[146] It is perhaps possible that this latter idea of continuation is what some persons really mean when they speak of the Incarnation in this way. But even Manson holds that the Church does truly extend the Incarnation, however the concept may fail to illuminate our thinking. By the 'more profitable' explanation of the Church as the continuing ministry of Christ, he does not mean merely that Christians follow the pattern of humble service which so thoroughly characterized the ministry of Jesus. Rather, he explains that the Church is a 'continuation *by the Messiah*' of that ministry, and so the instrumental value of the Church again becomes evident.

Nevertheless, this kind of moderation is still insufficient to prevent the idea of identification of Christ and Church, which some theologians consider to be untenable. And they oppose the doctrine of the Church as the extension of Christ's Incarnation for two reasons.

First, if the Church is the extension of the Incarnation, we must revise our belief concerning the nature of the Incarnation. For the christological judgement which is raised against this notion is that Jesus Christ was incarnate only once. 'The Word became flesh and dwelt among us' for a time, but after that the dwelling of the Word was not flesh but Spirit. 'For Christ also died for sins once for all,' according to 1 Peter 3^{18}; and in Hebrews 9^{26} the thought is continued: 'He has appeared once for all at the end of the age.' With such finality, such *Einmaligkeit*, the idea

[146] *The Church's Ministry*, p. 20.

of any extension of the Incarnation cannot be reconciled, unless the crucial word degenerates from its meaning of 'becoming flesh' and is understood as the continuing but invisible spiritual presence of Christ.[147]

Moreover, it is pointed out by Torrance that it is a fallacy to impute to Christ an incompleteness of Incarnation which must be made up by the *ekklēsia*. He does not disparage the idea that the Church participates in the wholeness of Christ, enjoying the relation of *koinōnia* with Him and the blessing of His abiding in the Church; 'but because that *wholeness* is already whole', he insists, 'there can be no talk of an extension of the Incarnation or historical continuity of the Body of Christ.'[148] Here he raises the question of Christ's self-sufficiency, which was the point at stake in the interpretation of 'fulness' in Ephesians 1^{23}, and which is of critical importance for the whole christology of the New Testament. This is not a questioning of the belief that the presence of Christ really constitutes the Church, for upon this most Christian theologians can agree. But as to the mode or manner of Christ's presence, the words of F. J. Leenhardt lend strong support to the contention made by Torrance: 'All that is visible of the Church is not Christ. Christ is not in the ecclesiastical Body as He was in the fleshly body at the time of His Incarnation.'[149]

In the second place, certain theologians criticize this belief as unwarranted because of the embarrassing implications which must result as logical consequences if the Church is truly the continuation of Christ's Incarnation. Even though he was not reluctant to regard being-in-Christ and being-in-Church as virtually synonymous, P. T. Forsyth balks on the idea now being considered. He feels that the inevitable end of such a doctrine must be the Roman Catholic dogmas of the Mass and the Papacy. This is 'the Catholic form of the engaging fallacy of liberalism', he observes: the fallacy that Christ is simply God-in-man for all men.[150] In order to refute the notion that Christ loses His identity in the Church and can be contained by the Church, Forsyth must deny what he considers to be the false teaching that the Incarnation is prolonged in the Church.

[147] cf. J. E. L. Newbigin, *The Reunion of the Church*, p. 60.
[148] In *Scottish Journal of Theology*, II.1(1949).88.
[149] In *La Sainte Église Universelle*, p. 88.
[150] *The Church and the Sacraments*, p. 77.

Newbigin brings to light another *impasse* to which this idea inevitably leads. One of the functions of the Church is to proclaim the Gospel in preaching, to bear witness to the life of Jesus as the revelation of God and the accomplishment of redemption for mankind. But 'if the Church is in itself, as an institution, the incarnation of God', he reasons, 'then there is no need for it to point beyond itself to Christ—as true preaching must do'.[151] And is it necessary to press a description of what happens to the Church when it neglects the preaching of the Word and points to itself rather than to the Lord of the Church, Jesus Christ?

Another essential element of the Church comes into jeopardy as soon as the idea of the extension of the Incarnation is actually applied to the life of the Church. This is the *humility* of the Church, its obligation to be, like its Lord, 'in the form of a servant'. When Johnston attacks the use of the phrase in question, therefore, he charges: 'It lacks the essential humility of the Church as at best an Apostolic society, witnessing to the Revelation but always imperfectly. This is true whether one is thinking of the empirical institutions of the Church or the Church in its ideal nature.'[152] As Reinhold Niebuhr, brooding over the un-Christlike pretensions and actions of many an ecclesiastical body, writes: 'The deification of the Church is spiritually dangerous, however conceived. The Catholic doctrine that the Church is an "extension of the Incarnation" represents a significant shift of emphasis from the Pauline-Biblical doctrine that the Church is the "body of Christ". For when conceived as the body it is clear that it remains subject to the laws of historical reality.'[153] Even the worthiest motives of the historical Church are subject to corruption from within, he would insist, and Jesus' kind of humility—that which really makes a man the greatest of all—can easily be turned into its opposite, which is spiritual pride. Can the Church be the extension of the Incarnation and still harbour members of the Body of Christ who are sinful?

This perplexing problem of sin in the Church is the one to which Newbigin finally appeals as a refutation of the extension idea. He writes: 'Even the man in Christ is a sinner. This fact alone makes the analogy of the Incarnation an extremely

---

[151] *The Reunion of the Church*, p. 61.
[152] Files of Commission I, W.C.C., Geneva.
[153] *The Nature and Destiny of Man*, II.144f.

misleading one. What is characteristic of the Church as a human society is not merely that it is visible and tangible as Christ was in His flesh, but that it is sinful, which He was not.[154] To deny that sin exists within the Church, even in its highest manifestations, would be foolish and hypocritical. Paul did not charge that the gross sins of the Corinthians kept them from being part of the Body of Christ. Even while being the Body of Christ, the sinless One, the Church 'is also the congregation of sinners, and is itself sinful in action', remarks Bonhöffer.[155] And Martin Luther once observed, '*Das Antlitz der Kirche ist das einer Sünderin!*'[156] And, to borrow another favourite phrase of Luther's, the duality of the Church is evident in the fact that it, like the Christian man himself, is *simul justus et peccator* justified and a sinner at the same time.

To recognize the sinfulness of the Church, and still to hold tenaciously to the notion of the extension of the Incarnation, seems to drive a person to the awkward position of asserting that only the 'inner being', the divine or invisible nature of the Church, continues to embody Christ. This would be what G. Dehn rightly calls a 'docetic ecclesiology', one which sees only an appearance of the Body of Christ in the Church. But, he continues: 'The Word truly became incarnate, and so also the Body of Christ, the Church, is found in the actual conditions of human life.'[157] Among these conditions it is subject to sin. Indeed, as Brunner asserts, it is 'permeated with sin'. He goes on to explain that this sinfulness did not intrude upon the Church incidentally in its history; it belongs to the very nature of the Church.[158] Both on historical and theological grounds is he justified in saying this: historically, because perfect sinlessness has never been known in the Church; theologically, because the Church, like a person within it, in spite of having been redeemed, is still short by far of final sanctification.

These theologians, then, would urge their colleagues to exercise much caution in ascribing to the Church, in even its highest form or conception, the title of 'extension of the Incarnation', unless it is clearly understood how much the literal meaning of the phrase implies.

(4) Two more aspects of the problem of the meaning of the

---

[154] *The Reunion of the Church*, p. 62.   [155] *Sanctorum communio*, p. 125.
[156] Quoted by E. Rietschel, *Das Problem der unsichtbar-sichtbaren Kirche bei Luther*, p. 22.
[157] *Man and Revelation*, p. 129.   [158] *The Divine Imperative*, p. 526.

Body of Christ today remain to be discussed. The first involves a controversy over the idea that the Church is literally an organism, as the word 'Body' suggests. The second is related to it, for it concerns the fundamental inner condition of the Church, which is the *koinōnia* of all its members.

(*a*) The phrase 'Body of Christ', when applied to the Church, spontaneously calls to the minds of most people the image of an organism. We are not interested in the imaginative attempts made in former times to find in the various groups or personages within the Church the counterparts to the different limbs and organs of the human body. Neither are we concerned with the misguided efforts to read back into the mind of Paul a knowledge of anatomy and biology which he could not have possessed. The figure of the Body of Christ can stand on its own validity without these artificial supports of spurious exegesis.

As we have noted well already, there are opposing sides to the question of the literal meaning of the Body. According to the nature of one's interpretation of the New Testament language and theology, the Body of Christ is either a very suggestive, though often limited and misleading, metaphor, or else it is the name of a supernatural entity, possessing both human and divine nature, which is related to Christ in a way which may be called 'mystical' or 'mysterious'. The same antithesis exists between the opposing concepts of the Church as an organism.

On the one hand, those who claim a 'Catholic' ecclesiology will agree with F. Heiler's statement that the Church is a 'living organism' in the real sense of the words, signifying the corporeality of the continuing presence of Christ in the world.[159] In this organism we are made one with Christ, not individually, but as a whole people,[160] and in a manner which our finite reason cannot grasp. So Thornton writes: 'All that happened to the physical organism of His body (suffering, death, burial, and resurrection) now happens to us also. It happened to Him in the literal facts of history. It happens to us in a mystical order. . . . Our incorporation into Christ identifies us with the history of the new organism to which we now belong.'[161]

---

[159] Quoted and criticized by E. Foerster *Theologische Rundschau* (1932), p. 132.
[160] 'We still think of At-one-ment as something which transpires between God and an infinite number of separate selves, forgetting that it is the corporate union of the *People* with the Presence': W. J. Phythian-Adams, *The People and the Presence*, p. 263.
[161] 'The Body of Christ' in *The Apostolic Ministry* (K. E. Kirk ed.), p. 77.

If we look for a rational understanding of this 'mystery' of the Body, the speculations of W. J. Phythian-Adams may be helpful. He borrows the findings of evolutionary biology with regard to the development of lower organism to higher ones and applies the evolutionary principle to the social organisms.[162] For example, the remarkable co-operation and interdependence of a bee-hive or an ant-hill constitutes a low form of social organism; the lives of animals in families, packs or herds represent a higher form; and the communal life of human beings a still higher. So he concludes that on a still higher level the human participation in the life of the Body of Christ may be considered as the evolving organism of a recreative humanity, which is growing up into the fullness of Christ. Such a provocative theory merits a separate discussion, but it is introduced here only to emphasize the seriousness with which the idea of the Body as an organism is held.

Against this literal interpretation there have been raised strong voices of protest, stressing one argument or another, and some of these have already been treated in the preceding pages. But a protest of particular relevance to the Church's present situation, and of all civilization's situation, has been launched by F. W. Dillistone. Having reviewed the various reasons why some theologians are led to regard the Body of Christ as a living organism, he reaches the conclusion: 'It cannot, in fact, be too strongly emphasized that any organism-theory, whether in Church or State, interpreted literally and biologically, must result finally in the terrible extremes of modern totalitarianism.'[163] The course of recent history, both political and ecclesiastical, has furnished him with evidence which seems difficult to refute. He thinks of the way in which Christians have employed methods for restraint of personal freedom which are just as ruthlessly effective as the methods used by political dictatorship. And when the Church or State acts on the assumption that the social group is an organism, it follows that those parts which refuse or fail to conform to the required patterns for the whole must be suppressed or cut off.

But *must* this totalitarianism be the result of a belief in the Church as a real organism? A denial hardly seems possible. And yet, the argument of Dillistone can be refuted, so far as the 'terrible extremes' are concerned. The crucial question is not *whether* there is a totalitarian authority in the Church, but *which*

[162] op. cit., Epilogue, pp. 254-83.   [163] In *Theology Today* II.1 (1945).59f.

authority is pre-eminent. It is on this point that Phythian-Adams asserts that within the organic Body of Christ an 'entire surrender of our individual selves', of our very will, is necessary, but the surrender is to Jesus Christ and not to the corrupted will of any creaturely power.[164] Paul did not hesitate to call a Christian a 'slave' or 'servant' (*doulos*) of Christ,[165] nor should any persons consider his obligation to be wholly obedient to the divine will as an infringement upon his inherent personal liberty. Service and obedience to the Christian community should not be construed to be service under any authority but that of Christ.

From this latter point of view, which is unquestionably biblical in content, the charge made by Dillistone seems to have missed the mark. Ostensibly this is because he refers only to the temporal power of a person or group in a church, and not the power of Christ. If the organism-theory leads inevitably to a corrupt totalitarianism, which is contrary to Christ, that is surely to be opposed. But this is the true situation only when persons within the Church arrogate to themselves the place and authority of Christ. Historical evidence can be produced to show how this has often happened, to the great shame and detriment of the Church, but in itself it is not an adequate repudiation of the organism-theory as such. This has to be challenged on theological, rather than historical, grounds.

(*b*) When all this has been said about the Body of Christ—its meaning in the New Testament, its relationship to Christ as the Head, and its organic nature—we emerge from the tangles of theological discussion and argumentation, still somewhat confused and a little weary, and witness in the plain light of experience that rare quality which makes the Church truly the Body of Christ: the *koinōnia*. Just as the first Christians, when they became members of the Body, found that they had become bound to one another by common ties, which were even stronger than those natural ties of family, race, religion and nation, so this *koinōnia* has characterized the communal life of the Church in every generation of its history, varying in degree, to be sure, but never lacking altogether. We have already considered at length in Chapter Two how the *koinōnia* is regarded as a work of the Holy Spirit, as participation of persons in the gifts of God. The concept

[164] *The People and the Presence*, p. 265.   [165] 1 Corinthians 6^{22}.

of the Body of Christ does not alter this meaning, but supplements and enlarges it for our understanding.

The earliest Pauline references to the Body of Christ were intended to illustrate the mutuality of life in the brotherhood. As T. A. Lacey repeats the idea: 'Each one is so identified with the whole that each is a member of everyone. Union can be stretched no farther.'[166] Such is the organic life of the Church in its ideal: the life-in-union, life-in-love of those who are united in faith.[167]

But faith in Christ is not an external point of reference to which the *koinōnia* experience is directed. For Christ is present in the Body, at its centre of life and energy, the Head; and the calling of the Church is to live His life in such a way as to represent Christ truly in the world. To the extent to which the Church lives in compromise with the sin of the world and fails to reflect the life of the Spirit, it is a defection from its essential nature as Christ's Body. The seriousness of this responsibility is underscored by Thornton's interpretation of the ground of Christian ethics: namely that 'such virtues as truthfulness and chastity are urged by New Testament writers, not on the ground that they are what the individual owes to his own dignity, but because untruthfulness and unchastity violate the fellowship of the Body of Christ, transgress its fundamental law of *agapē*, and grieve the Holy Spirit, who is the bond of unity in the new community'.[168] When all ethical behaviour is placed under this judgement, when a person knows himself to be inseparable from the Church so long as his faith in Christ is sincere, when participation in the fellowship of the Christian community is recognized as participation in the continuing ministry of Christ upon earth, the meaning of the Body of Christ has been apprehended.

[166] *The One Body and the One Spirit*, p. 42.
[167] cf. W. N. Pittenger in *Christendom*, IX.2(1944).210, where he likens this concept to the Eastern Orthodox word, *Sobornost*.
[168] *The Incarnate Lord*, p. 276.

CHAPTER FOUR

THE WORD OF GOD AS THE CHURCH'S AUTHORITY

I. THE NEED FOR AUTHORITY

So long as the Church exists in the world, as the manifestation of the presence of Jesus Christ, it has work to do and many tasks to fulfil. It must live to worship God, to propagate the Gospel of Christ to all mankind, to serve those who are in need of comfort and help, and to provide for the spiritual well-being of all who are drawn into its fellowship. The Church does not exist for its own sake, but rather to accomplish the commission which was given to it by Jesus Christ. Just as He had to do the work which God had given Him, so the Church bears the continuing responsibility of being active and effective among men for the glory of God.

In the course of carrying out this commission, however, the Church is constantly being confronted by the problem of its authority. How is it to know the degree to which it is fulfilling the divine intention? How can it know with assurance that the message it proclaims to the world is based upon the authoritative source? How can its decisions and choices be so guided as to be in harmony with the will of its Lord?

Because Christians are well aware of the close but subordinate relationship of the Church to Christ, its Head, they repeatedly turn and look to Him for guidance and direction. They seek communication from Him, not in the sense of occult or mystical immediacy, but in the sense of understanding to as high a degree as possible the profound meaning of the divine revelation in Him. Otherwise expressed, they desire to know Him more perfectly as the Word of God and to recognize the fact that the Church stands always under the judgement of the divine Word, which in Christ Jesus was incarnate and living among men.

Not since the sixteenth century has the concept of the Word of God received so much serious attention in Protestant theology as it has during the past thirty years. This meaningful phrase, so frequently and emphatically used throughout the Bible, has at times been almost forgotten by theologians in some quarters of the Church, while by others it has been applied exclusively to the Bible itself. This application of the phrase is surely valid, but, as we shall see, it by no means exhausts the content of the Word. To a large extent the theology of the Reformation was based upon the recovery of the full meaning of the concept of the Word of God, not only for the individual's faith, but very decidedly for the Church as a whole. That a great many Protestants, representing various denominations and types of theology, have lately come to a new appreciation of the importance, indeed the primary importance, of the Word of God for the Church, is a vivid sign of the current trend toward the rediscovery of the genius of the Reformation.

A survey of recent thought on the subject of the Word of God reveals that no really significant advance has been made over the interpretations of the reformers themselves. But the amount of serious re-thinking about the meaning and centrality of the Word in the life of the Church is clearly discernible in contemporary theological writing.

II. WHAT IS MEANT BY THE WORD OF GOD

The basic meaning of any 'word' is that it is a bearer of communication between one person and another. This too is the fundamental meaning of the Word of God; it is God's communication to man, His self-revelation. On this simple definition there is consensus of agreement, but far more is implied by the concept than this. For in Christian faith the Word of God is known primarily as a Person and only secondarily in the form of spoken or written language. Jesus Christ *is* the Word of God, and it is scarcely conceivable that in Christian theology the Word should be regarded as being in any way distinct from Him. To say that Jesus Christ, in His earthly, human life, in His death, and in His risen life is the divine Word, above all other forms of it, is simply to restate the primary proposition of the Christian faith.

Even so, despite what seems to be so obvious for some, theologians of recent years have found it necessary to emphasize this concept of Christ as the Word, calling it to the attention of

Christians who have tended to forget the fact in their theology. The Word of God means the communication of God to men, not simply of a law or a particular message or doctrine about God, but of God Himself. God effected this but partially and imperfectly in pre-Christian history and the prophets, through the lives and speech of chosen men. It was in the Incarnate Word alone that His communication was perfect and whole.

But something else must be said about the Incarnation of the Word, lest the revelation be misconstrued as an abstract philosophical concept. That God reveals Himself in Jesus Christ means much more than a miraculous occurrence in history, which may be treated academically. Abstractly considered, the Incarnation cannot be called the Gospel; historically viewed, the life of Jesus is not the unique revelation of God's Word. But when the fact of Incarnation and all the events which constituted the earthly life of Jesus between Bethlehem and Pentecost are apprehended by faith, they are in the full sense the 'good news' of salvation and the perfect revelation of God's love, mercy, and forgiveness. While some theologians place the major emphasis upon the bare fact that the Word was made flesh in Jesus, they would do well not to forget that the consequence of this Incarnation is what really gives meaning to the fact. Nathaniel Micklem thus remarks rightly that the Protestant doctrine of the Word always implies the Gospel, and this may be summed up in two sentences of the New Testament: 'God was in Christ reconciling the world unto Himself', and 'God so loved the world that He gave His only begotten Son, that whosoever believeth on Him should not perish, but have everlasting life.'[1]

It is Jesus Christ Himself, then, and not any teaching or ideas about Him, who is the final Word for the Church and for all mankind. Here we are on the bed-rock of the Christian concept of authority. But when this is recognized as being true, how are we to understand the manner in which the Word of God comes to be known by Christians in every generation? Does God's communication stop with the withdrawal of Jesus from human sight, or is the Word which was Incarnate in Him still being given to men for their salvation? To find the obvious but very far-reaching answer to these questions we must turn attention to what Karl Barth calls the 'two-fold mediacy' by which the 'immediate Word

[1] *What Is the Faith?* pp. 62, 68.

of God' becomes known to us: preaching and the Scriptures.[2]

(1) The Word of God is known first in the preaching of the Gospel, the *kērugma*, or proclamation about Jesus Christ. Jesus Himself appears early in the Synoptic stories as a preacher, following upon His fervently preaching forerunner, John the Baptist.[3] No sooner had the disciples received the Holy Spirit at Pentecost than they began proclaiming the news of the resurrected Lord.[4] How else but by preaching can a man come to faith? asked Paul, for 'faith comes from what is heard, and what is heard comes by the preaching of Christ'.[5] 'Woe to me if I preach not the Gospel!' he exclaimed.[6] Nothing seems more apparent than that the entire history of the Church has exhibited the central rôle of such proclamation, whether by ordained preachers or laymen, whether in prepared sermons or personal testimonies and eloquent actions.

Such preaching is surely not a secondary, accidental aspect of the Church's life. Just the contrary, it is an indispensable element of the Church, the means by which God communicates with men, and as such it is properly called the Word of God. As Barth observes: 'The presupposition which makes proclamation to be proclamation and therewith the Church to be the Church is the Word of God. . . . The Word of God now preached means . . . man's language about God, in which and through which God Himself speaks about Himself.'[7] This may be said seriously in spite of the great spate of preaching in the Church which is a different sort of 'folly' from that which Paul described in his own preaching! Surely there is some preaching which is unworthy to be called the Word of God, and is recognized as unworthy by its failure to concern itself with the love of God revealed in Jesus Christ, i.e. with the Gospel. In the words of Brunner: 'God wills to do more than "say something" to us, or even than to "communicate" something to us: the content of His communication is Himself.'[8] If such be true, we see the temptations and dangers which are implicit in the holding to such a lofty concept of preaching; for a preacher can become obsessed either with his utter unworthiness to be a vessel of the Word, or with the position of authority which his place in the pulpit seems to give him. Obsession with either extreme is, of course, in opposition to the

---

[2] *The Doctrine of the Word of God*, p. 136. [3] Mark 1^{14} and parallels.
[4] Acts $2^{14\text{ff}}$.   [5] Romans $10^{14, 17}$.   [6] 1 Corinthians 9^{16}.
[7] *The Doctrine of the Word of God*, pp. 98, 106. [8] *Revelation and Reason*, p. 109.

idea that preaching is a form of the Word. For it is not the act of preaching itself which is the Word, but that to which the act bears witness, Jesus Christ: the events of His unique life, His words, His death and resurrection.

Moreover, the failure to apprehend the meaning of preaching as the Word of God, whether in the form of a full sense of unworthiness or in the form of too much self-confidence, often is due to a misapprehension of the work of the Holy Spirit. The disciples testified to the belief that they preached in the power of the Holy Spirit,[9] and were just as certain that it was the Spirit who made possible the reception of their proclamation.[10] Difficult as such a doctrine may be for many modern minds, it is true to the New Testament to declare that no preaching by itself, even preaching about Jesus Christ, is in itself the Word of God, until the Spirit actively interprets the message.

Since the time when Melanchthon[11] and Calvin[12] sought to guard against all preaching which does not bear the Word of God, by insisting that the preaching be 'right' and 'sincere', it has been the distress and weakness of the Church that much of its preaching has failed to proclaim the Gospel of Jesus Christ. But when we take the biblical standpoint and consider the pseudo-preaching of that which does not communicate the Word of God, we recognize that this is not preaching at all, but another kind of discourse, which may well be religious, ethical, and inspirational, but which is still not the Word. If the Word is in the preaching, then, it must be borne in mind that true preaching is only that which concerns itself intentionally with the proclamation of the Word in conjunction with the Holy Spirit.

(2) *The Word of God is also the Holy Scriptures.* The relation between the written word and the Word of God may not be so close as that between the oral word and the Word. As Brunner holds, the earliest basis of the faith of the Church was nothing which Jesus wrote, nor even the written records about Him, but the spoken testimony of those who knew Him.[13] Even so, he continues, 'the Christian Church stands and falls with the written New Testament' because these books and letters are the legible form of the witness to God's revelation in Christ. To this the content and the whole intention of the New Testament are

[9] 1 Corinthians 2^4. [10] ibid., 2^{12}, 1^3. [11] *Augsburg Confession*, Art. VII.
[12] *Institutes of the Christian Religion*, Book IV.1.9. [13] *Revelation and Reason*, pp. 125-7.

directed: 'That which was from the beginning, which we have heard, which we have seen with our eyes, which we have looked upon and touched with our hands, concerning the word of life.'[14]

This is not to say that *only* the New Testament may be called the Word of God, although some spiritual descendants of Marcion in the present time may be tempted to feel this, if not to express it. Without relying upon typological interpretation or forcing historic and prophetic materials into a strictly Christian mould, we can still produce abundant evidence from the Old Testament to demonstrate that it merits full recognition by Christians as part of the written Word of God.[15] The fact that Jesus Himself, as well as the primitive Church, regarded and used the Old Testament as their authoritative Scriptures should be sufficient warning for those who would have it entirely supplanted by the New Testament.

This is not the place to raise the pertinent questions of criticism of the biblical text, but it is important to consider the problem of the justification for speaking of the Bible as the Word of God. This always is seen to be a matter of faith rather than of historical and scientific criticism, of biblical content rather than text and form. Obviously one cannot regard the Bible as a singular means by which God reveals Himself without maintaining a certain attitude of faith toward the Bible. By faith the Bible is accepted as the canon, or rule, in such a way as to distinguish it from similar literature, which cannot be claimed as the Word of God. History and criticism can only show that the canon *was* accepted as authoritative, but they cannot prove that one *should* accept this canon. The only alternative to the highly relativistic attitude toward the authority of the canon, to which all purely rational inquiry must lead, is the attitude of faith, which declares that Christians did not make the Bible a canon, but that 'the Bible constitutes itself the canon . . . because it has imposed itself as such upon the Church and invariably does so'.[16] This judgement of Barth's is recalled by the statement of C. H. Dodd, that the Church 'did not at first regard these writings as specially authoritative because they were canonical; they became canonical

---

[14] 1 John 1¹.
[15] cf. G. Aulén, *The Faith of the Christian Church*, pp. 367f.
[16] K. Barth, *The Doctrine of the Word of God*, p. 120.

because they had already made good their authority'.[17] Although problems of authenticity and authorship were undoubtedly considered important, and still are, the more essential factor in regarding the Bible canonically was, and still is, the sufficiency of its witness to the revelation of God for the salvation of men. As in all preaching, so in regard to the Bible, the written word is only *imago verbi*, suggesting what is meant by revelation, but the Word of God is the actual meaning itself.[18] Therefore, for the Christian it is not correct to say that the Bible is the Word of God because it makes that claim for itself, nor because the Church has decreed it so in defining the canon. Instead, the Word of God communicated in the Bible is that which authenticates the written word as 'Holy' Scripture and gives validity to the canon.[19]

Two misunderstandings of the idea that the Bible is the Word of God are still in wide currency today, both of which are vulnerable on the ground that they enclose the Word in a rigid and static form. The first of these is what Brunner calls 'an academic view of the nature of revelation', by which he means that, accordin to this attitude, the Word is considered to be revealed and final doctrine.[20] Rather than being received as the Gospel of God's mighty acts, His love and Incarnation, the revelation is interpreted as a body of religious doctrines which must be accepted and believed without doubt or reservation. From this viewpoint, the function of the Bible is to substantiate the articles of a creed, rather than to convey the Word of God, of which the creed is an exposition.

The second misconception of the Word is that which makes the written Bible fully identical with the Word of God, bringing the doctrine of literal inspiration and infallibility to the apex of its development. By so narrowing the meaning of the Word that it must be confined to the written page, some Christians have not only been obliged to distort the literal meaning of passages of the Bible and mechanize the concept of revelation, but they have

---

[17] *The Authority of the Bible*, p. 196. W. L. Knox points out that disputes about authority usually overlook the leading rôle of religious experience in the believer—the apprehension of God through the Person of Christ—and to a large degree, the canon was established on the basis of the proven ability of the books to satisfy this experience; cf. *Essays Catholic and Critical* (E. G. Selwyn ed.), pp. 104-7.
[18] cf. E. Brunner, *Revelation and Reason*, p. 119.
[19] cf. K. Barth, *The Doctrine of the Word of God*, p. 245; E. Lewis, *A Philosophy of the Christian Revelation*, p. 50: 'The writings are the creation of a prior fact, and are so many attempts to describe, preserve, proclaim, and interpret the fact.'
[20] *Revelation and Reason*, p. 118.

violated the Second Commandment by worshipping the book rather than God who gives the Word by the medium of the book.[21] That this form of 'idolatry' is widespread in Christianity today—so much so that many antagonists of the Christian faith think that it is *the* approved attitude toward the Bible—is not easy to explain. The craving for objective authority, the sincere belief that biblical faith and verbal inspiration are interdependent, a strong element of conservative sentimentality, and other reasons may be proffered. Basically, however, this biblicism is inherent in the type of theology of which it is a part. And instead of serving as a protection of the Gospel against the destructive forces of radical criticism, it becomes in itself a virtual foe of the Gospel, by obscuring the relevance of the Word to human experience, and by rendering the Bible even more vulnerable to hostile criticism.

The assertion that the Word of God is to be found in the Bible is by no means an admission of the doctrine of literal inspiration of the Scriptures nor of the belief that specific doctrines are therein revealed. Even Barth, whose theology is so biblical throughout, will not yield to these beliefs. The Church believes the Bible to be the Word of God, he writes, but 'she does not mean by this the book, as a book, or the opinions and lines of thought of its authors.... She means by the Word of God Him to whom this book and this book alone bears testimony.'[22]

As in respect to preaching, so also with the Bible: the sensible form is always subordinate to the content, the spoken proclamation and the written page derive their meaning as the Word of God only so far as they testify to God's revelation of Himself in Jesus Christ. He is the Word, who is only served by the preacher and the book. And their service to Him in every generation of the Church is actualized by the power of the Holy Spirit, who interprets the record of events in the history of Jesus Christ and makes them to be revelation.

In summary, then, the 'Word of God' is a phrase which is fraught with richest theological meaning for the Church. The Incarnate Word, the Gospel He brings, the proclamation and writing testifying to Him—all comprise the Word in the full sense,

---

[21] *Revelation and Reason*, cf. N. Micklem, *What Is the Faith?* p. 34, where he shows that biblicists really use the Bible to support their theology rather than as a basis for finding theology and faith.

[22] *The Knowledge of God and the Service of God*, p. 178.

which is made known to us today and in all time by the Holy Spirit. The differences in emphasis and interpretation of the Word in its several forms are not relevant to the present discussion, which is intended to illuminate only the question of how the Word of God constitutes the basic authority for the Church.

III. HOW THE WORD OF GOD IS THE CHURCH'S AUTHORITY

At the base of most of the contemporary thought about the nature of the Church is the problem of the ultimate authority for the faith and practice of Christians. This problem may not always be explicitly recognized, being overshadowed by more 'practical' matters of importance; but it is, nevertheless, implicit in any question concerning the essential faith, life, and order of the Church. One recent writer, R. E. Davies, has asserted that the problem of the Church's authority is truly the central one for modern theology.[23] There are some, of course, who seriously doubt that Protestants should even concern themselves with this matter, for they cast their eyes upon the actions of the Roman Church, with its claim to infallible authority within itself, and feel thankful that they are free to do and believe as they think best. The weight of tradition, the credal symbols of the councils, the pronouncements of the Roman *curia*, and the *ex cathedra* utterances of the Pope, when held to be the ultimate authority, are all repugnant to the Protestant mind. Insistence upon them as expressions of God's own will is looked upon as the height of human pretension and arrogance, as well as the Protestant faith's greatest enemy.

It is well known, however, that uncontrolled liberty proved to be too great a responsibility for many Protestants, and that they welcomed submission to other forms of objective authority. In doing so, they persuaded themselves that they had not forfeited their liberty, but in fact they had done so. It is necessary only to mention the authorities to which countless Christians still bend their wills. The Bible is considered legalistically as a 'casebook' for religion, wherein the specific answers to all problems of faith and practice may be located. The historic creeds, Nicene and Athanasian, are often regarded as binding upon the faith of

[23] *The Problem of Authority in the Continental Reformers*, p. 9. He concludes that the problem was not really solved by the theology of Luther, Calvin, and Zwingli, but that they pointed the way toward a deeper conception of the Word of God.

some Protestants, while others virtually attribute the same authority to such documents as the *Augsburg Confession*, Calvin's *Institutes*, the *Westminster Confession*, and the like. It is apparent that men and women *want* to be able to acknowledge an infallible authority, and to varying degrees in modern Protestant Christianity, these writings and formulations of belief have been so acknowledged.

It cannot be denied, and should not be desired to be denied, that there is in each of these *an* authority for the Church. But how, on theological grounds, can it be maintained that they constitute *the* authority? The conviction of some theologians today is that the final seat of authority which is intelligible to people of the Church is not to be seen in any of these exclusively. There is a higher authority still: and this is the Word of God, Jesus Christ, the Word made flesh, whose Gospel is proclaimed by word of mouth and testified to in the Bible.

The assertion that the Word of God is the authority for the Church demands certain clarifications. To avoid all legalism, we must reaffirm that the Word in this connexion does not mean just the written text of the Bible as such, even though it surely includes the Bible. Neither does it mean just the words of Jesus' teaching, since appeal to these alone can also lead to legalism. As Newbigin comments on this matter: 'We have to avoid the error of citing the authority of Christ after the manner of the Scribes and Pharisees, and so using His Name but reversing His method. By refusing to cite "authorities" and by confronting men with His own unique authority, He placed upon men the terrifying responsibility of discerning between truth and falsehood. . . . (The Church) must in each new generation so learn Christ that it may feel the constraint and hear the command afresh through the Spirit, and that it may know with what authority it faces a world whose rules obstinately question its right to speak.'[24] This 'terrifying responsibility' is never relieved for the Christian, since it is both the price and the glory of his freedom. It is in connexion with this responsibility, then, that the belief in the guidance of the faithful by the Holy Spirit is so pertinent.

In the preceding pages, the meaning of the Word of God, as presently regarded as the authority for the Church, was briefly developed. Admittedly, this concept of the Word's including

[24] In *The Church's Witness to God's Design* (W.C.C.), pp. 22f.

Jesus Christ, the proclamation and the Bible, is too broad for some Protestants. Even so, one is rather pleasantly astonished to discover that there is a high degree of unanimity on this definition among theologians of various denominations and schools of theology. For example, it is not a Reformed, nor a particularly 'Barthian' denomination which makes the following statement, but the Methodists of England: 'The Word of God thus interpreted as Christ Himself, living on earth, crucified, risen; Christ Himself as preached; Christ Himself as revealed in the pages of the Scriptures—this Word of God calls the Church into existence, and perpetually sustains it.'[25]

Again, members of the Dutch Church, in considering the authority for a new order in their denomination, firmly state that 'in the Church the Word of God, His revelation, is the starting point for every humanly framed Church order. . . . Concerning every form which history has bequeathed to us we must ask whether it is a response to the revelation in the Word of God.'[26]

In recent discussions on the ecumenical level there has also been a frank recognition of this authority of the Word. At Edinburgh, for example, when the Second World Conference on Faith and Order convened in 1937, a thoroughgoing attempt was made by representatives of nearly all Protestant denominations to clarify their concept of the Church. Among the statements in their *Report* are the following:[27]

The Word is the appointed means by which God's grace is made known to men, calling them to repentance, assuring them of forgiveness, drawing them to obedience and building them up in the fellowship of faith and love (II.v).

We concur in affirming that the Word of God is ever living and dynamic and inseparable from God's activity. . . . God reveals Himself to us by what He does, by that activity by which He has wrought the salvation of men and is working for their restoration to personal fellowship with Himself. . . . In the fullness of time the Word of God is manifest in Christ, our Lord, the Incarnate Word, and His redeeming work; that is, in His words and deeds, in His life and character, in His suffering, death, and resurrection, culminating in the gift of the Spirit and in the life which He gives to the Church which is His body (III.i).

[25] *The Nature of the Christian Church according to the Teaching of the Methodists*, pp. 19f.
[26] *Vorarbeiten für eine neue Kirchenordnung in Holland*, Files of Commission I, W.C.C., Geneva.
[27] *Faith and Order, Edinburgh* 1937 (L. Hodgson, ed.), pp. 346f.

A testimony in *words* is by divine ordering provided for the revelation uttered by the *Word*. This testimony is given in Holy Scripture, which thus affords the primary norm for the Church's teaching, worship and life (III.ii).

Due to the presence of theologians from as different extremes as the Baptist and Orthodox churches, there was, naturally, no full consensus expressed on this *Report*, but the majority favouring it was still a diverse group, and their agreement is significant.[28]

The importance of this common belief is that it indicates the extent to which Protestants are disposed to seek their authority in the Word of God, which is not only the Book, but also the Person and the proclamation of the Gospel. Some, indeed, withheld approval on the basis of the absolute adequacy of the Scriptures; while others held out for recognition of the authoritative interpretations of tradition, which, they believe, 'complete' the teaching and witness of the Bible. In either case, there is no reservation as to the authority of the Word, but only as to the real meaning of the Word, whether it is to be defined narrowly or broadly.[29]

The general admission is that Christ gives life to the Church, which is His Body, drawing into fellowship all those who have heard and responded to the Gospel. Since the Church could not exist except for Christ, it is He, the Word Himself, the Head of the Body, upon whom the Church is wholly dependent. In the words of N. Micklem: 'The Church, again, is wholly subject to "the Word" of which it is both the witness and the product. Obviously the Church can have no authority over against the Word that created it.'[30] This is the comprehensive principle of authority which is normative and ultimate for the worship, teaching, and action of the Church.

The close connexion between the ideas of the Church as the Body of Christ and the Word of God as the authority of the Church is now evident. Neither of these conveys much meaning to us unless it is conceived as a concrete reality, rather than as an

---

[28] cf. the various dissenting opinions, ibid., pp. 154-72, 347.

[29] William Robinson in *The Ministry and the Sacraments* (R. Dunkerley, ed.), pp. 254-8, shows how over-emphasis on either the Bible itself or the Church's traditional authority contradicts the intention of the Word of God, since both are necessary expressions of the Word.

[30] *What Is the Faith?* p. 105; cf. K. Barth, *The Knowledge of God and the Service of God*, p. 172: '. . . when we inquire about the true Church and consider preaching, the sacraments and the ordinances of the Church, it is Jesus Christ Himself as the Word of God, who has to be the subject of our inquiry.'

abstract, speculative, or mystical idea. The Body is the Church in its most profound sense. The Word is Christ in His most profound meaning. Both are present in the experience of the Christian; and the former is wholly dependent upon and responsible to the latter. 'Christ is actually the Word of God,' writes Barth, 'contemporary in prophecy and in the apostolate and contemporary in the proclamation of His Church. If He is contemporary here, if He *makes* that step, we are necessarily here faced with the knowledge of the sole rule of the Word of God in the Church.'[31]

But how are we to understand this rule in all specific situations? It is this simple, prudent question which raises the walls of dispute between the various factions of the Church. We are again faced with the problem of the 'terrifying responsibility' of which Newbigin spoke. But if Christ be the divine Word, and hence the final appeal of the Church, this terror is not so overwhelming as we might think. For the Christians of the primitive Church, as well as of all generations of Christian history, and particularly of those since the Reformation—these Christians have believed that the power which leads us into knowledge of the Word, in whatever form, is the Holy Spirit. This conviction is a primary pillar of faith, and, as we have seen in Chapter Two, is of the utmost importance for the life of the Church, not least of all with respect to the authority of the Church. In one of the earliest instances in which the Church exercised authority over its members, the decision was rendered on the ground that 'it has seemed good to the Holy Spirit and to us. . . .'[32] This attitude has prevailed whenever confidence in the work of the Spirit has not been subordinated to human wilfulness. So, in their unanimous statement concerning the authority for all sacramental doctrine, the Theological Commission of the Faith and Order Movement asserted that 'His Will is made known to us through the Holy Spirit who enables us to interpret Scripture as expressing the living Word of God to every age, and has constantly guided the Church and moulded its tradition in so far as it has walked by faith in its living Lord'.[33]

To some observers, at least, it would seem that exclusive dependence upon the infallible authority of a tradition or council

---

[31] *The Doctrine of the Word of God*, p. 171.   [32] Acts 15^{28}.
[33] *The Ministry and the Sacraments* (R. Dunkerley, ed.), p. 9.

of the Church, on the one hand, or upon an allegedly infallible text of Scripture, on the other, must amount to a mistrust or outright denial of the belief in the real *testimonium Spiritus Sancti*. If such dependence does not amount to this, it implies that the work of the Spirit is limited to the sphere of those who hold either the one view or the other.[34]

Authority must not mean authoritarianism in the legal or ecclesiastical sense. If the slave of Christ is still the most free of all men, it is inconceivable that he should be the slave of any authority which does not fully harmonize with the will of Christ. 'Real authority requires real freedom as the only environment in which it can live,' asserts Rawlinson.[35] For according to Paul, a Christian is led by the Spirit, he is not coerced, since the man in Christ has been set free from all legal bondage.[36] Being so led by the Spirit into apprehension of the meaning of the Word of God, the Church cannot yield to the opposing dangers of utter relativism or absolute authoritarianism, neither of which is in accord with the will of Christ.

So then, as a general principle, it is the responsibility of the Church in every specific problem of authority, whether in worship, faith, or social action, to seek that course of thought or practice which comes closest to being in full accord with the Word of God, known in Jesus Christ and the Scriptural testimony to Him. This involves faithful submission to the direction of the Holy Spirit and fervent appeal in prayer for His guidance. It also demands the bringing into service to the Word of all rational assets, intellectual acumen, and spiritual wisdom, since the Word of God is perfect truth and must always be sought as such.

Infallibility in all matters of authority is an ideal kind of wisdom which has not yet been delegated to mankind. The Tree of Eden is still jealously guarded. Were ultimate truth for all of life within man's grasp, there would be no cause for any question over the authority of the Church. But the authority which the Church *does* have now, in virtue of God's Word, is not so partial that it need be considered insufficient for the continuation of the life, order, and faith of the Christian community. The Body of Christ has not been left in the world without the proper direction

---

[34] It is remarkable that the same Bible which provides infallible directives for one group can provide contradicting directives for another. cf. W. L. Knox in *Essays Catholic and Critical* (E. G. Selwyn, ed.), p. 100.

[35] *Authority and Freedom*, p. 17.   [36] cf. Romans $8^{2, 14}$, Galatians 5^1.

for its maintenance and growth. The Body can think, decide, and act, for it has in its Head 'the mind of Christ', however distorted and misunderstood it may be by the minds of imperfect men.[37] The task of the Church, therefore, is not to wield the authority of the Word of God for its own glorification, but in all matters faithfully to serve the Word.

[37] cf. T. A. Lacey, *The One Body and the One Spirit*, p. 60.

CHAPTER FIVE

THE SACRAMENTS AND THE MINISTRY

Part One—The Sacraments of the Church

I. VERBUM VISIBILE

ACCORDING to the immemorial usage of Christianity, faith in the Word of God and service to it have been expressed by the perpetuation of the Sacraments. Despite the wide range of opinion as to the exact nature of the Sacraments, the spiritual descendants of Luther, Calvin, and the evangelical reformers have generally followed the belief of Augustine, that the true Sacrament is the *verbum visibile*, the Word in visible form and action. Apart from this integral association with the Word of God, the Sacraments cannot stand as independent entities. For Protestant thought, the Word and the Sacraments are always considered in the closest possible connexion. In accord with such an attitude, we may proceed to a short consideration of the meaning and place of the Sacraments in respect to the nature of the Church.

II. THE MEANING OF HOLY COMMUNION AND BAPTISM

It is well known that there are many conflicting doctrines of the Sacraments within the Church, and that some groups are determined to defend their views staunchly, if not at times almost belligerently. Some of these differences relate only to the outward forms of ritual observance and emphasis; others concern the basic purpose and effect of the Sacraments, the exact number of them, and the necessity for observing them; others centre on the problem of the necessity of faith on the part of the individual participant; still others hinge on the meaning of God's grace, the efficacy and validity of forms of administration, and the requirement of a proper ordination for the officiating minister. The scope of this present study is not wide enough to include an adequate presentation of the dogmatic background and recent theological justification

THE SACRAMENTS AND THE MINISTRY 121

for each of these different doctrinal ideas. Instead we are interested in discovering how recent thought on the Sacraments has tended to create a higher degree of agreement among Christians, and also to shed more light upon our understanding of the essential nature of the Church.

Far better than a survey of the independent writing which has been done on this problem is the book entitled, *The Ministry and the Sacraments*,[1] which collects and compares the theological convictions of representatives of all the major Christian denominations. The most striking feature of this comprehensive book is the great extent of honest agreement to be found with regard to the nature of the Sacraments. These items of agreement are outlined in the Report of the Commission, with only the Orthodox members failing to give unqualified assent. The Report does not intend to define a Sacrament categorically.[2] The nearest it comes to definition is to observe 'that an unfailing characteristic of all Sacraments is an external action dealing with material things to which a spiritual significance is attached by Divine institution'.[3] However, beyond this very general description, which is certainly basic for any sacramental concept, the Report lists four major beliefs about Sacraments, which support the particular doctrines of almost every denomination.[4]

(a) It is agreed, first, that every sacramental act is accomplished

---

[1] Prepared in 1937 for the Faith and Order Movement by the appointed Theological Commission, the members of which are: A. C. Headlam (Chairman), R. Dunkerley (Secretary), N. Arseniew, R. N. Flew, Fr. Gerke, H. Hermelink, W. Manson, O. C. Quick, W. Robinson, H. Neufield, R. Will, and B. Vasady. Several other theologians contributed essays to the symposium, giving a full cross-section of doctrines currently held.

[2] For such definition, cf. O. C. Quick, *The Christian Sacraments*, p. 108: 'A sacrament is a ritual act, using a certain form and matter, which both represents some universal relation of human life to God through Christ, but also, in thus representing all life, makes life worthy to be thus represented.'

Also, A. Dun in *Christendom*, IV.4(1939).502-14: 'A sacrament is an act of the Church in her character as the "Body of Christ" in which the action of God in Christ toward men is carried on and man responds by making himself party to this divine action.'

P. S. Minear in Files of Commission I, W.C.C., Geneva, writes that Sacraments may be defined in part 'as whatever means the Spirit adopts for communicating participation in the death and resurrection of Christ'.

K. Barth, *The Doctrine of the Word of God*, pp. 61f., draws his working definition from Question 66 of the Heidelberg Catechism, restating it as follows: '(A sacrament is) the symbolic act consummated in the community of the Church according to the directions of the biblical witness to revelation, which accompanies and confirms preaching, an act, the aim of which as such is to attest the event of God's revelation, reconciliation, and calling, which not only fulfils, but already proves the promise.'

[3] ibid., p. 23.   [4] ibid., pp. 24f.

in fact by our Lord Jesus Christ. The function of a minister is only to be the instrument for Christ, acting on His behalf in the ritual he employs. The universality of this belief is indicated by the reference to a paragraph from Thomas Aquinas, who confirmed the same idea.

(b) 'God is not bound to His Sacraments'—*Deus non alligatur sacramentis*—is likewise an ancient and universally accepted doctrine. That Almighty God should be limited by any sacramental institution would be a scandal to the Christian faith. On the other hand, while God is not so bound to the Sacraments, it is believed by many that we human creatures are.

(c) The efficacy of the Sacraments lies in the fact that 'by means of them Christ, through the Holy Spirit, effects His Grace in the soul'. With this belief Christians exclude the erroneous idea that the Sacraments are a refined form of magic. The minister does not dispense grace by his own will and discretion. The recipient's attitude of faith is a necessary condition of the Sacrament, even as the personal work and influence of Christ, who reaches men through the Spirit. Both are present, divine action and human response.

(d) The minister represents the whole Church, and not just an authority of his own, when he administers the Sacraments. In this respect, as always, the minister is the servant of the Word of God; and his action is important only in so far as it serves the ends which God, by the operation of His Word, intends.

These four points are by no means ideas of recent coinage, for they derive from the common treasury of faith, which the reformers and their successors held in high value. They are noteworthy, therefore, because they form the basis for so much contemporary thought on the Sacraments. Their importance is very evident, for example, in the Scheme of Union on which the Church of South India was recently constituted. These four principles are solidly embedded in the statement of the Scheme on the Sacraments, to which all the participating denominations could give full assent.[5]

Further attempts toward definition and doctrinal explanation of the Sacraments, however, usually bring to light the important differences which still obtain. The question of the true number of Sacraments does not seem to be a serious one for Protestants: except for members of the very 'Catholic' wing of Anglicanism, the

[5] J. E. L. Newbigin, *The Reunion of the Church*, p. 170.

two recognized Sacraments are Baptism and the Holy Communion.

A very definite problem persists with regard to the validity of Sacraments, however, illustrating a sharp cleavage between the 'Evangelical' Protestant doctrine and that of the 'Catholic' Protestants. The consensus has already been noted in respect to the action of Christ in the Sacraments, giving His grace to the faithful participants, and also in respect to the minister's representing the whole Church when he administers the Lord's Supper and baptizes. Although these two beliefs are commonly held in principle, variations in interpretation prove that the consensus is only theoretical. And the key word of the problem is 'validity'.

This word, when applied to the Sacraments, simply has no meaning for some theologians. If there is a valid Sacrament, then according to logic there must be an invalid one. But J. S. Whale reasons as follows: 'The Sacraments are God's action. God—if He be acting at all—cannot be acting invalidly or irregularly.'[6] To be consistent, one would have to speak of a Sacrament in contrast with a similar action which lacks the intention and meaning of a Sacrament: but never of 'valid' and 'invalid', for the latter word implies an imperfection of divine action. Although the word 'valid' is generally employed in sacramental discussion, therefore, it is helpful to keep in the mind the dangerous implications of its opposite.

Whale's objection is met by others who point out that, while the Sacraments have meaning only in so far as they are divine action, they are dependent in some degree also upon the spiritual state of the persons participating in them. It is a misconception so to emphasize the necessity of faith, for example, that the value of the Sacrament is made to depend entirely upon the recipient.[7] Likewise, to ascribe the Sacrament wholly and exclusively to God is to deprive it of real meaning for the human beings who take part in it.

The nature of the problem is made clearer if we distinguish between the words 'valid' and 'efficacious', as they are applied to the Sacraments. The former has the basic meaning of 'firm' or 'assured'.[8] Only by choice need it have the same meaning as 'efficacious', as it apparently does in the judgement of J. S. Whale. The efficacy of the Sacraments is thus a matter of the divine

---

[6] In *The Ministry and the Sacraments* (R. Dunkerley, ed.), p. 218.   [7] ibid., p. 27.

[8] Greek *bebaios* is equivalent to Latin *validus*; cf. O. C. Quick, *The Christian Sacraments*, p. 156.

initiative, the giving of grace in the Word visibly perceived, and the reception in faith. Validity, on the other hand, is concerned with the proper performance of the outward signs of the Sacraments, as authorized in the New Testament.

According to this distinction, a given performance of a Sacrament may have real efficacy so far as the faithful person experiences the grace of God in it, but it would still not be valid unless it complied with certain essential conditions and forms. A graphic example is to be seen in the following situation: During the last days of the demolition of Warsaw by the Nazis, two Methodist ministers awaited death in a dark sewer, deep under the ground, where they had been hiding for several days. In the darkness one of them found a crust of mouldy bread; the other found a tin cup to hold the unclean water. Repeating from memory Jesus' words of institution, they participated in the Communion of His body and blood. None would doubt that their faith was sincere and their intention right, nor that they received in that act of worship the gift of divine grace. Theirs was an efficacious Sacrament. But was it also valid? Some would assert that, lacking the proper element of wine, theirs was not a valid Sacrament. Others would insist more dogmatically that, lacking the ordination at the hands of a Bishop in the historic succession of the apostles, neither they nor any other ministers lacking such orders were ever in position to administer a valid Sacrament.

According to those two Polish ministers' belief, there was probably not the slightest doubt that their Communion was both efficacious and valid. Their Methodist doctrine, like that of many evangelicals, would conform to the statement of R. N. Flew: 'The only "valid" Eucharist is one where the promised blessing is given and received, where the Risen Lord grants and renews that personal communion with Himself to the believing soul for which the soul was made. In this sense the word "valid" really means "effectual".'[9] And although there are prescribed forms for observance of the rite, the primary question is whether 'the worship rendered therein to God be in spirit and in truth'. The divine action and the faithful attitude of the worshipper are thus the only really indispensable sacramental requisites.

A somewhat different view is held by D. Mackenzie of the Reformed, or Presbyterian, tradition.[10] He draws a distinction

[9] In *The Ministry and the Sacraments* (R. Dunkerley, ed.), p. 237. [10] ibid., pp. 206f.

THE SACRAMENTS AND THE MINISTRY 125

between the 'institutional validity' and the 'efficient validity' of the Sacrament. By the former he asserts the necessity of the observance of the forms which are traced back to the institution of Jesus: the bread and the wine, the prayer, the commandment to continue the rite, etc. These all have a symbolical meaning which is not merely desirable but truly necessary for the participants. However, greater importance still is attached to the 'efficient validity' of the Sacrament, which depends upon faith, love, and godly intention on the part of those who take part.

To all of these attitudes the more rigorous doctrine of the Sacraments, such as that of the Anglicans, stands in opposition. Only a few theologians would be so narrow as to declare that all sacramental observance except their own is really invalid, much less ineffectual. Rather than denying the reality of the Sacraments in the widest area of Protestant usage, they deem them *irregular*, that is, not according to their Church order.[11] Nevertheless, when by Church order is meant the necessity of a ministry which claims the apostolic succession as its authority, as it does mean for Anglo-Catholics, the tolerant attitude toward sacramental practice in other denominations seems rather inconsistent. Then it is held that such other practice is somehow imperfect and inferior because it is not in accordance with an ecclesiastical order for which Christ Himself is believed to be the authority. (The profound and far-reaching implications of this doctrine will be treated more adequately in connexion with the question of the ministry of the Church.)

Toward a better understanding of the Holy Communion, scholars in recent years have found that the interpretations which have the widest currency in both Catholic and Reformed Churches today are not exactly the same as those which were recognized in the early Church. Although their findings do not concur in such a manner as to show Christians *the* true and adequate interpretation of the Sacrament, they serve as a reminder of the perils of holding to a rigidly dogmatic and exclusive view.[12] Examining the earliest written records concerning Christian

[11] cf. O. C. Quick in ibid., p. 129. also his discussion in *The Christian Sacraments*, pp. 129-58, and in *Faith and Order, Edinburgh* 1937 (L. Hodgson, ed.), pp. 324f.
[12] The writer cannot here treat specifically the many important studies which have recently been made. The best summary and bibliography may be found in the article by E. Lohmeyer, '*Vom urchristlichen Abendmahl*' in *Theologische Rundschau* (1937), pp. 168-227, 273-312. Also valuable is *Eucharistic Faith and Practice, Evangelical and Catholic* by Y. Brilioth.

sacramental practice and belief, the scholars have adduced evidence that several views of the Holy Communion were current in the early Church. Some held it to be a simple, family-type meal expressing fellowship; others, following Paul, related it to the Last Supper and the sacrificial death of Jesus; still others felt the rite to be an expression of faith in the eschatological return of Jesus; and beliefs varied also with respect to the meaning of the elements and the nature of Christ's presence at the Communion.

These findings are well worth studying in the context of our present discussion, for they illuminate the fact that the task of clarifying the meaning of the Sacraments, particularly of Holy Communion, has still to be accomplished. The four classical interpretations—Roman Catholic transubstantiation, Lutheran consubstantiation, Calvinistic equation of substance with power, and Zwinglian memorialism—have been accepted in various modern communions with little modification. As for the distinctively Protestant denominations, it is unhappily true that modern rationalism has almost driven out a frank recognition of the profound mystery of the Sacrament, a mystery, as Wilhelm Stählin remarks, 'that once embraced and filled the whole life of the Christian Church'.[13]

This mystery is most persistently before us whenever we try to understand the belief that Christ Himself is present in the Holy Communion. It is thought by many Protestants today that they cannot believe in the 'real presence of Christ' in the Holy Communion without conceding the truth of the Roman doctrine. But this is all a matter of interpreting the meaning of the phrase. And the widely held belief of Protestant theologians is that a denial of Christ's presence—not His *material* presence—negates the whole significance of the Sacrament. As P. C. Simpson asserts, the Evangelical concept of Communion insists more strongly upon the real presence than does the Roman Catholic doctrine, for Christ is not limited to elements on the altar, but is present spiritually in and among all communicants. 'It is Christ who *speaks*, who *blesses*, who *breaks*, who *gives*,' he declares.[14]

Basically it is not a question of whether Christ is present, but of how. 'Anyone who could deny the Real Presence of Christ in the Sacrament,' writes C. A. A. Scott, 'would place himself in the

[13] *The Mystery of God*, p. 79.   [14] *Church Principles*, p. 107.

curious position of saying that Christ is present with His people in all places and in all circumstances except in the Sacrament.'[15] Protestants are agreed that Christ is not made actual flesh and blood on the altar by miracle. On the other hand, attempts at rationalization of the manner of His presence have always led to the purely memorial meal associated with Zwingli's interpretation, or else to the impenetrable darkness of mystery wherein the unaided reason loses its competence. Then the evidence rests upon the faith of the communicant, his knowing of Jesus Christ through the Word previously revealed, and his testimony to an experience of Christ's transforming power in his life. If Christ be not present, offering Himself to men for their redemption—not being offered to God by the priest!—the continuance of this Sacrament in the Church could hardly be justified, except as a dramatic and symbolic aid to worship. But the fact with which theologians have to deal is that countless Christians do see in this Sacrament a sign, or exhibit, of Christ's presence; and their task is to relate this fact to the Gospel in general. If we try to construct a theology on the basis of the sacramental presence alone, we must work in the realm of pure theory and ultimately confuse the issue even more.[16]

The present quest for a theological understanding of the Church has to be made largely by way of thought on the meaning of the Sacraments. 'If the sacramental element is largely neglected,' writes A. Dun, 'there is a danger that religion will tend to become chiefly a traffic in ideas. God communicates and informs, but does He act and confirm?'[17] The general conviction is that God does act and confirm through the Sacraments of the Church; but concerning the necessary conditions through which this action and confirmation take place there is still divergence of opinion and belief.

Thus far we have been specifically concerned more with the Holy Communion than with Baptism. It is evident from contemporary practice in the Church as a whole that a clearer conception of the theological and religious significance of Baptism than is now generally held must be gained by those Christians whose denominations or confessions teach no comprehensive doctrine

---

[15] *The Church: Its Worship and Sacraments*, p. 102.
[16] C. M. Jacobs in *The Ministry and the Sacraments* (R. Dunkerley, ed.), p. 143.
[17] In *Christendom*, IV.4(1939).514.

of this Sacrament. If Baptism is also a *verbum visible* and a means of grace, it has obviously been to the spiritual loss of some denominations that the rite has been so neglected or else stripped of its sacramental reality.

The fact that Baptism in the apostolic generation was an experience of the utmost importance for faith and the Church needs no defence here. But today, except on the fringe of missionary expansion, the situation of the early Church no longer obtains. It is theologically correct to say with D. Bonhöffer that whoever is baptized belongs no more to the world, serves it no more, and is no longer subject to it, since he belongs to Jesus Christ alone and relates himself to the world only through Christ.[18] But only a small percentage of baptized Christians can honestly declare that their Baptism has meant so much in their lives, particularly if they were baptized in infancy.

How far we have departed from the New Testament idea of Baptism as a dying and rising with Christ,[19] or a purifying bath,[20] or an act of repentance and forgiveness and the receiving of the Holy Spirit,[21] or a regeneration by water and the Spirit,[22] is evident in the general practice of the Churches. Adult Baptism is often treated only as a declaratory act of faith, while infant Baptism has degenerated to the perfunctory rite of 'christening'. Where in either of these misuses of the rite is there any recognition of the action of God, addressing the person in His Word?

Awareness of the seriousness of this situation has spurred some theologians to take anxious but critical looks at their respective doctrines of Baptism, and to try to relate these doctrines to the larger problem of the nature of the Church.

What is the cause for so much contemporary confusion with regard to the meaning of Baptism? Of the various answers which can be offered, few seem to fit so well as that offered by W. J. Phythian-Adams.[23] Our theology of Baptism, he contends, has become grievously distorted because the Church many centuries ago abandoned the biblical understanding of the Sacrament. John the Baptist preached a greater than himself, who would baptize, not with water, but with the Holy Spirit and with fire.[24] This first spiritual Baptism was Pentecost, specifically identified as such by the historian, Luke.[25] And although the apostles

---

[18] *Nachfolge*, p. 155.   [19] Romans 6^4.   [20] Ephesians 5^{26}.   [21] Acts 2^{38}.   [22] John 3^5.
[23] *The Way of At-one-ment*, pp. 100-3.   [24] Mark 1^8 and parallels.   [25] Acts 1^5.

retained the practice of using water, it was the receiving of the Spirit which really gave meaning to Baptism. In subsequent ritual practice, Baptism was divided into two actions: the presbyter using water and the Bishop laying on his hands to invoke the Spirit. Then, as the Bishops became farther removed from local ministry, the second part of the rite was usually deferred, becoming eventually the Sacrament of Confirmation. But the general belief remained, (largely due to the etymological meaning of Baptism, from the Greek *baptizein*, 'to wash' or 'dip') that the water Baptism included that of the Holy Spirit as well. The Reformation confused the situation even more by abandoning the episcopal office. It was necessary, then, to attempt to interpret theologically infant Baptism with a subsequent, non-sacramental Confirmation, or even harder, adult Baptism which differed very little from that of John the Baptist, with more thought of water than of the Spirit.[26] The baptismal practice in many Churches reflects all too graphically this defection from the biblical ideas, which Phythian-Adams regards as being absolutely necessary to recover. It is not unlikely that a failure to make this recovery could lead eventually to the Sacrament of Baptism's falling into desuetude in a large area of the Church.

Especially critical, moreover, is the problem of the theological justification for infant Baptism. The prevailing conditions with respect to the baptizing of babies, whether in established or free Churches, are appalling to anyone who holds it to be a Sacrament. 'The contemporary practice of infant baptism can hardly be regarded as anything short of scandalous,' charges Brunner.[27] By this he does not mean to refute the whole practice of baptizing infants, but only to deny the flagrantly irresponsible misuse of the rite. But how can the baptizing of infants still be justified and defended? Do the traditional explanations still carry weight for modern Christian belief and practice?

That the New Testament says nothing explicitly about the baptizing of little children is incontestable. There are certain passages which do seem to give support to the practice. Althaus cites 1 Corinthians 7[14] as an example of Paul's belief that children

---

[26] The opposite extreme is achieved in the practice of the Quakers, who dispense with water and ritual altogether and believe that the Baptism of the Spirit comes personally and immediately to each believer.

[27] *The Divine-Human Encounter*, p. 132.

of baptized parents are holy rather than unclean.[28] If parents are called to be baptized, so are children, he believes. Thus Paul also related how he baptized the whole household of Stephenas, ostensibly including some infants or small children.[29] By and large, however, it is generally agreed that these texts are inconclusive. While this fact is rigorously emphasized by Barth in his case against infant Baptism,[30] it is admitted by Flemington only in connexion with his further belief that the Church's subsequent practice in baptizing infants was a legitimate working out of the New Testament teaching.[31] In current discussion, therefore, greater weight must be placed for the defence of the practice upon theological, rather than scriptural, grounds.

Theologians of various communions are not hesitant to assume this defence. Aulén begins by asserting that Baptism is primarily 'an expression and an action of the *gratia praeveniens Dei*',[32] by which God on His own initiative gives persons the opportunity to be saved. The Baptism of infants, therefore, is an even more striking expression of this divine prevenient grace than adult Baptism is, since the element of faith on the part of the infant is unthinkable. This is a rather extreme concept of the effect of Baptism, and for many critics it would approximate an almost magical view of the rite. On the other hand, it would be unfair to Aulén, and a misunderstanding of the Lutheran doctrine, to suppose that this concept of prevenient grace is applied to Baptism in the Roman Catholic sense, which can hardly be anything but magical, as the practice of Baptism *in utero* clearly shows. Aulén is more concerned with the free and loving initiative of God than with the mechanical effects of the rite itself. 'For the baptism of infants shows us how our membership in the Church has its basis not in our own endeavours, and efforts, but solely in the divine Love and grace, and therefore also how this membership is quite independent of human judgement and decisions. At the same time this kind of baptism acts, and must act, as a living

---

[28] *Die christliche Wahrheit*, II.349; cf. O. Cullmann, *Die Tauflehre des Neuen Testaments*, pp. 20f.

[29] 1 Corinthians 1^{16}. Only sentimentality can lead a theologian to consider Jesus' summoning of the little children (Mark 10^{14})) as a warrant for infant Baptism; cf. M. Goguel, *L'Église Primitive*, p. 325.

[30] *The Teaching of the Church regarding Baptism*, p. 49.

[31] *The New Testament Doctrine of Baptism*, pp. 130f.

[32] In *The Ministry and the Sacraments* (R. Dunkerley, ed.), p. 157f; cf. Aulen's *The Faith of the Christian Church* for extended discussion.

conscience in the Church, impressing upon her her duty to take care of the baptized and to give them a Christian education.'[33] The complementary factor to divine grace is not the faith of the child, which is impossible, but the duty and responsibility of the family and the Church.[34]

Not far from Aulén's confidence in God's free grace is the view of P. T. Forsyth, who declares that 'Baptism is something that *happens* to the man (or child) at the Church's hand. . . . The baptismal act in which he enters the Church, like the birth whereby he enters the world, is something done rather on him than by him.'[35] This is not to discredit the need for real faith on the part of the adults, but to emphasize again the power and initiative of God. Therefore, in respect to infants, 'Baptism *unto* faith has as good a right in the principle of the Gospel as Baptism *upon* faith'.[36] When this is not admitted, Forsyth continues, and the faith of the individual is made the sole condition for Baptism, the rite which is a Sacrament is reduced to a mere confirmation of experience and nothing more.

'Whatever else infant Baptism may or may not do, it at least speaks of Grace,' remarks Edwin Lewis.[37] It is this which fundamentally constitutes its sacramental character. The Baptism of infants signifies their entry into the household of faith, but not their full possession. 'But to deny that it signifies even entry until there is a full recognition on the part of the baptized person of all that is involved in the rite, is both to make the rite a farce—at least in the case of infants and children, and, one surmises, in the case of many adults—and to limit the operation of Grace to the human understanding and will.'[38]

Certainly none of the theologians who has thus supported the practice of baptizing infants could be accused on theological grounds of having insufficient regard for the necessity of faith in the Christian life. In their understanding of Baptism, however,

[33] In *The Universal Church in God's Design* (W.C.C.), p. 25.
[34] W. Elert points out in *Der christliche Glaube*, p. 501, that it is this responsibility of the Church rather than of the individual which shows the difference between the conception of the Church as a totality (*Gesamtkirche*) and the Baptist conception of the autonomous individual Church (*Ortsgemeinde*), the former being the congregation of the baptized, the latter of the faithful only.
[35] *The Church and the Sacraments*, p. 194.
[36] ibid., p. 211.
[37] In *The Ministry and the Sacraments* (R. Dunkerley, ed.), p. 481.
[38] ibid., pp. 481-2.

they recognize no obstacle to the baptizing of infants, for they cannot ascribe to God an indifference toward the little children He has created, as though He maintained a neutral attitude toward them until they could respond to Him in faith. In their view, then, Baptism is still considered a 'sealing' of the promises of God. 'The idea that the ceremony alters God's attitude to the child or determines its eternal destiny is not far from superstition,' warns N. Micklem: 'The Sacrament is not given to assist God, but to comfort us.'[39]

The foregoing attitudes express a real belief in Baptism as a work of God and not merely as a symbol of dedication. However, unless one does recognize the symbolic value of the rite, he is tempted to regard Baptism as a rather mechanical means of divine grace. Modern difficulties with regard to Baptism, according to O. C. Quick, 'have arisen because neither the orthodox nor their critics have sufficiently realized that the change from adult-baptism to infant-baptism as the normal practice of the Church should have involved a shifting of emphasis from the instrumental to the symbolic aspects of the Sacrament.'[40] The rite is instrumental to the extent that the grace of God is given, but not to the extent that original sin is blotted out or that salvation is guaranteed. Its symbolic value lies in the fact that it symbolizes the ultimate end of salvation for which life is intended, and in so doing, 'symbolizes also by anticipation all those many purifications from sin and gifts of new life, of which the progress toward the final salvation is made up'.[41] Instrumentality and symbolism are thus equally important in the concept of the effect of Baptism. And Quick is convinced that God intends all persons —infants if in Christian families, adults otherwise—to enter the Church by 'this same sacramental door'. However, he does not condone the rigorous dogma that only baptized persons can be saved, since God must not be thought to be restricted by His own Sacraments.[42] While Baptism is not absolutely necessary, it is the normal and accepted manner of entrance into the Christian faith and the Body of Christ, and it is a uniquely dramatic testimony of the Gospel.

Theologians of those denominations which do not practice infant Baptism (notably the Baptists and the Churches of Christ)

---

[39] *Congregationalism and the Church Catholic*, p. 56. [40] *The Christian Sacraments*, pp. 168f.
[41] ibid., p. 173. [42] *The Christian Sacraments*, pp. 178-81.

can agree in principle to most of the preceding interpretations, except, of course, in respect to infants. They must insist upon the condition of conscious faith in this Sacrament, just as much as in the Holy Communion. 'Infant Baptism obscures the fact that salvation is by faith alone, independent of all priestly ministrations and ecclesiastical rites,' says A. C. Underwood.[43] This protest is just as much a denial of the priestly conception of the Church as an affirmation of the primacy of faith. Both aspects of the protest have been countered by the practice of their fellow-evangelicals, however, and unfortunately no genuine reconciliation of the opposing beliefs concerning infant Baptism seems probable.

III. THE WORD OF GOD INCLUDES THE SACRAMENTS

Such is the nature of recent thought on the meaning of the two Sacraments, which almost all Christians, with the exception of a few,[44] hold to be necessary to the continuing life of the Church. It is Baptism which marks the admission of a person to the Body of Christ, placing upon him the seal of God's call and promise for him. And in the repeated observance of Holy Communion, the participant benefits by several effects: he is vividly reminded of the death and resurrection of Christ, of the real and acting presence of Christ today, of the essential *koinōnia* of the Church, and of the eschatological hope for the fulfilment of the Church in the Kingdom of God. These are some of the meanings of the Sacraments which must be preserved in the practice of the Church.

It has already been noted that the Sacraments and the Word of God have been kept traditionally in the closest proximation, because the Sacraments are believed to be the visible and tangible forms of the Word. This close association is assumed and emphasized in much theological writing. But can it be said that the Word of God and the Sacraments are of equal value or necessity for the Church? Few Protestants, although most of the Catholic Anglicans, would subscribe to the doctrine that 'valid' Sacraments (i.e. performed by the ministry of the historic episcopate) are what give the Church visible character, and are

[43] In *The Ministry and the Sacraments* (R. Dunkerley, ed.), p. 224.
[44] Quakers, Salvation Army, and many individuals.

therefore pre-eminent in the *esse* of the Church.[45] In theological circles where this doctrine is accepted, it is apparently seldom thought necessary to speak of the Word of God in connexion with the Sacraments.

On the other hand, where the influence of Luther is still strong, and to a somewhat smaller degree among Calvin's descendants, it is the Word of God—the Gospel of Jesus Christ known in the Scripture and preaching, interpreted by the Holy Spirit—which is the one, indispensable keystone of the Church.

We err when we try to make distinctions between oral proclamation and the Sacraments, writes Althaus, since both of these are subsumed under the one, living Word of God.[46] In this vein, C. M. Jacobs points out that 'the Sacraments are neither more nor less than a means or method by which the central message of the Gospel is brought close to individual lives. They do nothing that this message may not conceivably do without their intervention.'[47] And another Lutheran, H. Hermelink, states this attitude still more positively: 'The Sacrament is *verbum visibile*, which has no special meaning of its own, nor one apart from the Word of God. It gives no higher or more intimate communion than the Word of God in the teaching of His Church. . . . Given the preaching of the Word of God by the minister on the one hand and the believing congregation on the other, which together constitute the Church of Jesus Christ, the outward form of things does not matter. They are, as our fathers said, "*adiaphoron*".'[48]

Between the extreme emphasis upon the Sacraments in Anglican theology and the extreme devotion to the Word of God in Lutheran theology there is considerable ground for controversy, but such a controversy would surely not be fruitful for a better

---

[45] O. C. Quick, *The Christian Sacraments*, p. 138. This is identical with the view expressed by G. Florovsky of the Orthodox Church, to the effect that 'the sacraments constitute the Church': in *The Universal Church in God's Design* (W.C.C.), p. 47. But Newbigin remarks that no Church, even Catholic and Orthodox, except in periods of degeneracy, separates the Sacraments wholly from the Word. 'We cannot without violating the Church's real nature make the sacramental order alone decisive and say that by this the Church is constituted': *The Reunion of the Church*, pp. 68f.

[46] *Die christliche Wahrheit*, II.332.

[47] In *The Ministry and the Sacraments* (R. Dunkerley, ed.), p. 138.

[48] ibid., pp. 153, 156. The notable work of Karl Holl shows how Luther gave the Word the primary place in the Church, above the Sacraments. '*Durch das Wort ist die Kirche gegründet worden und wird sie noch immer erhalten*,' wrote Luther (*Weimar Ausgabe*, III.545.25); cf. '*Die Entstehung von Luthers Kirchenbegriff*' in Holl's *Gesammelte Aufsätze zur Kirchengeschichte*, Vol. I.

understanding of the nature of the Church. Neither party would wish to exclude either the observance of the Sacraments or the proclamation of the Word of God from the common practice of the Church. But *if* there should arise the question of pre-eminence between these two, as rarely happens, the greater weight by far of Protestant belief would favour the Word. It is the Word, as we have seen, which, as the expression of God's will, is the final authority for the Church. Recognizing that there are some tremendous objections to this doctrine, chiefly in the fact that the numerical majority of Christians on earth cling to the belief that this authority is inherent in the hierarchy of the Church itself, Protestant theologians are still convinced that the living Word, known to men by revelation and the Holy Spirit, stands high above the pretensions of those who would arrogate to themselves, however sincerely, the prerogatives of God. 'Church, ministry, and sacraments alike rest upon the Word of God,' concludes Micklem, 'and the minister has no authority whatever except the authority of the Word which he has been commissioned to expound.'[49] To challenge this assertion, one who assumes the burden of proof must appeal to an authority which is still higher than the divine Word; and this always means putting other gods before the One whose Incarnate Word Christ is.

IV. THE WORD AND THE SACRAMENTS CONSTITUTE THE CHURCH

Holding in view this concept of the Word of God as the pre-eminent authority of the Church, which means a subordination of the Sacraments as instruments of the Word, we must still take into account the fact that both Luther and Calvin, and their followers unto the present day, stressed the centrality of *both* the Word and the Sacraments for the Church. Interpreted through Melanchthon in the *Augsburg Confession*, the Lutheran doctrine of the Church was precisely stated in Article VII, as 'the congregation of saints in which the Gospel is rightly taught and the Sacraments rightly administered'. In the *Institutes of the Christian Religion* Calvin says virtually the same thing, although with more specific reference to the hearing of the Gospel and the basis of the Sacraments in the commission of Jesus Christ: 'Wherever we see the Word of God sincerely preached and heard, wherever we see

[49] *Congregationalism and the Church Catholic*, p. 58.

the Sacraments administered according to the institution of Christ, there we cannot have any doubt that the Church of God has come into existence.'[50] Almost verbatim echoes of these related statements are to be found in the various confessions and articles of religion which form the basis for most of the contemporary Lutheran, Reformed (Presbyterian), and Anglican[51] doctrines of the Church.

The importance of this prominent Reformation principle is that it plays so dominant a rôle in much of the contemporary writing about the Church. This is particularly, though not exclusively, true of the Lutheran writing. And in the whole area of Evangelical Christianity, the principle has afforded a strong restraint against pietistic and liberalistic tendencies to reduce the nature of the Church to a religious fellowship, or to make moral perfection a condition equivalent to the preaching of the Word and the observance of the Sacraments.

This is clearly illustrated by the reaction of certain German Lutherans in 1933 to the corruptingly perverse beliefs of the *Deutsche Christen*, who wanted to make the Church an obedient tool of national political policy. In the *Betheler Bekenntnis*, Martin Niemöller and others steadfastly reaffirmed the principle that 'the only signs of the Church are the purity of proclamation of the Gospel and the right administering of the Sacraments'.[52] All else, including the moral goodness and the religious position of its members, is not a sign of the reality of the Church, but is the fruit of living faith within the Church.

To those who are not in agreement or sympathy with this typically Lutheran understanding of the Church, the definition seems rather narrow, as well as highly vulnerable to the deadly corruption of objectivization of the Word of God and the Sacraments, a state which for the Church can literally be a *rigor mortis*. This danger shall be examined presently. Meanwhile it should be

---

[50] Book IV.1.9. In Book IV.1.12 Calvin writes that the preaching and administration must be 'pure', and this adjective seems to be favoured in modern references to the reformer's doctrine.

[51] Although Article XIX of The Thirty-nine Articles of Religion rests upon the Word and Sacraments, it is not considered a binding definition by many Anglicans.

[52] K. D. Schmidt, *Die Bekenntnisse und gründsätzlichen Aeusserungen zur Kirchenfrage des Jahres* 1933, p. 122. To make even clearer their dependence upon the Word and Sacraments, these 'confessing' churchmen of the *Kirchenkampf* went on to reject these other conceptions of the Church: that it is an invisible ideal; that its unity rests upon uniformity of teaching; that there is any previously given authoritative pattern of organization; that no external order is necessary.

noted that the Lutheran theology which is genuine does not forget who it is who gives meaning to these two signs of the Church. As Regin Prenter, the Danish Lutheran, remarks, 'It is the glorified Christ, in reality, who preaches, who baptizes and who invites to His table,' and this He does through the communion of saints, the Christians on earth, who constitute His Body.[53] Since this is true, the Church can forget its utter dependence upon Christ only at the peril of ceasing to be His Church, and becoming instead a religious society with a message and rites which have lost their meaning.

From this christological attitude toward the Word and the Sacraments the Church may at times depart in the direction of objectivism, on the one hand, or subjectivism, on the other. As Prenter remarks in another context, it is generally the great temptation of Catholicism to gravitate toward a false objectivism, and of Protestantism to slide toward a false subjectivism.[54] At the former extreme, the pronouncements, forms of worship, and Sacraments of the Church are, in effect, considered to be sufficient unto themselves. At the latter, all these are meaningful only in so far as the immediate experience of Christians interprets them. Neither extreme in the absolute sense is compatible with either Catholic or Evangelical Protestant belief, but they are aberrations which are not uncommon. 'Both subjectivism and objectivism in one way or another lead to the result that man makes himself God,' declares Prenter, 'either in deifying his visible Church institutions or in deifying his invisible thinking or religious experience.'[55]

But there have been instances in which the objectivization of the Word and the two Sacraments has taken place within *Protestantism*, and this has not gone unnoticed by critical theologians. Three decades ago Hermann Mulert reminded the Germans of Luther's famous epigram, that the devil himself could preach rightly and administer the Sacraments.[56] So long as the rightness of the preaching and the sacramental practice is regarded as something objectively established, rather than as

[53] In *La Sainte Église Universelle*, p. 125; cf. the previously noted statement of Barth, that when we consider preaching and the Sacraments, 'it is Jesus Christ Himself as the Word of God, who has to be the subject of our inquiry'.
[54] *The Ecumenical Review*, I.4(1949).387; cf. G. Aulén, *The Faith of the Christian Church*, pp. 364-6.
[55] *The Ecumenical Review*, I.4(1949).388.
[56] In the *Harnack-Ehrung* (Leipzig), p. 294.

being constantly in direct relation to Jesus Christ, Luther's quip about the devil is true.[57]

Such being the truth about Luther's own belief, Emil Brunner holds Melanchthon responsible for the objectivization of the Church and the hardening of the Word and the Sacraments into institutional concepts.[58] Since the time of Melanchthon's formulation of the *Augsburg Confession*, observes Brunner, the two marks of the Church have really meant 'pure doctrine', rather than the living Word, and 'correct administration', instead of faithful observance of the two visible manifestations of the Word. What Melanchthon wanted was just what some modern theologians also want: objective criteria for all the practice of the Church. In keeping with this desire, as C. Damour testifies, Melanchthon regarded the Church as an institution (*Anstalt*), a 'machine for salvation' (*Heilsmechanismus*) on the Roman Catholic pattern.[59] 'In this way,' continues Brunner, 'the personal concept of the Church—which is the only New Testament one—is obscured by the Objectivist concept of institution; and the revolutionary perception of Luther—that the Church is nothing other than a fellowship of persons, namely, the believers who through their present Lord, their Head, are connected with a body—was again lost.'[60]

This is not intended simply as a historical judgement upon Melanchthon, which could be of only academic interest, but as a judgement upon the (sometimes unintentional) acceptance and continuation of his doctrine in certain Protestant Churches today. It may be true, as Karl Heim writes, that this institutional doctrine of the Church and Sacraments, epitomized in Roman Catholicism, 'satisfies the hunger for objectivity, which, in an age of relativism like our own, is the deepest longing in the hearts of men'.[61] But that it satisfies such a hunger is hardly an acceptable justification for it. Submission to this kind of static authority, objectivized either in the Bible, or in Church doctrine, or in priestly control of the Sacraments, really means disobedience

[57] In the *Harnack-Ehrung* (Leipzig), p. 306.
[58] *The Divine-Human Encounter*, pp. 144ff. W. Niesel in *Evangelische Theologie* III (1936).321, takes Brunner to task for misunderstanding the meaning of 'teaching' (*doctrina, Lehre*). It means teaching of salvation in Christ, he says. But whether all Evangelicals have so understood it is still an open question.
[59] *Die Epochen des Protestantismus*, pp. 9, 27.
[60] *The Divine-Human Encounter*, p. 145; cf. H. Asmussen, 'Kirche Augsburgischer Konfession,' *Theologische Existenz Heute*, XVI(1934).29: Word and Sacraments must not be regarded 'juristically', he maintains.
[61] *Spirit and Truth*, p. 26.

to the final authority of the Word of God and refusal to accept in faith the responsibility which the Word lays upon each Christian, to live by grace rather than by law.

The antithesis of objectivization of Word and Sacraments in Protestant faith is found in the subjectivization of the same to the point where neither preaching nor sacramental action is deemed necessary. So, when speaking of the reformer's doctrine of the Word and the Sacraments as marks of the Church, S. Cave concludes: 'We dare not make even these two signs an exclusive test, for that would be to unchurch the Society of Friends, whose members show that they truly belong to Christ'.[62] To those tolerant theologians of the majority of denominations, who believe the Word and Sacraments to be essential to the Church, the position of the Society of Friends (Quakers), the Salvation Army, and many modern liberals has been a great embarrassment.

The attitude of the Quakers is well stated in this exerpt from a 1944 book of discipline:

Friends do not feel the need of symbols when the realities symbolized are achieved (in the experience of worship). They do not find that Jesus commanded that the 'sacraments' be observed as perpetual ordinances of his Church. They have furthermore been impressed by the endless controversies and divisions over them and by the historical variations in practice. The baptism, which they consider to be essential, is that of the Holy Spirit; the communion which they most earnestly desire is participation with Christ, the Bread of Life, and the spiritual apprehension of God as the source of life and power.[63]

When the Spirit of God is believed to be omnipresent, so that through the Spirit there is 'immediate contact with God', and when there is no recognition of the biblical basis for believing that Jesus desired the Sacraments to be perpetuated, the Quakers see no obstacle to viewing all of life as having 'sacramental character', and no reason for observing only the two Sacraments.

In this crucial matter they have received the support of one who speaks from a strictly Calvinistic standpoint, Auguste Lecerf. 'The sacraments have been instituted to confirm and seal faith,' he writes. 'Strictly speaking, faith may be living, even if it does not enjoy these aids. They are necessary, not for the *esse* but for

---
[62] *The Doctrines of the Christian Faith*, p. 253.
[63] Quoted by H. J. Cadbury in *The Nature of the Church* (American Theological Committee), p. 81; cf. also the statement by Quakers in *Convictions* (L. Hodgson, ed.), pp. 21-31.

the *bene esse* of faith. The doctrine of the sacraments is fundamental only in the restricted sense that it is necessary for the normal life of the Church. This is the reason why we do not consider that the Society of Friends must be excluded from visible catholicity.'[64]

This is a judgement to which a great many Protestants today would subscribe their names. It reflects the modest humility which ought to be implicit in the Church of Christ; it recognizes the fruit of the Spirit among those who have faithfully sought His guidance; and it acknowledges the reality of a worship in spirit and truth which can claim with full sobriety the 'real presence' of Christ, though without word or action.[65] And in return, the Quakers are fully tolerant of those who hold to a stricter sacramental doctrine, and are quite ready to appreciate the high value which others place upon the two Sacraments and their proper observance.

But is the tolerant attitude, which would admit that Sacraments are necessary only to a certain extent, beyond which spiritual immediacy suffices, really justifiable? O. C. Quick condemns this attitude on what seems to be a rational and pragmatic ground; namely that only the spiritually *élite* can sustain their worship without the aid of Word and Sacraments, and the Church is not intended to be the community of the select few.[66] However, Quick does not appeal, as might be expected, to the theological proposition that the Sacraments are so divinely ordained that they are to be considered indispensable.

This more rigorous view is espoused by J. S. Whale. He admits that recent biblical scholarship has strengthened the Quakers' position on the origin of the Sacraments. However, he cannot acknowledge that the Quakers' conception of sacramental life is adequate, for such an acknowledgement would reduce the elements of the Holy Communion to *nuda signa*, bare signs, which can be dispensed with at will. These elements are much more important than that, he maintains. They convey the realities of the divine grace and action themselves.[67]

[64] *An Introduction to Reformed Dogmatics*, p. 361.
[65] cf. *Faith and Order, Edinburgh* 1937 (L. Hodgson, ed.), p. 256.
[66] *The Christian Sacraments*, p. 178. He refers to the fact that Quakers have never been a missionary body, remaining small in number, and have never succeeded in incorporating people of poorer classes; cf. W. J. Phythian-Adams, *The Way of At-one-ment*, p. 105.
[67] In *The Ministry and the Sacraments* (R. Dunkerley, ed.), p. 217.

Here meet two conceptions of sacramental reality which can hardly be reconciled, for each appeals to the faith and experience of those who, in common, base their attitude upon the living and written Word of God, looking for guidance in the New Testament and by the Holy Spirit.

The Quakers will readily admit that their faith involves a high degree of subjectivism. But with this does not go the admission of Prenter's judgement, that they thereby make themselves identical with God by 'deifying (their) invisible thinking and religious experience'. By 'subjectivism' they only mean their effort to avoid the 'confusion between symbol and reality, which too often leads, as they think, to an undue concern for the symbol'.[68] The Quakers make their strong witness to the reality of a thoroughly spiritual worship, convinced that they are scripturally and theologically justified in keeping their position, regardless of the antagonism of all who, with equal conviction, believe the Quaker position to be wrong. And rather than attempting to cut the knot in too facile a manner, it is perhaps best in this matter to trust, as the Edinburgh Conference found fit to do, 'that the Holy Spirit will show to us . . . His will'.[69]

Despite the persistence of the Friends' witness to the reality of the unspoken Word and the invisible Sacrament, we have seen in the foregoing pages that, during the past thirty years, largely due to the revival of interest in Reformation theology, but also because of the significant attention given to problems of Church reunion, the theologians of Protestantism have been deeply concerned with the nature and meaning of the Word of God and the Sacraments of Baptism and Holy Communion. Their concern has been an impetus to extensive and profound study, which has not yet effected a consensus of belief nor a reconciliation of half-forgotten doctrinal differences, but which has brought into the full light of day the facts which, to a large degree, divide and estrange Christians from one another.

[68] *Faith and Order, Edinburgh* 1937 (L. Hodgson, ed.), p. 354.
[69] C. Heath in ibid., p. 246.

Part Two—The Ministry of the Church

1. A MATTER OF FAITH OR OF ORDER?

Possibly the most perplexing problem in the current study of the Church's nature is that of the meaning and authority of the Church's ministry. For many persons, indeed, this appears to be the only problem to discuss, because they assume that, once the ministry has been properly defined and recognized, all other aspects of the Church's being can be readily explained. On the other hand, it is felt by many that, until a definite concept of the nature of the Church has been attained, the problem of the ministry should be held in abeyance. And whereas some believe that the ministry is *the* basis for understanding the Church, others at the opposite extreme assert that the Church can live quite well with no ministry at all. Between what may be termed the 'hierarchical' and the 'anarchical' views of the ministry, which are the opposite poles of thought, exists a wide area of mixed opinion, admitting more or less importance to the commission, function, and authority of the ministry.

A reading of the voluminous literature concerning this problem, which has been published since 1918, indicates that the various arguments belong as much to the field of Church history as to theology. Appeal for one view against another is largely based upon the documents of Apostolic, Patristic and Reformation periods of history, and the ministerial practice therein described or commended. To treat such literature adequately, even to present a digest of its complicated findings, would require many more pages of writing than are permissible in this book. Our primary interest shall be in the theological rather than the historical problem of the ministry, although some historical references will inevitably have to be made, since the matter cannot be abstracted from the actual life of the Church.

Some will perhaps question the assumption that there can be any theological problem of the ministry, since they hold all matters of Church order to be concerned merely with the outward organization and economy of local churches. The problem of theology arises, however, when we perceive, as so many Protestants do, an inherent connexion between the work of the ministry and the divine message and purpose of salvation in the Word of God. Whatever the titles given to the minister or the authority ascribed to him, the ministry is necessary in the Church, as Phythian-Adams reminds us, to 'do what St. Paul says it was given to do, viz., "perfect" the At-one-ment of the personal relationships of Christians in the one Body'.[70] To this end, it is held, the ministers are ordained and the ministry perpetuated. Inasmuch as the many denominational representatives at Edinburgh could agree that 'the ministry was instituted by Jesus Christ . . . and is a gift of God to the Church in the service of the Word and Sacraments',[71] it is clear that those who consider it to be no more than a convenient means of administrating the affairs of a Church are in a minority.

The place of New Testament exegesis in this discussion must not be underrated either. Whatever other claims the various factions may make with regard to the validity of their doctrines of the ministry, they all believe themselves to be in accord with the spirit, and often with the letter, of the Bible. That Catholic Anglicans, Presbyterians, and Quakers can all justify there various conceptions of the ministry by reference to the New Testament must be a source of much comfort for the avowed antagonist of the Church! This is probably why Reinhold Niebuhr would prefer to pass over the whole question, as he indicates when he writes: 'The "order" of a Church, its rites and its polity, belong clearly to the realm of the historically contingent. Failure to recognize this fact naturally leads the Catholic wing of the non-Roman Churches to insist that its order is the only possible one for an ecumenical Church. The logic of this sinful spiritual imperialism conforms to the logic of sin generally.'[72] But in spite of this popular attitude which Niebuhr articulates, there are many in the Protestant theological tradition who feel obliged to struggle with problems of order and ministry in order to clarify their own beliefs and to seek a common understanding with those who hold opposing ones.

It is impossible to catalogue the views of the ministry which are held by Protestant theologians into such well-defined categories

---

[70] *The Way of At-one-ment*, p. 98.
[71] *Faith and Order, Edinburgh* 1937 (L. Hodgson, ed.), p. 356.
[72] *The Nature and Destiny of Man*, II.225.

that each would appear to be wholly distinct from the others. There is a great deal of overlapping opinion. In our treatment of the subject, therefore, we shall simply begin with the most flexible and pragmatic concept of the ministry and move on toward the more rigid and hierarchical.

II. THE PRIESTHOOD OF ALL CHRISTIANS

Basic to the distinctively Protestant idea of the Church's ministry is the idea that all true believers in Jesus Christ are priests in their own right, independent of the sacerdotal mediacy of an established priesthood. There is good reason for holding such an idea, since there is sound authority for it, both in the New Testament and in the teaching of Luther (who was not the authority himself, but only the interpreter of it). The classic reference in 1 Peter 2^9 urges the Christians to regard themselves as a 'royal priesthood'; and in Hebrews 8^1 the sufficiency of Jesus as the one high priest for mankind is assured. Moreover, the intensely personal relationship between God and man, which is so implicit in the teaching of Jesus, substantiates this doctrine of the universal priesthood.

In recent usage, however, the idea has become grossly distorted by an unavoidable merger with the equalitarian political philosophy of Western democracy. And the resulting concept of the priesthood of all believers amounts to the belief that in the sight of God it is 'every man for himself'.

If this distorted doctrine were the real principle for Protestantism, there would not only be no need for a ministry in the Church, but no need for the Church itself. The wrong understanding of the doctrine as strictly individualistic is exposed by Althaus in his treatment of Luther's ideas.[73] The office of a priest, he writes means: to come before God, to pray for others, to intercede and offer oneself to God, and to proclaim the Word of God. This cannot be done in isolation from other persons, however; so the priesthood of all believers means that each Christian is a priest *for others*, not for himself. Rather than expressing a radical individualism for Christians, this doctrine is a most emphatic testimony to the communal unity, the interdependence of all Christians, and the *koinōnia* of the Church.

But how does this affect one's attitude toward the ministry?

[73] *Communio sanctorum*, p. 69.

THE SACRAMENTS AND THE MINISTRY 145

In the first place, remarks Kattenbusch, it means that there can be no inherent difference between the ministry and the laity, religiously speaking. In virtue of their faith, both have the right and obligation to serve the Church, but it would be presumptuous to contend that God is more favourably disposed toward one than another.[74] In this he has the support of leading biblical scholars, notably, C. H. Dodd, who interprets Paul as recognizing no distinctions between clerical and lay ministries, but only between the spiritual 'gifts' (*charisma*) or talents for service, which Christians receive from the Holy Spirit.[75] In the Church all persons are indeed priests, but they are to be distinguished by gifts and functions rather than by hierarchical stations. And even these marks of functional distinction do not involve any differences of worth or eminence in the sight of God.

This has recently been stated graphically by Barth: 'There can be no talk of higher and lower orders of specific services. There is differentiation of functions, but the preacher cannot really stand any higher than the other elders, nor the bell-ringer any lower than the professor of theology. There can be no "clergy" and no "laity", no merely "teaching" and no merely "listening" Church, because there is no member of the Church who is not the whole thing in his own place.'[76] And since the pastor is just a member of the congregation, he is not authoritatively superior to others.

This principle, which was so crucial in the Reformation, if properly understood, has a momentous importance for the Church. It is both the weakness and the strength of Protestantism, observes Karl Heim, that it is the only religion in history which has made priests unnecessary.[77] It is only 'division of labour' which makes it necessary to have clergymen in the Church. 'The clergymen can do nothing which could not be done by any living member of the community,'[78] except for the talents he has been given.

In the second place, continues Kattenbusch, this principle of the universal priesthood takes out of the hands of the clergy the

---

[74] *Die Doppelschichtigkeit in Luthers Kirchenbegriff*, p. 86.

[75] *The Epistle of Paul to the Romans*, p. 195, with regard to Romans 12. Paul's idea of the ministry is debated by scholars now, particularly when the Pastoral Epistles are regarded as Pauline. 2 Corinthians 5²⁰ is often cited as a statement of Paul's ministerial consciousness: 'So we are ambassadors for Christ, God making His appeal through us.'

[76] Files of Commission I, W.C.C., Geneva: first draft of Barth's article for *The Universal Church in God's Design*.

[77] *Spirit and Truth*, p. 151.   [78] ibid., p. 177.

major responsibility for the proper maintenance of the Church and gives it to the whole community of members. It is their duty, not the pastor's alone, to make sure that the preaching and witness of the Church are truly in accord with the Word of God, and so they have a kind of 'power' over the pastor.[79] This is a concept which is highly acceptable to Evangelical Protestants, although it hardly needs to be pointed out that, even in those denominations which adhere to it in principle, many churches have become 'pastor-centred', and the congregation has not assumed its full responsibility.

In view of the doctrine of the priesthood of all Christians, it may well be asked whether the act of ordination can have any real meaning. Inasmuch as the reformers refuted the doctrine that ordination is a true Sacrament, it is not inconsistent to assert that, in general, ordination is an act in which the Church accepts and gives approval to a man who has been personally called by God to the ministry. This is the fundamental idea which is held by the various Reformed and Evangelical Churches, and it is considered to be in harmony with the New Testament example.[80] As Heim declares: 'On Protestant principles it is no longer possible to think that religious authority can be transferred by anointing or by any other ceremony.'[81] If the 'inward call' of Christ to be His minister is not an authentic commission, adds Walter Lowrie, nothing can be gained or added by ordination: it is not even necessary to receive thereby the authority of the whole Church, as some maintain, for the authority of the Head of the Church is all that is needed.[82] Any further authorization on the part of the Church implies a deficiency in the authority already bestowed by Christ, which is just the commission to be a servant, as He was in a perfect sense. Upon this basis, one may say with T. L. Haitjema of Holland, that a group of Christians on an isolated island of the ocean could acknowledge a faithful man of their number as their minister, and that he could administer valid Sacraments and perform all necessary duties,

---

[79] *Die Doppelschichtigkeit in Luthers Kirchenbegriff*, p. 104.
[80] Despite some critics' contention that it is not authentic, the story of the selection and ordination (by laying on hands) of the seven deacons (Acts 6) is the earliest example in the Church; cf. 1 Timothy 4^{14}, Acts 13^3. E. Schweizer says that Paul regarded ordination as only a recognition of the gift of grace already received: *Das Leben des Herrn in der Gemeinde und ihren Diensten*, p. 114.
[81] *Spirit and Truth*, p. 176.
[82] *Problems of Church Unity*, p. 212.

THE SACRAMENTS AND THE MINISTRY 147

according to his gifts, bestowed by the Spirit.[83] A side remark of Brunner's expresses the Protestant concept even more radically, although not definitively: 'The pastor—that is to say, the believing Christian who has the advantage over the others of a thorough theological training . . .'[84]

Some of these quotations, if taken as complete and normative for Protestant thought, would seem to indicate so severe a minimization of the act of ordination that it might well be dispensed with altogether. Instead, they express the extremes to which theological statements about the ministry *can* go, and they perform the polemic function against the Catholic doctrine of the priestly class. In actual practice, however, the synods, conferences, and local churches of denominations which hold these views exercise varying degrees of care in examining the candidates for the ministry, and perform their ceremonies of ordination with much solemnity and sincerity, believing that God does work through the Church's ministers for the spiritual care of persons and the propagation of His Word.

III. THE SERVANT OF THE WORD

With regard to the actual function of the minister, no other description better applies than the phrase *minister verbi divini*, 'the servant of the Word of God'. The fundamental, literal meaning of 'ministry' has always been *diakonia*, or *leitourgia*, i.e. 'service', of which the life of Jesus was the epitome. 'There is in the New Testament scarcely one title of service which did not previously exist as a title for Christ Himself,' observes E. Schweizer.[85] And all of the many specific duties which a modern minister must fulfil are gathered together in this one duty, to carry on His task of bringing the Gospel to the people. But the Protestant minister rejects the claim of the Roman priest, that he is in a full sense an *alter Christus*. As Anders Nygren describes the function of the ministry, it is not to lead people to God by offering prayers and services, but rather to bring the Word of God to the people, whom God Himself seeks in His love.[86] 'It is right, therefore, to speak of the minister as representing Christ to his people,

---

[83] In *The Ministry and the Sacraments* (R. Dunkerley, ed.), p. 172.
[84] *The Divine-Human Encounter*, p. 141.
[85] *Das Leben des Herrn in der Gemeinde und ihren Diensten*, p. 32.
[86] '*Vom geistlichen Amt*' in *Zeitschrift für systematische Theologie* (1935), pp. 40-2.

but only in Christ's way, in the form of a servant,' concludes Daniel Jenkins.[87]

The concept of the minister as the servant of the Word is so general, however, that by itself it cannot tell us what form the ministry should take or what prerogatives belong to the minister. While the minister in principle must conform to Jesus' pattern of service, he must also in practice know what his position in the Church is; and there should be a clear understanding on the part of the Church as well with respect to his position. It is just this understanding that is often not clear, and the problem of clarification of the minister's status and identity is a difficult one.

Any student of the New Testament knows that it is virtually hopeless to find therein one indisputable, unchangeable pattern for the Church's ministry. Several kinds of function or office in the Church can be justified by appeal to one or more references in the New Testament. Since it was held in the primitive Church that varieties of function derived solely from the gifts of the Spirit 'for building up the Body of Christ', the ministry may be said to have included every Christian in the Church. Not only were apostles, prophets and teachers so recognized, but evangelists, pastors, administrators, healers, speakers in tongues, almsgivers, etc.[88] This is not to overlook the fact that there were certain leaders in the Church during the first century, with particular respect being paid to the original disciples and to James. Paul could also speak of himself as a spiritual father of the Corinthians, and exercise on necessity a degree of discipline over them.[89] It would hardly have been possible that the groups of Christians, with their many problems of communal living, their common worship, their questions about Jesus Christ, and their missionary zeal, to have continued long without delegating duties according to individual gifts and recognizing certain men and women as really worthy for the full-time ministry. All of these ministries were considered equal in principle, although in practice the differences of gifts had to be recognized.[90]

But two questions must be asked about the New Testament ministry. First, did these differences of gifts soon account for certain specific offices, some of which may still be considered to be

---

[87] *The Gift of the Ministry*, p. 39.
[88] cf. Romans 12^{6-8}; 1 Corinthians 12^{28}; Ephesians 4^{11}.
[89] 1 Corinthians 4^{15}, ^{21}, 5^{5}.   [90] cf. A. V..Ström, *Kyrkans Väsen*, p. 22.

normative for the ministry of the Church today? And, more important to ask, were these offices so essential that only by their preservation and perpetuation through the ensuing centuries could the authentic character of the Church be retained?

With regard to the first question, most modern denominations would affirm that their ministries are substantially in accord with the *diakonia* of the New Testament, if not in exact duplication of offices, at least in the actual function. Even the Society of Friends claims to reproduce the original ministry of the 'prophets' of the primitive Church; and their prophets today, speaking by the Holy Spirit, along with the elders and overseers (literally *episkopoi*), constitute a three-fold ministry with New Testament origins.[91] Presbyterians hold that their office of presbyter is an identification of the offices of bishop, presbyter, and pastor, as named in the New Testament.[92] Others having their deacons, elders, and bishops can also find New Testament counterparts to these offices. None of these, however, except those claiming the apostolic succession of bishops, makes of its ministerial office a theological principle, which would connect the authority of the office to the peculiar authority of the original apostles. As Hans Asmussen says, the modern minister is not sent in the same way in which Peter, James, John, and the others were sent by Jesus; only in virtue of the fact that he preaches the same Word and administers the same Baptism can he claim a kinship with the apostles.[93] By this he apparently does not mean to minimize the importance of the ministry, but only to point out its limitations of authority.

The modern Protestant minister looks to the New Testament for guidance in his preaching, pastoral care and service to the community; he finds his faith strengthened by the witness of the apostles, and his desire to serve his own brethren quickened by their love and devotion to theirs. He sees there the one indefatigable ministry of the Word of God. But he does not expect to find there a support or proof for the claim that his orders carry an apostolic authority, derived from Christ Himself, in virtue of his having been the recipient of the same power which Christ granted to the original apostles, and which has devolved upon

[91] In *Convictions* (L. Hodgson, ed), p. 25. No ordination is observed, however.
[92] In *The Ministry and the Sacraments* (R. Dunkerley, ed.), p. 177.
[93] In *Rechtgläubigkeit und Frömmigkeit*, III.95f.

generations of clergy by transmission through the succession of bishops. If the minister can know his task to be the faithful service to the Word, he is not worried about other credentials for his authority.

IV. APOSTOLIC SUCCESSION

In pondering an answer to the second question posed above, we are involved in the complex problem of the apostolic succession of bishops. For the many Protestants who live in areas where neither the Orthodox nor the Anglican Churches have much influence, this is a remote and somewhat unreal problem. But churchmen in England, in particular, have long been familiar with the issues at stake. And in recent years, spurred by the ecumenical movement and the increasing pressure for reunion, theologians of both the Church of England and the English Free Churches have placed apostolic succession in the centre of their discussions. Churches outside England have also been drawn into the debate, because the Anglicans and Orthodox, having played so prominent a rôle in the ecumenical movement, have still steadfastly refused to compromise their position on the necessity of episcopacy. This resoluteness strikes a non-Anglican Protestant as being either narrow-mindedness or sheer obstinacy, largely because he cannot understand the presuppositions on which the doctrine of episcopal succession is based. Likewise, the Catholic Anglican regards the Free-Churchman as obstinate, if he is informed, because the latter will not accept a doctrine which seems to be so incontestably substantiated by the history of the Church.

At the root of the whole matter lies the problem of apostolicity. It is the common belief of Christians that the Church is apostolic. Just as the original disciples were made apostolic when they were 'sent' by Jesus, the Church was sent as a redeemed people who should serve Him for the redemption of the world. Brunner's analysis of the rôle of the apostle shows how the Church too became apostolic: 'The Apostle stands on the borderline where the history of revelation becomes the history of the Church; he has a share in both. . . . The Church comes into being only because the Apostle comes forth from his secret intercourse with God and turns to others, giving to them in the third person what God Himself gave him in the heart in the second person. The existence

THE SACRAMENTS AND THE MINISTRY 151

of the Church is based on this Apostolic act of turning toward man. Thus the Apostolic word precedes the Church as its foundation.'[94]

If there were in the New Testament a dependable definition of an apostle and a description of his function and place in the Church, we should be spared a great deal of the speculation and theorizing, over and above well-established historical date, which have claimed the energies of such competent scholars of this century as R. Sohm, K. Müller, A. von Harnack, C. Gore, J. A. Robinson, H. Lietzmann, A. C. Headlam, F. Heiler, B. H. Streeter, and G. Dix. In spite of the vast amount of labour expended upon the study of primitive sources, there has not yet appeared a really satisfactory explanation on which all scholars can agree as to how the personal commission given by Jesus to the apostles[95] was transmitted to others. So far as dependable literature is concerned, there extends from the late first century to the end of the second century a dark 'tunnel', as it has been called, through which the Church historian must grope and stumble with uncertainty. How was it that the authority which the apostles alone could claim, in virtue of their having seen the risen Lord and received His commission, is again claimed by a bishop in the third century when he ordains a man to the priesthood?

The Anglo-Catholic scholar, Gregory Dix, relying largely upon 1 Clement 44 and *The Apostolic Tradition* of Hippolytus, reconstructs the process in an ingenious way.[96] Christ authorized the apostles to be His plenipotentiaries, giving them a position corresponding exactly to the Jewish idea of *shaliach* (i.e. one who represents *with full power* the man who sent him).[97] The leaders of the primitive Churches were the elders, also called 'overseers or *episkopoi*, but they did not receive the authority of Christ from the apostles. Rather, the apostles chose certain 'apostolic men' such as Timothy and Titus, and transmitted[98] the *shaliach*-authority

[94] *Revelation and Reason*, pp. 122f.
[95] cf. John 20^{21}, 'As the Father has sent me, even so I send you.' Hoskyns, *The Fourth Gospel*, pp. 545f., says of this verse: 'The controversy whether the commission is given to the Church as a whole or to the apostles is irrelevant. There is no distinction between the Church and the ministry; both completely overlap. . . . Both are inaugurated together. There are as yet no converts. . . . The Christian community was, at its inception, a community of Apostles.'
[96] In *The Apostolic Ministry* (K. E. Kirk, ed.), Chapter 4.
[97] cf. K. H. Rengstorf, *TWNT*, I.397-448: *shaliach* in the Hebrew Old Testament corresponds to *apostolos* in the Septuagint.
[98] But T. W. Manson, *The Church's Ministry*, p. 36, argues on the basis of Hebrew usage and law that a *shaliach* could not delegate his authority to anyone else.

of Christ to them, empowering them to ordain others. In time this power came to reside with the permanent office of bishop, which had gathered to itself the ruling function of the elder as well. After the third century the apostolic commission was firmly guarded and passed on by the episcopacy alone, and so it has come down to the present time.

The evidence which Dix adduces for this theory is more extensive than that which was available to Charles Gore; but his dogmatic conclusion harmonizes with Gore's assertion that Jesus Christ constituted in the Church 'an authoritative ministry in the persons of His Apostles, which was intended to be permanent and which did in fact propagate itself in various grades of ministry, so that the three-fold ministry[99] of Church history is in fact, by succession, the only representative of the original apostolate, and all who desire to adhere to "the Body of Christ" must adhere to this (episcopal) ministry'.[100] All those Protestants who broke away from the succession of Roman episcopacy, therefore, repudiated their inheritance in the Church of Christ, namely the benefits of authentically administered Sacraments. The Orthodox Churches possessed this authority from the first. And inasmuch as the Church of England (and perhaps the Church of Sweden) did not really abrogate their episcopal orders at the time of the Reformation, the Anglicans still lay claim to their possession of the true apostolic ministry.

It is wrong to think that all Anglicans are fully persuaded that this reading of the history of episcopacy is the only right one. B. S. Easton, for example, asserts flatly that 'precisely how the Christian succession began is unknown and unknowable'.[101] And there are a good many others who aggressively oppose the rigid claim that no ministers called and ordained outside this succession share the apostolic commission of Christ. Their opposition is not based solely upon a different understanding of the history of the ministry, but also upon a different conception of the nature of the Church and the relation of Christ to the Church.

A strict Anglo-Catholic would find his belief well expressed by A. G. Hebert in this sentence: 'That which is of the *esse* of the

---

[99] That is, bishops, elders (priests), and deacons.
[100] *The Church and the Ministry*, Revised edn. (C. H. Turner, ed.), p. 392.
[101] *The Pastoral Epistles*, p. 226.

THE SACRAMENTS AND THE MINISTRY 153

Church is the essential core of the Ministry, namely the Apostolic Commission, which the Bishop alone holds in its fullness, and is empowered to hand on.'[102] Too many implications may not be drawn from this conviction without violating its meaning, however. Because the apostolic ministry is thought to belong to the 'being' (*esse*) rather than the 'well-being' (*bene esse*) of the Church, it does not follow that the whole being of the Church depends upon this ministry, so that a Church without such a ministry is inconceivable.[103] In fairness to the Anglo-Catholic theologians, it must also be noted that the apostolic commission is not considered a personal possession of any bishop, so that he can wield it at will, apart from his place in the Church. As O. C. Quick carefully explains: 'Capacity to exercise authority, and *a fortiori* capacity to transmit it, must reside in the office held rather than in the person of him who holds it.'[104] Failure to recognize these two reservations of the doctrine has been responsible for even further confusion in this very complex problem.

The Anglo-Catholic is not concerned about hypothetical questions of how the apostolic commission and witness in the Church ought to be or could be continued, apart from the episcopacy. Neither does he feel the need for reconciling the doctrine of succession with the faith in Christ's continuing presence through the Holy Spirit, for he discerns no contradiction between the two. He believes that he is defending, historically and theologically, the actual fact that in such a way Christ intended His authority to be continued in the succession of bishops, and that the history of the Church has demonstrated how well His intention has been realized. As K. E. Kirk believes, the Church can base its confidence for its victorious mission in the world only upon the claim that the ministry 'derives from the Lord Himself in the days of his flesh'.[105] Since this claim must rest upon the historical succession of the unbroken episcopacy, of which other Protestant bodies do not pretend to be a part, it is unfortunately necessary to conclude that all non-episcopal denominations are outside the visible Church of Christ.

This uncompromising interpretation of episcopacy is not shared by a majority of Anglicans, however, who consider 'the

---

[102] *The Form of the Church*, p. 113.
[103] H. Burn-Murdoch, *Church, Continuity and Unity*, p. 109.
[104] *The Christian Sacraments*, p. 143.   [105] *The Apostolic Ministry*, p. 52.

only necessary outward condition of a valid ministry (to be) the solemn commission of the Church through those appointed by it to ordain', while the episcopacy itself is no more than 'a valuable witness to and safeguard of the Church's unity and continuity'.[106] They do not feel that in order to accept and treasure the historic episcopacy it is necessary to regard it as the sole channel by which the authority given by Christ to the apostles is conveyed to the Church today. Many would agree with the conclusion of A. C. Headlam, himself an Anglican bishop, when he wrote: 'It is, then, not because I believe that the historical episcopacy is necessary for valid orders, but because I believe that it is necessary to secure Christian unity, that I hold that it must be the rule of a reunited Church.'[107] This opinion, growing out of ecumenical discussion, is based only upon prudential considerations, however, and substantiated by the bishop's own extensive knowledge of the history of episcopacy.

But is the problem only one of history and practical order of the Church? Some leading Anglican theologians think it is not, for the claims of the Anglo-Catholics really involve deeper theological questions of divine grace and justification, as well as of the nature of the Church itself.

With regard to grace, C. F. D. Moule writes that those who discuss the Christian ministry must hold either one of two different doctrines: either they think of grace 'primarily in personal terms, as a right relationship between God and man created by God's undeserved generosity', or else they 'think impersonally of authoritative status'.[108] The former is surely the meaning of the Gospel in the New Testament and the interpretation which Paul made of the redemptive work of Christ. But the latter concept is inherent in the Anglo-Catholic doctrine of episcopal succession, in which the primary concern is for the authentication of the credentials of the minister who mediates grace vicariously for Christ. A too rigid adherence to the principle of apostolic succession may thus be another form of the error of objectivization, of which we have already taken note. According to the New Testament, the priesthood and its function properly belong to all the people of the Church, but there is no priesthood within the

---

[106] J. P. Hickinbotham in *The Ministry of the Church* (S. Neill, ed.), p. 34, drawing upon Article XXIII of the *Thirty-nine Articles of Religion*.
[107] *The Doctrine of the Church and Christian Reunion*, p. 269.
[108] In *The Ministry of the Church* (S. Neill, ed.), p. 45.

royal priesthood of the people.[109] If this be recognized, it seems hardly possible that a ministerial order which restricts the work of Christ through His Spirit by regarding His commission as once-given and self-perpetuating in the continuum of history, can take very seriously the elementary Christian faith concerning the freely-given grace of God.

It is difficult for some to see, moreover, how the prominent doctrine of 'justification by faith alone', proclaimed by the reformers and espoused by the Anglican Church,[110] can be consonant with the implications of the claims made by Anglo-Catholics. A few of their spokesmen not only prefer not to accept this doctrine but openly disavow it in the light of their emphasis upon the episcopacy. Though he is perhaps not typical of all who hold this view of the ministry, Gregory Dix declares: 'Where the doctrine of 'justification by faith alone' is held, no question of Church order can be anything but entirely secondary, even meaningless. No external institution of any kind can ever be regarded as in itself *necessary* for the living of the redeemed life.'[111] No statement could indicate more clearly than this does how deep a theological gulf separates the Catholic Anglicans (so far as they share this view) from the remainder of Protestantism, with which they are conventionally, but erroneously, classed.

It is just on this doctrine of justification that Stephen Neill rests his contention that the very 'Catholic' writers of *The Apostolic Ministry* do not speak for the theology of the whole Anglican Church.[112] 'Those of us who reject the doctrine of the Church and ministry set forth in *The Apostolic Ministry* reject it, not on grounds of minute differences on points of archaeological interpretation, but because we cannot recognize as Christian the doctrine of God, which seems to underlie this imposing theological edifice.'[113] Of all the criticisms aimed at the rigid doctrine of succession, this one, if valid, carries the most cogent force.

There is reason for the Anglo-Catholics' deprecation of such doctrines as those which disregard altogether the order and form of the Church and regard it solely as a fellowship of the Spirit.

---

[109] The New Testament nowhere calls the minister of the Church 'priest'. Only the people at large are so named, 1 Peter 2^9, or Christ Himself, Hebrews 4^{14}; cf. W. J. Phythian-Adams, *The Way of At-one-ment*, p. 74.
[110] Article XI of the *Thirty-nine Articles of Religion*.
[111] In *The Apostolic Ministry* (K. E. Kirk, ed.), p. 301.
[112] *The Ministry of the Church*, p. 20.
[113] ibid., p. 28.

But some of their fellow Anglicans are driven to protest against an ecclesiastical system which would virtually require the restriction of the Spirit's activity to the duly constituted and ordained clergy. This is the gravamen of T. O. Wedel, who writes of the doctrine of succession: 'The Spirit is no longer, as clearly in the New Testament, a corporate possession of the whole Body of Christ, but a gift monopolized by and in a ministerial succession. . . . The Spirit is a corporate possession. How can it be monopolized by a single organ of the Body?'[114] It may even be asked why those who hold to the most extreme view of succession see the need for any indispensable relationship between the Spirit and the Church. Assuming the truth of the concept of the Church as the Body of Christ, consisting of persons called, inspired, and bound together by the Holy Spirit, does it not follow necessarily that, if Christ's commission of authority to the apostles were transmitted by the episcopal laying-on of hands, Pentecost need never have happened to the Church? This is the critical question posed by Newbigin, and he feels that the Anglo-Catholic apologist cannot refute its implications.[115] Communion with the living Christ in the Spirit is then no longer essential for the life of the Church, since the really determinative factor is the authenticated apostolic authority, historically delegated, rather than the Spirit-motivated free faith of all who believe in the Lord Jesus Christ as the Word of God.

As an explanation of the pertinence of these criticisms, it must be observed again that the critics have no hostility whatsoever toward the idea of apostolicity. Reformed theologians are just as willing to acknowledge the apostolate's primary importance for the Church as the most thoroughgoing Catholic. Barth makes it abundantly clear that Christians do not have any ground for contesting the fact that there is one, and only one, apostolic authority in the Church.[116] And from this it follows that apostolicity is really an essential mark of the Church, as traditional Catholic thought has always maintained. But wherein does this apostolicity lie? In the testimony of the apostles, to be sure. However, the division between Catholic and Protestant doctrine now appears: for 'the testimony does not draw its authority from the fact that it is the Apostles who bear it, as traditional Catholic

---

[114] *The Coming Great Church*, p. 144. [115] *The Reunion of the Church*, p. 163f.
[116] *Die Theologie und die Kirche*, p. 292.

teaching seems to suggest, but the Apostles have authority only in so far as they forget themselves in being faithful witnesses to Jesus Christ'.[117] Upon this testimony the Church must inevitably rest, for it is the proclaimed Word, which was eventually written and given to the Church, which perpetuates the apostolicity of the laity and ministry alike.[118] Thus Leenhardt concludes: 'The Church is apostolic because it is the messenger of the Gospel. Its apostolic function will be fulfilled only if it takes the succession of the apostles, not simply as messengers, but as messengers of the authentic Gospel.'[119]

From the Reformed and Evangelical points of view, it is this interpretation of apostolicity which really belongs to the *esse* of the Church. Where the Catholic Anglicans (and 'High' Lutherans) have gone astray, implies P. C. Simpson, is in confusing what the Church *is* with what the Church *has*.[120] The Church *is* the community of those who believe in Jesus Christ and faithfully live by His will. The Church *has* outward institutional forms, ministry and order, which are the possessions of the Church but not its basic attributes. When the possessions are so magnified that they are regarded as indispensable to the very nature of the Church, the unavoidable result is always 'ecclesiastical materialism'.[121] It is not the desire of Protestant theologians to belittle the order of episcopacy, therefore, but to insist stoutly that it is not the episcopacy which makes the Church to be what it is.

Neither is it the desire of these theologians to deny the real necessity of continuity in the Church, from the apostolic generation through the present. As Leonard Hodgson has pointed out: 'The fundamental cleavage in Christendom does not lie between those who hold differing views on the nature of the continuity of the visible Church, whether, for example, it is maintained by episcopal or presbyteral succession or by the continuous life of the whole body handing on the true faith from one generation to another. It lies between those who hold that there must be some such continuity of the earthly body and those who hold that this is unnecessary.'[122] In respect to this cleavage, the

---

[117] D. T. Jenkins, *The Nature of Catholicity*, p. 24.
[118] J. E. L. Newbigin, *The Reunion of the Church*, p. 164, defends the thesis that the 'whole people of God' is apostolic in commission. J. Moffatt, *The Presbyterian Churches*, p. 111, declares that the 'apostolic ministry of presbyters' is faithful to the will of Christ.
[119] In *La Sainte Église Universelle*, p. 87.   [120] *The Evangelical Church Catholic*, p. 33.
[121] ibid., p. 28.   [122] Unpublished seminar notes, Oxford, 1949.

Protestants of whom we have been speaking stand on the side of those who cling to the apostolic succession of bishops. While not rejecting the principle of continuity, however, they maintain that the true succession from the apostles to the present has depended wholly upon the preservation of the Word of God, the Gospel of Jesus Christ known to us in the apostolic Scriptures and the preaching.

P. T. Forsyth thus asserts that the real successor of the apostolate was the canonical New Testament,[123] and G. S. Hendry concurs when he writes: 'It is the transmission of the Canon in this positive sense from faith to faith throughout the generations that constitutes the true apostolic succession.'[124] These testify to the continuity of the written Word. But the Word faithfully proclaimed and observed in the Sacraments means the same kind of continuity, as R. Prenter proposes: 'Especially where there is correct preaching, Communion and Baptism, there is the true and indubitable apostolic succession.'[125]

Stated in still another way, it is the whole Gospel and the fellowship that it continually calls into being which preserves the authoritative testimony of the apostles.[126] 'There extends from the beginning of the Church down to the present', remarks Karl Holl, 'a *successio fidelium*' which is the response of all generations to the ever-present Christ.[127] It is this understanding of Church continuity which is normative for Protestantism, and it is the only kind which its many theologians can acknowledge as the divine mode of succession, as opposed to that which is contingent upon the episcopacy.

Where Christ Himself, the living Word, is not regarded absolutely as the One who gives the Church both apostolicity and continuity, it is hardly possible that any theologian who draws his ideas from the New Testament can agree to any other principle. As T. W. Manson states the case: 'Our contention is that the Church as the Body of Christ is apostolic in the sense that the apostolic ministry inaugurated by the Lord in the days of His flesh is continued in Him through her in the new period of world-history inaugurated by the Resurrection. . . . If that is the right

---

[123] *The Church and the Sacraments*, p. 59.
[124] In *Scottish Journal of Theology*, I.1(1948).41.
[125] In *La Sainte Église Universelle*, p. 129.
[126] N. Micklem, *Congregationalism and the Church Catholic*, pp. 54f.
[127] *Gesammelte Aufsätze zur Kirchengeschichte*, I.298.

way of looking at the matter, it means that we ought seriously to consider whether it would not be a good thing to dispense with the misleading term "Apostolic Succession", which carries with it the idea that someone has died and left his rights and property to someone else. Ought we not to be laying the whole emphasis on the fact of continuous life, unflagging strength, and unceasing work? And if we do that, can we find, and need we seek, any other basis of continuity than the Risen Christ Himself?'[128]

If there is to be a reunion of the broken fragments of the Church on earth, as Christians pray there shall be, it will have to include a common agreement as to the Church's principle of continuity. On this there is already a common meeting ground which is wide enough to accommodate many denominations, namely the faith in the abiding Word of God, which is the revelation on which the Church is based. Compared to this, the matter of ministerial succession seems to be of much less importance. 'Our protest is not against that which episcopacy represents,' writes Micklem, 'but only against that view which would make Word and Sacrament contingent upon the office, not the office on the Word.'[129] The coming years can tell how intransigently some Christians will continue to regard ministerial office as higher than the Word of God, which remains for all time the ultimate authority of the Church. It is very unlikely, and probably not even desirable, that there shall be uniformity of ministerial order or of sacramental doctrine and practice in the Church Universal. Such uniformity could, in fact, stifle the vitality of the Church and bring about an even greater measure of spiritual debilitation than presently exists in our divided denominations. But to the extent that these differences, which now obtain, prevent the spread and intensification of Christian fellowship and hinder the witness of the Gospel to mankind, they can under no circumstances be justified. This applies as strongly to the ministry as to other aspects of the Church on which deep-rooted disagreements persist. The Word, which has gone forth from God, shall not return unto Him void, but shall accomplish that which He pleases. The requirement and privilege of the Christian faith call for unconditional service to that Word.

[128] *The Church's Ministry*, p. 54.   [129] *What Is the Faith?* p. 215.

CHAPTER SIX

SALVATION IN THE CHURCH

I. THE PROBLEM FOR MODERN CHRISTIANS

A GOOD DEAL of explanation is required in these times to convince the ordinary Protestant layman, or many a minister, that the Church is, as some theologians have said, 'the sphere of justification' and the 'realm of redemption'. To a generation which has been taught to believe that these deepest elements of a man's destiny are the private concern of an individual and his God, such phrases sound too much like echoes of a pre-reformation ecclesiasticism. Moreover, the very words 'justification' and 'redemption', as well as their corollary, 'salvation', have been greatly diluted in the vernacular of both pulpit and pew. Somehow the modern man finds it much easier to believe that his purpose in life is to become well 'integrated' psychologically, than to be justified, redeemed, and saved.

In this chapter no effort toward a dogmatic definition of the word 'salvation' may be made, since a biblical understanding of the word is presupposed. Rather, the problem is: How are we to grasp the idea that the salvation of the individual person is to a large extent dependent upon his being in the Church? And even stronger: How can many Protestant theologians hold to the traditional doctrine that outside the Church there is no salvation? If these beliefs seem to be anachronistic to many Protestants, as they no doubt do, we are obliged to study the relevant ideas in the theology of those who hold them, and so to evaluate them.

Some preliminary discussion is unavoidable, however. In the first place, it is necessary to look at the twin concepts of 'Church visible' and 'Church invisible', which are so popular in books and speeches about the nature of the Church. Secondly, the problem of what constitutes true membership in the Church must be discussed, for there is wide diversity of opinion with regard to this matter, ranging from the idea of demonstrable membership in the Church visible to that of spiritual membership in the Church invisible. No concrete consideration of salvation in the Church is possible until some attempt has been made to comprehend the meaning of these terms. It will be seen that certain viewpoints relating to these problems are in irreconcilable opposition to others, and no easy syntheses are to be expected. However, the chances of finding a common meeting ground will be much more favourable when these various positions have been briefly defined.

II. THE 'VISIBILITY' AND 'INVISIBILITY' OF THE CHURCH

If we were to follow the advice of Gustav Aulén, we would immediately abandon this discussion in the belief that it would be just one more confusing addition to an area of thought which is already hopelessly confused. He writes: 'As regards the terms "invisible" and "visible" Church, I think that theology would do well if it refrained from using them.'[1] The reason he offers is not that the words are meaningless, but that they are invariably misapplied. 'These terms,' he continues, *'when contrasted with each other*, have never contributed to the lucidity of the idea of the Church.' In this latter statement he is probably right. Nevertheless, by rejecting the two terms we would not come any nearer a solution of the problem confronting many Christians, namely that there is an aspect of the Church which is empirical, temporal, and corruptible, as well as an aspect which is spiritual, eternal, and incorruptible.

Furthermore, new terms would have to be invested with the same meanings as visible and invisible to express this distinction. Eduard Schweizer, for example, suggests that in place of these terms we employ the phrases, 'Church in the sense of law' and 'Church in the sense of faith'.[2] These substitutes do carry more specific connotations, but they still lend themselves very conveniently to the kind of contrasting which Aulén deplores, and their final contribution might be no better than that of the others.

In a similar manner, Hans Lilje tries to resolve the tension between these terms by declaring that the Church is neither visible nor invisible, but is 'hidden' (*verborgen*).[3] As such, it can truly be known only in faith. This is also a pregnant idea, and one of which N. Micklem has written the following: 'The

---
[1] In *Theology* (March 1949), p. 82f.
[2] *Das Leben des Herrn in der Gemeinde und ihren Diensten*, p. 124.
[3] In *Allgemeine evangelisch-lutherische Kirchenzeitung* (1935), p. 919.

hiddenness, the *incognito*, in the life of Christ has its reflection in the hiddenness, the *incognito*, in the life of His disciples. As the incarnate life of God was hidden in man, so the regenerate life of man is hidden in God. Though Christians may let their light shine before men, and many of the triumphs of the Cross are for all to see, yet the life of the Church is a hidden life.'[4] This principle can be applied readily to such 'hidden' aspects of the Church's nature as the faith and love of its members, its relation to Christ, its destiny in time and eternity, etc. But it is still difficult to see how this idea makes any substantial or unique contribution toward an understanding of the Church which would warrant its supplanting the more conventional terms. Rather, the hiddenness of the Church, like the distinction between law and faith, serves as a useful complement to the notion of the Church seen and unseen.

Bearing these warnings and distinctions in mind, we may still proceed to an analysis of the ways in which the terms 'visible' and 'invisible' have been applied to the Church in recent theological literature, also remembering that much of this modern thought reflects or restates ideas of a former time.

(1) Martin Luther's distinction between the visibility and invisibility of the Church, which was due largely to this need for distinguishing between the hierarchical structure and the community of faithful persons,[5] still dominates and directs much current thought. But in Luther's theology, which is being so extensively re-evaluated in this century, the meaning of these terms signified more than a differentiation between the hierarchy and the personal fellowship in the community of saints, which would allow two opposing forms of the Church to be recognized. As Eric Wahlstrom points out, the words 'visible' and 'invisible' do not refer to two Churches, but to two aspects of one and the same Church.[6] It is misleading, then, to employ the adjectives in direct connexion with the Church, as 'visible Church' and 'invisible Church', for this suggests a duplicity which is foreign to the thought of Luther. Rather, we should speak of the

---

[4] *What Is the Faith?* p. 208. Likewise, Paul Tillich says that we must always consider the 'latent' and 'potential' Church as implicit in the manifest Church: in *The Christian Answer* (H. P. van Dusen, ed.), p. 39.

[5] cf. Paul Althaus, *Communio sanctorum*, p. 90.

[6] In *The Nature of the Church* (American Theological Committee), p. 41; cf. K. Barth, *Die Theologie und die Kirche*, p. 290: 'According to Protestant doctrine, the invisible and visible Church is one and the same, not two species of one genus, but two predicates of the same subject.'

SALVATION IN THE CHURCH 163

'visibility' and 'invisibility' of the one Church, if we are to avoid this misconception.

In a like manner, the intended distinction of terms can be dangerously distorted if one tries to visualize the two aspects of the Church as two concentric circles, the inner representing the invisible group of truly Christian members at the core of the wider, visible circle of doubtfully faithful members.[7] This concept of invisibility, expressed by the phrase *ecclesiola in ecclesia*, or small Church within the Church, belongs to the moral perfectionism of the Pietists rather than to the basic thought of the Reformation.[8] Moreover, as E. Rietschel believes, there is no justification for interpreting Luther's doctrine to mean that the true members of the Church are invisible, for this would make it nonsense even to speak of the Church on earth as being the Church of Christ.[9] The Church would then indeed be a *civitas platonica*, an ideal about which men could speculate, rather than a reality for both experience and faith.[10]

When the three misconceptions of duplicity, *ecclesiola*, and platonic idealism have been summarily dismissed from the discussion, it remains to be asked what is really meant by the visibility and invisibility of the Church. And according to one contemporary view, which stems from Luther but is not peculiar to Lutherans, the meaning is that the essence of the Church is no more visible to an outsider than the faith of a particular Christian is visible to someone else. The Christian man can be seen, but the relationship of faith and love between him and God can by no faculties be perceived externally. The Church is likewise an empirical body of people, worshipping in groups and confessing their membership when apart. As a visible entity it stands over against everything else in the world, which is *Nichtkirche*, as H. Lauerer calls it.[11] But this visible form of the Church, and even the public manifestation of Christian love and fellowship, can give merely a hint of that divine and spiritual nature of the Church which is perceptible only by faith. It is this which makes the distinction necessary, writes Brunner, between

[7] cf. O. Zänker in *Credo Ecclesiam* (H. Ehrenberg, ed.), p. 79.
[8] cf. J. Wach, *Sociology of Religion*, p. 175, where he attributes the use of this phrase to Spener, the father of Pietism.
[9] *Das Problem der unsichtbar-sichtbaren Kirche bei Luther*, p. 28.
[10] cf. K. L. Schmidt in *TWNT*, III.537.
[11] '*Sichtbarkeit der Kirche*' in *Luthertum* (1939), p. 65f.

the Church of faith and the worshipping congregation.[12] Were it not so, the confession of belief in the Church in the Creed would be insupportable. 'The Creed does not say *video ecclesiam*, but *credo ecclesiam*. Everybody can see the society or system of societies which we call the Church. But nobody can know whether that society is the Church. . . . It is also true of the Church that outsiders cannot say of her, Lo here! or Lo there!'[13]

The essential mystery of the Church must always consist of the tension between its divine and human aspects, the mundane and the heavenly. It is at once the body of sinful men and the Body of Christ. And this apparent dichotomy, which so often confronts Christian thinkers and disturbs their complacency, defies a thoroughgoing and satisfying rationalization. This concept of the visibility and invisibility of the Church, manifesting itself in the world and yet concealing its spiritual identity from all who lack the eyes of faith, is not a rational explanation of the mystery, but only a description of it. And although other descriptions may vary, as we shall see, the mystery is not thus to be dissolved. It is enough to say, with W. Künneth, that the Evangelical concept of the Church rests upon this mysterious and indissoluble bond between invisibility and concrete form.[14]

(2) The same two characteristics of the Church have been interpreted somewhat differently by theologians of the Reformed tradition, as compared to those of the Lutheran. Although based by and large upon the distinction which Calvin draws between the whole visible Church of professing Christians and the invisible Church of 'saints', who are known only by God Himself,[15] these recent interpretations have taken various forms.

Maurice Goguel indicates that the meaning of the Church has been two-fold since the beginning in New Testament times: on the one hand the empirical group of Christians assembled for worship; on the other hand the transcendent reality, which is neither in time nor space, and including all Christians who have ever lived on earth or will live, and hence to be fulfilled only when history itself is fulfilled.[16] It is this thought which is expressed

---

[12] *The Divine Imperative*, p. 531.

[13] H. Sasse, Files of Commission I, W.C.C., Geneva; cf. the distinction made by a group of American theologians between the Church as 'empirical' reality and as 'invisible Fellowship'; in *Christendom*, VII.1(1942).31f.

[14] In *Luthertum* (1934), p. 359.   [15] *Institutes*, Book IV.1.7.

[16] In *Le Problème de l'Église*, p. 8.

conventionally in the doctrine that the *communio sanctorum*, of which the Creed speaks, is the whole company of believers or elect in heaven as well as on earth. The Church, being *one* in essence and *universal* in dimension, cannot be contained within spatial or temporal limits. And, as P. Carnegie Simpson testifies, 'that part of the Church which is visible on earth in no wise differs from that part invisible in heaven, or from the Church in its entirety, in respect of its constitutive principle; it differs only in its manifestation'.[17]

This view of the Church enjoys such a wide acceptance, being acknowledged generally by theologians in various denominations,[18] that it is often taken to be the *one* meaning of the term 'Church invisible'. The full implication of the idea is not always apprehended, however, unless one recognizes how inextricably it is bound to the doctrine of election and salvation. For it makes little sense unless it is understood as a corollary to the doctrine that God has chosen those whom He has saved on earth, and has placed them on parity with those whom He already has with Him in heaven. And inasmuch as it is God alone who knows who these chosen and saved are, only He can know the limits of the Church invisible. This doctrine is not to be used as a principle for discrimination of true and false membership of the Church invisible on earth, for such is not the given prerogative of men.[19]

The idea of invisibility, therefore, while expressing the transcendence and unity of the Church, is nevertheless a great temptation for Protestants, especially, to disparage the temporal structure and life of the Church as being inconsequential, or else to arrogate to themselves the power of deciding who do or do not belong to the blessed company of the saints. The results of the inability to resist this temptation have been manifest in Church history and have been largely responsible for such present-day discrediting of the Church's invisibility as there is.

Micklem describes how such temptation may be overcome, so that the sinful occupation of separating the saved from the unsaved on dogmatic or moral considerations is shown up as a blasphemous pretension. He writes: 'The Church visible on earth is a company of weak and sinful and ignorant men and

---

[17] *Church Principles*, p. 35.
[18] cf. the two Faith and Order Movement books (L. Hodgson, ed.): *Convictions*, pp. 45f., 55, 115; and *Edinburgh* 1937, p. 345.
[19] cf. G. Aulén, *The Faith of the Christian Church*, p. 351.

women, divided amongst themselves, showing many evidences of the spirit of the world, and organized in institutions like those of society at large. The Church invisible on earth is that same company of people viewed as those who belong to the covenant of grace, have received the Holy Spirit, and are members of the Body whose Head is Christ.'[20] In virtue of this explanation of the distinction between visibility and invisibility, Micklem keeps from admitting the unscriptural idea that the visible Church is essentially a different Church from the invisible and inferior to it. And this, as we have seen, would be an untenable interpretation of the Church's being both visible and invisible.

Instead of delimiting the nature and membership of the Church visible and invisible, we are on firmer ground when we can understand, as Robert Will does,[21] that these two aspects are not separate entities, both of which constitute the Church, but that visibility and invisibility are concepts which serve as aids to a better apprehension of the mystery of the Body of Christ, embracing heaven and earth.

(3) The pertinence of Aulén's warning, that these terms lead to contrasting concepts of the Church and more confusion, is evident when we read the criticisms made by some theologians against any idea of the invisibility of the Church. These come largely from Anglicans, and they seem to show a lack of understanding of the idea which the Reformed and Lutheran theologians are trying to express. For example, A. E. J. Rawlinson writes: 'To maintain that the true Church is invisible is to evacuate the doctrine of the vocation of the Church of its meaning. The whole conception of the "invisible Church" in the Lutheran and Calvinist sense is simply unusable, whether from the point of view of theology or from the point of view of the practical pastor of souls.'[22] Similarly, L. C. Lewis declares: 'Anglicans feel that historically the doctrine of the Invisible Church has generally been the expression of discouragement and frustration in efforts to reform the Church.'[23] T. O. Wedel also points out, rightly, the long recognized fact that the idea that the Church is invisible has no basis at all in the New Testament.[24]

---

[20] *What Is the Faith?* p. 209.
[21] In *Revue d'histoire et de philosophie religieuses*, XII(1932).484f.
[22] *The Church of England and the Church of Christ*, pp. 18f.
[23] In *The Nature of the Church* (American Theol. Comm.), p. 86.
[24] *The Coming Great Church*, p. 53; cf. G. Gloege, *Reich Gottes und Kirche im Neuen Testament*, p. 390.

Why do these men and others rise to oppose the doctrine of the Church's invisible nature? Negatively, they wish to suppress the 'platonic' notion that only the invisible, spiritual Church is the true one, and that all visible aspects, including even the worship and *koinōnia* of the Christian community, are not evidences of the true Church. Their justification for this attitude would not be disputed by their Reformed brothers, who, like Carl Damour, assert that the Church is either visible or it is not the Church.[25] C. C. Morrison also abhors the notion of the invisibility of the Church and thinks it the grand delusion of Protestantism, even though he writes as a Protestant: 'The Reformers did not intend to sacrifice catholicity. They believed in the Church as the body of Christ, and it was in the name of this august conception that they condemned Roman Catholicism as unworthy of so lofty a title. But they set up a conception of the Church as a "spiritual" body, in contrast to the objective historical body. Their purified Church was held to be continuous with the *invisible* Church which had maintained a "spiritual" existence since apostolic days. . . . The only kind of Church which protestantism could have was an invisible Church, a Church in idea. And this was because its conception of salvation was also transcendental.'[26] It is by no means the Anglicans alone, therefore, who are discontent with the doctrine that the visible elements of the Church are secondary.

Positively, these critics of the Church invisible want to insist upon the necessity of the sacramental forms which bind visible human beings into the visible Church, though necessarily in an 'invisible way'.[27] Here again it is difficult to see how there is a really fundamental disagreement between such an idea and the Reformation principle that the true Church is found where the Word of God is preached and the Sacraments administered to the congregation of the faithful. There are variations of emphasis upon the importance of the visible forms and the invisible faith, to be sure, but these are not to be thought of as constituting such radical divisions as some seem to think.

In an interesting and illuminating manner, Wilhelm Stählin remarks that the two ancient heresies of Docetism and Arianism, which had to do respectively with the 'invisibility' and 'visibility'

---

[25] *Die Epochen des Protestantismus*, p. 229. cf. W. Niesel in *Evangelische Theologie*, III(1936).320.
[26] In *Christendom*, II.2(1937).279-81.
[27] cf. E. L. Mascall, *Christ, the Christian, and the Church*, p. 151.

of Jesus Christ, are now being repeated to some degree in the modern views of the Church.[28] The Docetists are those who say that the true Church includes nothing but the spiritual, invisible elements of the transcendent world. The Arians on the other hand want to exclude everything from the true Church which cannot be explained by rational and empirical categories. Both of these extreme poles of thought require modification, however, and between them there are diverse ideas of the true Church, some nearer one pole and some nearer the other. The extremists would maintain that the Church is either an invisible ideal or else it is a visible reality, with no admixture of the two concepts on a middle ground. The great majority of Protestants recognize none the less that the Church is characterized by both one and the other. So Walter Lowrie writes with insight: 'What remains of the visible Church when we have taken from it all its invisible part, its spiritual reality, is really nothing more than a denomination.'[29]

The two aspects constitute the wholeness of the Church, just as the corporeal and the spiritual constitute the wholeness of a man. This understanding ought to be a prerequisite for all discussion of the nature of the Church. It is not consistent with Christian ethics to regard a certain man as being *only* a good soul, or *only* a material body. The whole man is both, and is so to be known and understood. So it is also with the visibility and invisibility of the Church.

III. MEMBERSHIP IN THE CHURCH

One of the most pressing needs in theology today is to discover an idea of Church membership which at least the majority of Christians can fully accept. But on few issues is there more unhappy evidence of the denominational distinctions which keep the Church in a state of schism than on that of membership. It is necessary, therefore, when considering this problem from theological viewpoint, to recognize clearly the beliefs underlying denominational practice in receiving people into the membership of their Churches, and to ponder whether these beliefs apply as well to the Church which is the one Body of Christ.

Joachim Wach, treating the problem sociologically, constructs

[28] *The Mystery of God*, p. 131.   [29] *Problems of Church Unity*, p. 29.

SALVATION IN THE CHURCH 169

a scale to illustrate how different denominations vary between strict exclusiveness and liberal inclusiveness in their concepts of Church membership.[30] The exclusive are those which demand either credible profession of faith or assurance of personal salvation and sanctification, or both. The broad and inclusive want to accept not only the individual on the basis of faith, but to include as well his whole family, social community, and eventually the widest areas of society. These sociological observations also have relevance to the theological problem involved, and Wach's distinction may be kept in mind as a very general way of considering the denominational differences.

At the time when the German Churches were obliged to decide the extent to which the *Deutsche Christen* were members of the Church, D. Bonhöffer reached the conclusion that the whole question of dimensions or boundaries and qualifications for membership is essentially foreign to the theology of the Church.[31] Since the Reformation, the question of what the Church *is* has been separated from the question of who belongs to the Church, he remarks. And unless the latter question is left open, to be considered only in the light of the former, a wholly legalistic concept of the Church is unavoidable. And although only the more rigid theologians hold that the decisions of the Church regarding membership are binding and ultimate, a good many others, holding more flexible ideas on the subject, would still not agree with Bonhöffer, who seems to doubt that the Church has interest, much less authority, in determining who are truly members and who are not. He has support in this view, however, from such men as P. S. Minear, who feels disposed to leave the whole question in the hands of God. He asserts that 'the boundary is never closed, never frozen, never within the province of men to determine'; and this is because 'an individual enters the Church, not when he accepts certain abstract ideas of eternal truth, nor when he promises to contribute certain values to the Ecclesia, but when God, active in Christ, bestows grace as a gift of the Spirit'.[32] In this appeal to the convoking work of the Holy Spirit as the action which makes persons members of the Church, Minear has a basis for thought which is incontestably biblical.

[30] *Sociology of Religion*, p. 149.
[31] In *Evangelische Theologie* (1936), pp. 214-18.
[32] *Eyes of Faith*, pp. 92, 94.

And no one who takes the faith of the New Testament seriously would dare suggest that such work of the Spirit, by which persons are chosen to belong to the People of God, can be limited by the decisions of other men of the Church.

In spite of the truth which is embedded in the idea of the unrestrained action of the Spirit in calling people to faithful membership in the Church, it is of little use in the practice of the Church visible to reject any and all recognizable norms of membership. This seems to be a principle applicable only to the 'hidden' or invisible Church, if those terms are used in the absolute sense. And when appropriated by churchmen of a very liberal and tolerant viewpoint, this principle can so dilute the concept of membership as to make it impossible to identify the Church on earth at all. Thus, in a statement which perhaps implies more than the author intended, C. E. Raven writes of the Church,[33] that it is 'the fellowship of those who live in Christ, and by Him are incorporated into His body', but then goes on to say that 'those that are led by the Spirit of God, be they Jew, Turk, infidel, or heretic, are within its membership; all mankind belongs to it if having eyes they see, if their lives display the fruits of the Spirit, if they have love one toward another'. This view has the merit of trust in the divine election through the Spirit, as well as of a plenitude of charity toward all men. And yet, one wonders how the Church could continue to exist in society if this were its norm, except perhaps as an expression of the ideal of 'the great human family', as a spiritual entity existing only in the mind.

The vagueness of this idea of membership is more clearly perceived when contrasted to a view which is diametrically opposed, such as that held, for example, by most Baptists. In their belief and practice they adhere to the rule, so implicit in the thought of Schleiermacher,[34] that the one test of membership is the conscious experience of rebirth. According to one spokesman, W. O. Carver: 'Baptists believe that the Church is entered by the experience of regeneration wrought by the Holy Spirit in connexion with repentance and faith on the part of each believer.' But the Church does not 'include "all who name

---

[33] *Jesus and the Gospel of Love*, p. 447.
[34] '*Die Kirche bildet sich durch das Zusammentreten der einzelnen Wiedergeborenen zu einem geordneten Aufeinanderwirken und Miteinanderwirken,*' *Der christliche Glaube*, §115.

SALVATION IN THE CHURCH 171

Christ's name", for some of these may be mistaken about their experience and some may have inadequate experiences or even impure motives in claiming that name'.[35] This is not a contrast between Troeltsch's well-known 'church-type' and 'sect-type', but rather between the type of denomination which can recognize no real prerequisite for membership and that which has a very positive idea of what that prerequisite is, knowing on what basis to accept or reject applicants for membership. Both of them testify to the two elements which are indispensable to Christians: the calling of God through the Spirit by the revealing of His Word, and the response of the individual in faith. But they tend to isolate these elements from one another, emphasizing too exclusively either the one or the other.

This is why the majority of Protestant denominations in both theology and practice prefer to incorporate into their beliefs both the action of God and the response of man, and, so far as possible, find evidence that this 'transaction' has taken place, or, in the case of children, will take place. This would possibly be called 'legalism' by Bonhöffer, and it is undoubtedly a precarious view, which can easily be interpreted legalistically. Common knowledge of the misuse of Church discipline, whether in Roman Catholic, Puritan, or other bodies, has demonstrated how it may be corrupted. Nevertheless the exigencies of the life of the Church in the world demand for most people some norm for knowing who is truly a member of the Church and who is not. At best, of course, this norm can be only a *relative* one, for the *absolute* one is known only to God. But because man cannot know everything, it must not be said that he can know nothing. And through the Word of God it is granted to man to know what his faith is, in contrast to the lack of faith or the corrupted faith of others.

Upon the basis of this fact, Brunner declares that the Church 'is not something which is added to the faith of the individual ... the Church is there when faith is there. The individual enters the Church the moment he enters into faith.'[36] And it is the Holy Spirit, of course, who makes such faith possible and real. The problem of moral perfection, or even of a conscious experience

---

[35] In *The Nature of the Church* (Amer. Theol. Comm.), p. 66. But this is no official expression of consensus of all Baptists.

[36] *The Mediator*, p. 615.

of regeneration, does not enter upon this scene. But the attitude of faith with which man responds to the loving revelation of God is the thing which counts, not only for the justification of the individual, but for his life in the Church. In accord with this principle, the Lutheran can describe the Church simply as the 'community of the faithful' (*Gemeinde der Gläubigen*)[37] and the Reformed can say with Barth that the Church is the fellowship of sinful men who are bound in living faith and obedience to His Word.[38] To allow one who does not give at least some evidence or profession of faith in Jesus Christ to be considered a member of the Church may be the antithesis of legalism, but it is also, from the human point of view, a thorough evacuation of the meaning of membership.[39]

For the normal practice of many denominations, the outward act by which a person enters the Church as a member is the Sacrament of Baptism. There are varying degrees of emphasis upon the meaning and efficacy of this rite, as we have already seen in Chapter Five, particularly with respect to the baptizing of infants and their inclusion in the Church. But no Protestants should attach any magical meaning to this Sacrament; and its primary significance is that it is a sign, or seal, God's testimony of His grace in calling the person into the life and fellowship of the Church. Since this is the commonly accepted view of Baptism, with a sure foundation in the practice of the New Testament Church, it is Baptism, either upon faith or unto faith, which has the widest recognition as the sign of membership in the Body of Christ.[40]

IV. THE CHURCH AND SALVATION

To speak of the Church as the effective means of salvation for men; or even stronger, to say that God saves men only within the Church, is a good way to incur the righteous indignation of many contemporary Christians. Deeply embedded in their faith is the strong conviction that, so far as a man's salvation is concerned, the Church is an unwelcome intruder between the individual and God. They find their sentiments well expressed in the words of

---

[37] cf. E. Rietschel, *Das Problem der unsichtbar-sichtbaren Kirche bei Luther*, p. 21.
[38] '*Die Kirche und die Kultur*' in *Zwischen den Zeiten* (1926), p. 363.
[39] The World Council of Churches testifies to this by making their requirement for membership the faith in Jesus Christ as Lord and Saviour.
[40] cf. C. J. Cadoux in *Essays Congregational and Catholic* (A. Peel, ed.), p. 67.

John Wesley: 'Church or no Church we must attend to the work of saving souls.'[41] For it has been, and still is, characteristic of a large share of Protestant theology to reject any idea that the Church might be integral and necessary in the saving action of God.

We are not concerned here to enter the involved debate as to the faults or merits of this anti-ecclesiastical, individualistic attitude. It is sufficient for the present discussion to recognize that this view is one to be seriously reckoned with, for it is sincerely embraced by literally millions of members of the Church. And for them the statement of R. A. Ashworth is a definitive judgement on the problem: 'The place of the Church in the thought of the Christian depends ultimately upon his convictions as to the manner which the grace of God comes into human life. . . . The congregationally organized bodies hold to the spiritual autonomy of the individual soul. . . . The Christian has immediate access to God through Christ who is the sufficient and only mediator. This rules out the doctrine that outside the Church there is no salvation.'[42]

It is taken for granted even by some leading theologians that this individualism is firmly rooted in the Reformation and is an integral part of the Protestant faith. The several theologians who wrote the pamphlet, *Catholicity*, thus observed that 'Lutheranism and Calvinism imply a doctrine of the union of individual souls in the way of salvation prior to their incorporation into the visible Church. Whereas in Catholic Christianity the order is: Christ—the visible Church—the individual Christian; Protestantism is unable to avoid the notion that the right order is: Christ—the individual Christian—the Church; as if entry into the Church were a secondary stage that follows and seals a salvation already bestowed upon individuals by virtue of "faith alone".'[43]

Passing a similar judgement upon the Reformation, as well as upon Protestant theology, C. C. Morrison asserts that the whole habit of Protestant thinking is dominated by the concept of

---

[41] Quoted by R. N. Flew in *The Ministry and the Sacraments* (R. Dunkerley, ed.), p. 231.

[42] In *Christendom*, V.4(1940).485.

[43] G. Aulén in *Theology* (March 1949), p. 82f., regards this as a greatly distorted description of Lutheranism, since even Luther (and Calvin) said the Church is the 'Mother' of every Christian and hence prior to the individual.

Christianity as a private experience, in the light of which it has built its theology, evangelism, missionary enterprise, and ecclesiology. The contrast with the Catholic principle is most vivid, he writes, for the Catholic regards the living Church as the locus of the saving relationship between God and man, while the Protestant believes that this locus is the individual's experience of the inner spiritual life.[44] Equally willing to attribute this line of thought to the reformers is Paul Tillich, who regards individualism as the inherent *Leitmotiv* of Protestant faith.[45]

Undeniable as it may be that such emphasis upon individual experience of salvation has been the hallmark of much Protestant thinking, it is far from self-evident that this constitutes the genuine point of view of the great reformers and their present-day descendants. One wonders whether the Anglican writers of *Catholicity*, Morrison and Tillich, have appreciated the temper of much Protestant theological writing in recent years. For prominent Lutheran and Calvinistic have taken pains to demonstrate that the Reformation on the principle of justification by faith was not intended to negate or even minimize the reality of the Church, and that both Luther and Calvin were, in fact, very conscientious protagonists of the Church. From the point of view of historical theology, it would be more valid it seems to trace the rise of individualism from the pietistic movements and the philosophy of rationalism, which engendered the self-consciousness of the single person in both the religious and political spheres. But this problem of how Protestantism came to be so individualistic is less important than the realization that individualism is still a strong factor in Protestant faith and that it has a far-reaching influence upon our idea of salvation.

To cast doubt upon the validity of the individualistic concept of faith is not to deny or reject the necessity of the faith of the individual. However enthusiastic one may be in setting forth the idea that the communal *koinōnia* life of the Church is essential and indispensable, he must not allow himself to forget that the life of the individual is also indispensable. 'There is thus at the heart of the Church's existence an ineradicable individualism,' writes Newbigin. 'Every man has to stand at the last before God and render his own account. The opposite of this true individualism is not fellowship, but the crowd and the clique, the place to

[44] In *Christendom*, II.2(1937).274-7.   [45] *The Protestant Era*, p. 226.

SALVATION IN THE CHURCH 175

which we run when we want to avoid personal responsibility.'[46] Stählin calls this alternative the 'convenient collective existence' to which Christians may fly in order to escape their personal problems of faith.[47] But let it not be thought that this collectivism, or crowd, is the same as the community of the People of God, whom He wills to save.

Rather than opposing the Church to individualism, therefore, we look upon the Church as the complement and summation of individual experience, which is still not equal to, but more than, the sum of the individuals who are members of it.

Consideration of the place of the Church in relation to the saving work of God through Christ demands a concept of the Church which is much higher than that held by radical individualists; and in all the foregoing discussion the evidences for this higher concept have been repeatedly set forth. What we are dealing with now is not the Church as the creation of men, but as the creation of God. The Church is that area of human life in which the revelation of God is received and proclaimed, and in which the Holy Spirit's work is concentrated.

Some modern theologians prefer to speak of the Church's primary meaning in terms of divine creation. 'The Church is the creation of God working with and through man in a free and historic process,' declares H. F. Rall. 'The Christian life is organic of its very nature; it is a life of love and truth and worship which cannot exist in isolation. So far as God gives this life, He gives the Church.'[48] That the Church is God's gift to man is not cause for deifying it, however. We are reminded by E. Thurneysen that the Church on earth is human through and through,[49] so far as we can apprehend its characteristics, and it is therefore never to be confused with God Himself. The earth and man are also creatures of God, and because of that relationship there is a radical distinction of a qualitative nature between the creation and the Creator.[50] We can recognize the fact that God is at work in the sphere of the Church, making His saving Word known by the Holy Spirit. But the Church as God's instrument is not to be identified with God, as some rapturous language about the Church seems at times to express.

[46] *The Reunion of the Church*, p. 80.   [47] *The Mystery of God*, p. 145.
[48] In *Christendom*, IV.2(1939).171.
[49] '*Kirche und Staat*' in *Zwischen den Zeiten* (1925), p. 191.
[50] cf. K. Barth, *Die kirchliche Dogmatik*, I.2.641.

'To confess the Christian Church is to confess the God who creates fellowship,' declares Aulén.[51] Does this not mean identification? some might ask. At first glance it seems to mean just that. However, it is at the most an identification of God's *action* with the Church rather than of His *nature*. If these two words can be kept in distinction from one another, a good deal of the misunderstanding with regard to high language about the Church can be avoided. God is love, we all believe. The Church is not love, however, but is the expression of God's loving action. It is God's freely given love, His *agapē*, by which He creates the Church and continually draws people into its fellowship by the Spirit. The existence of the Church is the clearest evidence of the fact that this divine action does take place in the course of history.

For clarity of thought on the creation of the Church it is desirable to make a distinction between the creation of the world and the creation of the Church. Edwin Lewis does just this when he thinks of the creations as two-fold: 'A primal creative act brought the world into being. A second primal creative act brought the Church into being, for the Church is inexplicable apart from Christ, and Christ is inexplicable apart from God.'[52] The Church is the 'new creation' of God; and just as the world of space and time bears witness to the creative act which made it, the Church continues to bear witness to the creative act of revelation in Christ. But this distinction is made even sharper, and probably comes nearer the truth, when we say that the world was *made* by God in the creative act and *redeemed* by Him in the creation of the Church. This is the idea preferred by Brunner, when he remarks that 'the Church is not based on the fact of Creation, but on that of Redemption, although Creation was designed with this end in view'.[53]

Therefore, the Church is not to be thought of as a finished product, but as a continuing, living fellowship, extending into each new generation the ministry which Jesus Christ began, and looking forward to its fulfilment in the Kingdom of God. This 'new creation' has a life, but not a life of its own. Neither is it the sum of the lives of all persons who belong to it, but the life

---

[51] *Den allmänneliga kristna tron* (*The Faith of the Christian Church*), quoted by N. S. F. Ferré, *Swedish Contributions to Modern Theology*, p. 189.

[52] *A Philosophy of the Christian Revelation*, p. 77.   [53] *The Divine Imperative*, p. 526.

SALVATION IN THE CHURCH 177

which the living God keeps giving to it. Were this source of power withdrawn, so that the merely human resources were all that remained to the Church, it would immediately cease being the Church.

If the Church was created and continues to exist for the salvation of mankind, as these theologians believe, it is right to consider the Church as having the utmost importance for the Christian doctrine of salvation. The Church does not obstruct or appropriate for itself the saving work accomplished by Jesus Christ. Only when corruptly 'institutionalized' as a hierarchical order does the Church pretend to dispense or withhold salvation according to rule of dogma or sacramental practice. As Christ remains the revelation of God, unique and by Himself, the Church lives only to serve His own soteriological purpose in the world. So the existence of the Church of Christ stands or falls, writes Barth, according to the way men can recognize and believe the saving revelation in Christ.[54] As we have previously noted, the purpose of revelation is not to tell us something about God, but to bring to us men a knowledge of God Himself, 'in the face of Jesus Christ'. God's majesty and holiness are revealed, but even more His grace and love, in which alone men have hope of salvation.

The constantly recurring impact of this saving revelation of Jesus Christ upon the Church is what Barth calls the *Ereignis* (approximately translated 'event') which is indispensable to the life of the Church.[55] Since the Church has its origin and essence exclusively from the revelation of God, which is to say, from the power, counsel, commission, and direction of the Word of God,[56] it is this same revelation which keeps giving purpose and hope to the Church; and in the light of it, the Church constantly is being recreated, or re-formed, by the work of God. The necessity of this *Ereignis*, as it occurs in the experience and faith of the Christian community, thus making the community to be the Church, is a vivid reminder to us of the absolute dependence of the Church upon the revelation in Christ, as well as of its subordination to Christ. As Barth remarks, the Church is but a secondary 'token' of the revelation, of which the bodily flesh of Jesus was the

[54] *Die kirchliche Dogmatik*, I.2.604.
[55] In *The Universal Church in God's Design* (W.C.C.), p. 68.
[56] '*Gottes Wille und unsere Wünsche*,' *Theologische Existenz Heute*, Heft 7(1934).10.

primary, unconditioned token.[57] Even though the Church is secondary in this sense, however, the revelation which it believes and to which it bears witness is the same revelation of God, embodied in Jesus in a primary sense. And the ultimate meaning of this revelation for mankind, whether already within the Church or still outside, is the salutory, forgiving love of God.

When we say, then, that we believe in the Church or belong to it, we think not of an abstract bond of fellowship (important as this is) nor of an organization of faithful and friendly Christians. Rather, we believe in and belong to the Church which is the locus of man's confrontation of the revelation and saving grace of God,[58] the very place in human life where the grace of God in Christ is made known to us now.[59]

Modern thought of this type, relative to the divine intention for the Church, thus centres about the belief that God created the Church to be the continuing vehicle in the world by which His plan and purpose of salvation, testified to in the work of Jesus Christ, may be carried forward. There is nothing mechanical, automatic, or self-sustaining about the Church, however; it either lives by the constant supply of power from on high, or it ceases to exist. And this life, so far as it is discernible in the outward forms by which the Church is known to society, is manifest in its constant witness to God's self-revelation in Christ, and in the loving fellowship and unpresuming faith which this witness calls forth. Into this Church are drawn the countless believing persons who make up its membership. The ways by which they are drawn, the understanding of faith which they have, the motives by which they are guided, the ecclesiastical requirements they fulfil, and the estimate they have of the Church and the Christian life as a whole are different and even conflicting, according to many kinds of thought and experience. As devious and dissimilar as the basic habits and viewpoints of all the nations and groups of mankind may be, they are all represented by persons who belong to the Church of Christ. And this amazing unity-in-diversity, though interesting from a sociological point of view, is also a fact to be reckoned with theologically. For it testifies not only to the zealous evangelism of the Church's missionaries, but even more to the timeless purpose of redemption

---

[57] In *Revelation* (J. Baillie and H. Martin, eds.), p. 73.
[58] *Die kirchliche Dogmatik*, I.2.371.   [59] *Die Theologie und die Kirche*, p. 296.

which God is striving to accomplish by means of the Church, using free and responsible men to propagate the saving faith in His Son.

This recognition, that it is God who uses men for His purpose, and not men who kindly deign to serve God, should be a constant reminder of the Old Testament conviction that God can make use of whom He pleases for the accomplishing His ends. As Barth told the German Churches in the first year of the apostasy of some of them under the Hitler régime, if Germany—or all Europe—should deny the Church and reject their trust, then God can make His Church live in India or Japan or any other land as well.[60] It would hardly be consistent with the biblical, and therefore Christian, apprehension of God as the sovereign Ruler of the world to cast doubt upon this hypothesis, and to assume that the rôle of this or that individual, or this or that nation, is indispensable to God at any time.

In respect to this problem, we must deal with the complex doctrine of election, which is so closely connected to both the concept of salvation and the existence of the Church. This is not a popular doctrine at the present time; and in reading much contemporary theology of the Church it is apparent that the idea of election, or predestination, is more conspicuous by its absence than by its presence. In spite of this current neglect of the problem, except in certain theological circles of Calvinistic character, W. J. Phythian-Adams calls our attention to the fact 'that from one end of it to another the Bible teaches Election'.[61] This reminder is less to be expected from an Anglican, perhaps, than from a strict Calvinist like C. Van Til, who calls the doctrine of election 'the heart of the Reformed conception of the Church'.[62] As may well be expected, however, these two theologians have quite different understandings of the doctrine.

It is not necessary in this context to undertake a thorough review of the idea of election as it evolved in the Old Testament, in the Gospels, and in the theology of Paul, Augustine, and Calvin. It is enough to recognize the firm belief that God, in His inscrutable wisdom, loved Jacob and hated Esau, chose the People of Israel and rejected others, and showed His Mercy upon

---

[60] In *Evangelische Theologie* (1934-5), p. 293; cf. K. Heim, *Der evangelische Glaube und das Denken der Gegenwart*, III.253.
[61] *The Way of At-one-ment*, p. 47.   [62] *The New Modernism*, p. 276.

whom He willed. We do not have to become enmeshed in the many implications of this doctrine, as it affects individuals' experiences, but may limit ourselves to its implications for the Church.

As the study of the origin of the Church has indicated, the members of the New Testament *ekklēsia* were convinced that God had chosen them to be His own People. 'Once you were no people but now you are God's people,' wrote the author of 1 Peter 2^{10}. Paul declared that the Christians are the true Remnant of Israel, the living branch engrafted into God's olive tree, children of that promise given unto Abraham.[63] The Christians were reminded that God elected them before the foundation of the world to be holy and blameless as His sons.[64] They remembered also the words of Jesus: 'No one can come to me unless the Father who sent me draws him. . . . You did not choose me, but I chose you and appointed you that you should go and bear fruit.'[65] The consciousness of election in the New Testament is indisputable, not only with respect to individual salvation—as in Romans 8^{28-30}, for example—but even more with respect to the *ekklēsia*, all those who are 'called forth' by God.

By the simple act of ignoring the evidence, modern theology has to a large extent preferred not to think of the Church in terms of such election by God. It is not a doctrine which accommodates itself very nicely to our modern way of thinking. Particularly is it almost wholly incompatible with the democratic and equalitarian idealism of Western thought, which holds as axiomatic the belief that all religious claims are at best relatively true and at worst baseless pretension and superstition. Thus each religious faith, as the popular illustration goes, is a separate path leading up the mountain, on the peak of which all shall meet at the same point. The claim of the Jewish people still to be the chosen race of God is condemned as the height of racial arrogance. Still more would the claim of the Christian Church to this divine favour be considered intolerably presumptuous. Christianity teaches universal love and mercy, meekness and humility; how can it therefore remain consistent with these ideals and pretend at the same time to be the body of God's Elect? Such is the popular reaction, which needs no documentation, and against which the Christian can only raise the defence based upon faith in the

[63] cf. Romans $11^{5, 17}$, Galatians 4^{28}. [64] Ephesians $1^{4, 5}$. [65] John 6^{44}, 15^{16}.

SALVATION IN THE CHURCH

revealed intention of God. It is small wonder that few theologians have recently felt impelled or qualified to take up this element of New Testament faith and present it boldly before a sceptical society.

This is exactly what some are attempting to do, however, for they share the ancient Christian conviction that the counsels of God are to be trusted, not opposed, and they very deeply believe that the history of salvation (*Heilsgeschichte*) can be conceived only in terms of people in the community of faith, namely the Church. This is the meaning of Brunner's assertion that 'in the Christian understanding of community the individual and the community are so related that the one cannot be thought of apart from the other.... The *communio electorum*, the *ekklēsia* of the *klētoi*, is *the only true* community.'[66] Just as individuals are brought by the Spirit to have faith in Christ and are thereby bound together in community, so the community is not an end in itself, serving its own needs, but it serves the will of Him who calls it into being.

It has been argued that this belief is an arrogant one for the Church to hold concerning itself, that it is diametrically opposed to the humility which Jesus, as the humiliated servant, enjoined His followers to have. Undoubtedly it is a temptation to pride, and not all members of the Church by any means have been able to resist it. On the other hand, when rightly conceived, the belief in election gives neither the individual nor the Church the slightest ground for being proud. This election is nothing other than the expression of God's *agapē* for those who have no more merit than what He, the Creator, imputes to them. And though they may be tempted to appeal to this calling as an index of their worth, they will remember, writes Barth, 'that it is the "Call" itself which is their sanction, and not their appeal to their *calling*'.[67] However highly the Church may be regarded as the People of God, it has constantly to be reminded, as Paul reminded his brethren, that the glory belongs solely to God. For the opposite of election by God is rejection by Him, and this is a very real possibility which always looms before the Church as a judgement upon it. Instead of relaxing into a state of assurance and complacency, the Church is thus kept at all times aware of its responsibility in the world, to be exactly what its critics say its character

[66] *The Divine Imperative*, p. 300.   [67] *The Epistle to the Romans*, p. 323.

must be: the form of a humble servant. 'What the triumphing Church names "God" has never been veritably God. The Church is related to the living God only when it is in tribulation, when it knows that, in the whole expanse of its historical manifestation, it is rejected by God, and when it, nevertheless, holds on firmly pronouncing this terrible God to be God, but to be also much more and vastly different from this—to be, in fact, the God who can and will elect.'[68]

In so presenting the case of the divine election of the Church, Barth is consciously trying to refute the error which, he claims, the reformers did not altogether avoid. This is the error of human classification, of delimiting the elect from the damned, of regarding and applying the doctrine quantitatively, of presuming to have knowledge of the divine mystery itself.[69] But such misunderstanding is an inversion of the doctrine, for it supposes that God's election exalts the Church, whereas, in reality, it exalts only God and reminds the Church of its constant dependence and servility. Belief in election can, when distorted, inflate the ego of the Church and do the very opposite from that which it ought to do. But if the Church is the fellowship of the Elect, rather than the *élite*,[70] there can be no room for any feeling except faithfulness and gratitude toward God for His mercy.

In general, this is the concept of the election of the Church as it is held by some theologians today, although it can in no wise be called the prevailing or dominating interpretation, for it is considered too rigid by one side and too lax by the other. The one side cannot tolerate such a restriction upon man's freedom as election implies, even to seek out his own salvation; the other cannot bear the implications that God does not have exact knowledge of who are saved and who are reprobate.

The teaching of the Bible concerning election is thoroughgoing from start to finish, observes Phythian-Adams, 'but this does not refer to anything abstract or indefinite or (ultimately) individual, it means the concrete historical People of Israel,' now the Church.[71] His bracketing of the word 'ultimately'

---

[68] *The Epistle to the Romans*, p. 352.
[69] cf. *The Knowledge of God and the Service of God*, p. 78f. Van Til criticizes Barth on this point, holding that Barth dilutes the doctrine of election to such an extent that the category 'elect' has no meaning for men, except as aid to 'a process of growth on the part of the would-be autonomous man' (!): *The New Modernism* (C. van Til), p. 284.
[70] cf. P. S. Minear, *Eyes of Faith*, p. 92; N. Micklem, *What Is the Faith?* p. 216.
[71] *The Way of At-one-ment*, p. 47.

carries the very important idea that election, while concerning the individual, always points beyond the single person to the chosen People as a whole. Since the concepts of election and salvation are virtually inseparable for the Christian faith, the same idea is to be applied to salvation: the concern for the individual person is necessary, and yet there stands beyond the individual the community of which he is a part. The salvation of the individual is not ultimate, but that of the Church is. 'No one can be saved by himself,' remarks Nels Ferré, 'we are saved in, into and for Christian fellowship. . . . A member can naturally transcend the institutional level of the Church, but he can never transcend the Christian Church.'[72]

This understanding of the primacy of the community is based upon the ancient concept of God's covenant relationship to the People of Israel, a covenant which demands much of the individual but is not conditional upon his faith as an individual, so much as his membership in the community. 'Israel is not God's people because the Israelites individually are good men,' writes B. S. Easton; 'Israelites enjoy God's favour because they are members of Israel. It is the group that sanctifies, not *vice versa*.'[73] Also, in none of the Old Testament prophecies of the promised Deliverer 'is the Christ regarded as the Saviour of the individual as such. Always the Christ is to be the Saviour of the Church, and of the individual by his faithful membership in it.'[74] Inasmuch as the Church is the continuation of Israel, this principle loses none of its force for Christians.

V. RECOVERY AND REINTERPRETATION OF '*EXTRA ECCLESIAM NULLA SALUS*'

Although the Christian faith is a personal faith, calling for the decision of the individual to believe in Christ and placing upon each one the responsibility of loving obedience, and although evangelical pietism has magnified the individual concern for salvation until it has become the dominant principle for many Protestants today, theologians in increasingly greater numbers are coming to the rediscovery of the fact that God saves men and women in community rather than in solitariness. This rediscovery

---
[72] In *Protestantism, a Symposium* (W. K. Anderson, ed.), p. 280.
[73] In *Anglican Theological Review*, XXII(1940).157.
[74] H. L. Goudge, *The Church of England and Reunion*, p. 158.

is now taking place, according to F. J. Taylor, for several reasons: the pressure of persecution on some Christians; the need for community in the world, which is being constantly depersonalized; the experience of Christian solidarity in missionary territories; and in addition to these historical factors, the great theological revival in Protestantism since 1918. All these have demanded that Christians look once more to the fellowship of the Church as the place to encounter the saving Gospel. And it was unnecessary to manufacture some new idea of community to meet their need, for it has been implicit in biblical faith all along. For 'redemption from sin means an end of self-centredness and the reintegration of life around a new centre. That centre is Christ, but a Christ who can never be separated from His redeemed people, so that personal salvation means incorporation into the new community of which Christ is the very life. All subsequent Christian experience is corporate experience.'[75] Even the retreat to personal isolation and private experience, the attempt to attain the at-one-ment with God in a life of mysticism, carries with it the influence of the fellowship, which preserves and teaches the Word of God and testifies to the pervasive love of the Father for His children.

That this doctrine of salvation in the fellowship of the Church has displaced to some extent the idea of salvation in isolation, so far as the leading Protestant theologians of the present day are concerned, becomes more and more evident. There is a natural lag between Christian thinkers on the frontier of theology and the many ministers and laymen of the Churches, so this revived concept of the rôle of the Church in salvation has still not reached back to those who follow the theologians. But a dependable expression of this rediscovered belief is to be found in the Report of Section I (on the Church) to the Amsterdam Assembly of 1948: '*We all believe that the Church is God's gift to men for the salvation of the world.*'[76] Among the representatives in this section there were differences of opinion as to how to understand salvation in this way, but the general degree of unanimity is still very significant.

Advancing one step beyond this belief that salvation is given in the community of the Church, we come to the more exacting doctrine that only and exclusively in the Church can salvation

---

[75] F. J. Taylor, *The Church of God*, p. 17.
[76] *The Universal Church in God's Design* (W.C.C.), p. 213.

be found. The slogan which is taken from Cyprian's attack upon heretical Baptism, '*salus extra ecclesiam non est*,' is still very repugnant to the thinking of a vast number of Protestants today, for it has not been understood apart from its hierarchical context. Even when so singular an authority for much modern theology as Calvin could write that 'beyond the pale of the Church no forgiveness of sins, no salvation, can be hoped for',[77] the feeling of repugnance remains.

Perhaps such distaste for the doctrine rests as much upon the favourable attitude toward individualism as upon the unfavourable view of institutionalism. Whereas the former attitude has already been dealt with at length, it should be emphasized strongly that the latter, the distrust of institutionalism, is not essentially at odds with the Protestant understanding of the Cyprianic formula. For even the exponents of the 'High Church' theology of the Church are not so hierarchically-minded as to believe that the action of the priesthood can restrict the saving grace of God. L. S. Thornton sees this doctrine as being the most consistent with the Pauline concept of the *koinōnia*, since the essence of the Church is the common participation and 'sharing in the grace of our Lord Jesus Christ, the love of God, and the gift of the Holy Spirit'.[78] H. Burn-Murdoch interprets Cyprian's words just as follows: 'That phrase does not necessarily mean that no one can be ultimately saved who is not on earth in visible communion with the Church, but it does mean that God's grace is ordinarily given to us, not as mere individuals, but as members of a body.'[79] And V. A. Demant, commenting on the same phrase, says that it 'is not so much a warning to those outside as a proclamation of the nature of redemption'.[80] As such a proclamation, it is consistent with the thought of many theologians who cannot be accused of being advocates of a hierarchical concept of the Church.

A survey of Reformed and Evangelical writing of the past thirty years, so far as it relates to this doctrine, reveals the rather astonishing fact that some of the foremost theologians have been most articulate in declaring their belief in it. There are disagreements within definite theological circles, to be sure. The Lutheran W. Elert, for example, strongly opposes Calvin on this matter,

[77] *Institutes of the Christian Religion*, Book IV.1.4.
[78] *The Common Life in the Body of Christ*, p. 92.
[79] *Church, Continuity and Unity*, p. 6.
[80] In *Union of Christendom* (K. Mackenzie, ed.), p. 51.

and insists that the Church does not foster the children of God at all, since these must be born only through the Spirit of God.[81] Hence it would be contrary to what he holds to be the biblical teaching of salvation to say that it can not be received outside the Church. On the other hand, Paul Althaus specifically approves the idea, that so far as we can know, God's grace is given only within the bounds of the Church—though the ultimate dimensions and limits of the Church are known only to God.[82] In a like manner, E. Foerster, while admitting that Luther sometimes used the words of Cyprian, insists that Luther held none of Cyprian's ecclesiastical views, and that his meaning concerned only God's action in the *Gemeinde*.[83]

The words of Bonhöffer sound an even firmer note of assent: '*Extra ecclesiam nulla salus* is a true statement of the purpose of the Church. It is an expression of faith, not a speculative idea. Faith is bound to God's revelation of salvation; and it knows no other salvation but that of the visible Church. Salvation apart from the Church is for faith basically not recognizable and can therefore never become a point of doctrine.'[84] Notice that he guards against the tendency to weaken and etherealize this idea by saying that it is the Church in its visible manifestation in which salvation is found, and not just in an invisible, heavenly sphere. In this certainty he is at one with Aulén, who regards the Church as 'the indispensable prerequisite for God's grace to the individual'.[85]

The sharpest critics of this position would very likely be those who understand the Church more in terms of human association than of divine convocation. Certainly it is pointless to speak of salvation in the sphere of the Church unless its reality as the Body of Christ and the People of God be taken seriously and with appreciation of the theological content of these two titles. And in the circle of Lutheran tradition, as we have seen, are to be found exponents of that serious appreciation of the divine reality of the Church.

The same line of belief is held by theologians who represent points of view which, respecting other problems of theology, are at variance. Karl Barth is unequivocal in his conviction: 'The maxim *extra ecclesiam nulla salus* is still in force and still valid; it is

---

[81] *Der christliche Glaube*, p. 486. [82] *Die christliche Wahrheit*, II.340.
[83] In *Theologische Rundschau* (1932), p. 153. [84] In *Evangelische Theologie*, III(1936).231.
[85] N. S. F. Ferré, *Swedish Contributions to Modern Theology*, p. 191. G. Gloege, *Reich Gottes und Kirche im Neuen Testament*, pp. 347f., cites Schlatter, Scheel, and Spörri in support of this doctrine.

something *which not even the most profound humility will allow us to deny or qualify*,' he writes.[86] Strong emphasis itself is not enough to justify this statement, however, and the basis for Barth's position may be found in his teaching on the Church as the place in which God makes known His revelation for the salvation of the Elect.

The list of concurring statements might be extended to include references to Brunner, Newbigin, Morrison, Rall, Zänker, and many others, but their agreement need not be substantiated by quotation.[87] That this modification of Cyprian's doctrine has taken firm root in the soil of recent Protestant theology can hardly be doubted, individualists' protests to the contrary notwithstanding. 'Salvation' and 'Church' are words which cannot be divorced for the latter serves the purpose of the former, and both are of God rather than of men in point of origin.

Even where this doctrine is well established and understood, however, the essentially communal nature of the Church is not thereby inviolably protected. With his unusual insight, Phythian-Adams discerns the inadequacy of the Cyprianic aphorism, even when used in the modified, Protestant sense. While it is true that this concept of salvation in the Church has prevented 'outright atomism' among Christians, it remains in the last analysis 'an appeal to the individual's concern for his soul'.[88] This is always the case when men and women are motivated to enter the Church by their fear of damnation instead of by their love for one another and desire to share with the People of God the gift of salvation in Jesus Christ. 'For once you lose sight of the People,' he concludes, 'and of the chief end of its consecration, you begin to think of yourself and other individuals as reborn simply *in order to be saved.*'[89] When this kind of faith prevails, the corporate life of the Church, the *koinōnia* and *agapē*, are matters of secondary importance and are constantly in danger of being neglected, in which case the replacement of the Church by individualistic religion has already begun. This eventuality is one which Christians should regard with dread, and one which they can forestall only by matching their concern for personal salvation with their devotion to one another in the love of God.

[86] In *Revelation* (J. Baillie and H. Martin, eds.), p. 74.
[87] cf. Brunner, *The Divine Imperative*, p. 300; *The Word and the World*, p. 106; Newbigin, *The Reunion of the Church*, p. 28; Morrison, *What is Christianity?* pp. 211, 233; Rall in *Christendom* IV.2(1939).170; Zänker in *Credo Ecclesiam*, p. 87; Hodgson, *Faith and Order*, Edinburgh 1937, p. 348.
[88] *The Way of At-one-ment*, p. 50.   [89] ibid., pp. 51f.

CHAPTER SEVEN

THE CHURCH'S ESSENTIAL UNITY

I. RATIONALIZATIONS OF DISUNITY

IF EMPIRICAL evidence rather than biblical faith were the foundation of our concept of the Church, we would conclude quickly and without qualification that the Church is not essentially a unity. No one needs to be convinced that the Church presents to secular society the appearance of a house hopelessly divided within itself. The divisive forces, which have splintered the Church into its numerous and often conflicting parts, are as diverse as the many factors involved in the segregation of mankind itself into hundreds of different groups. Upon these causes and the divisions attributed to them we need not and cannot dwell, for even a minimum treatment would involve a long historical survey. Of immediate concern instead are the attitudes which recent and contemporary theologians have shown toward the fact of disunity in the light of the widely-held belief that the Church is in essence one.

The characteristic attitude of Protestants during the past thirty years has been, in the main, a steadily increasing impatience with sectarian divisions. The point has now been reached where this is considered by a majority of Protestants to be no more than a natural manner of regarding disunity. But many of these would be astonished to learn that this modern concern for reunion on so ecumenical a scale is something new in the history of the Church. The records show that since the earliest years of its existence, when the apostles divided over the issue of Jewish ritual and the Christians at Corinth preferred to belong to Paul or Apollos rather than to Christ, the Church has known only divisions and subdivisions. In our present generation that process is being reversed. Some strands of the cord which were unravelled three centuries ago are now being retwined, although the remaining frayed ends are still numerous, and the hopes for retwining all of these seem forbiddingly remote. But if we are able to appraise the trend according to its present manifestations, we can see that it moves distinctly in the direction of reunion, and away from the perpetuation of sectarian fragmentation.

No one is so unrealistic in his thinking as to believe that eventually all differences within the Church must be totally eradicated. This would not come within the realm of possibility, nor is it even the desired meaning of the unity of the Church. Human attitudes, sensitivities and habits are far too various to be standardized according to one universal Christian pattern. When we speak of disunity, therefore, it is not as the opposite of uniformity. Regin Prenter describes how there have been concerted but unsuccessful attempts made to establish higher degrees of uniformity within the Church.[1] The doctrinal uniformity of orthodox Lutheranism still allows different forms of organization; Roman Catholic organizational uniformity permits variations in doctrine and worship; and Eastern Orthodox uniformity of liturgical worship does not preclude diversity in doctrine and juridical views: yet even these have not attained full uniformity in all aspects of the Church's life. Almost complete uniformity of belief, worship, and order may be the ideal of some few, but it is argument enough against such a view to show that it is inconsistent with the teaching of the Bible. As G. Aulén asserts: 'Considering the conditions and manifestations of unity according to the New Testament, we must emphasize that unity is not uniformity—neither uniformity of doctrine, nor uniformity of organization and orders, nor uniformity of life and religious experience.'[2] A different concept of unity than this must be adduced as the norm by which the Church's prevailing disunity is to be judged. For the unity of the Church, based upon the conception of the Body of Christ, does not mean uniformity, declares G. Gloege, but unity within multiplicity.[3]

There are Christians, however, who believe that the unity of the Church is of such a fully spiritual, invisible nature, that the divisions which are a scandal to others are considered irrelevant by them. For instance, in a reply to the *Report* of the Lausanne Conference of 1927 it was affirmed: 'There is no widespread conviction among Baptists that the division of Christendom into

---

[1] In *La Sainte Église Universelle*, p. 102.
[2] In *The Universal Church in God's Design* (W.C.C.), p. 28.
[3] *Reich Gottes und Kirche im Neuen Testament*, pp. 417f. The *Einheit* of the Church is not *Einerleiheit*, but *Einheit* in *Mannigfaltigkeit*.

churches or denominations is of itself to be deplored nor that the organic union of all Christians is an object to be sought for its own sake.'[4] This is an attitude which is characteristic of many, but by no means all, who are a part of the Free Church tradition. Feeling no need for questioning the rightness of the distinctive interpretations of faith which identify their denominations, they are not bothered by the fact that a great majority of Christians do not share their beliefs. Transcending all the walls of division, they hopefully declare, is a 'unity of spirit and purpose' which God wills for the Church. They do not want this position to be misconstrued as a denial of the unity of the Church, however, for the Church is indeed one. 'And it makes no difference to this Oneness', writes C. A. A. Scott, 'that as a fact of history members of the Sacred Society have come to be grouped in separate organizations. It makes no difference that these different organizations severally emphasize different aspects of Christian truth or that they are organized under different forms of government. Below all such distinctions there remains the "Unity created by the Spirit". That is a unity which is not even threatened by such divisions, any more than the unity of the king's army is threatened by the fact that it is divided into regiments.'[5] How valid this analogy drawn from the army is for the unity of the Church is not self-evident. Nevertheless, that this statement well represents the attitude of many Christians cannot be doubted. The factors which constitute denominational walls within the Church are not seen to be limitations upon the Church's unity. For this is a wholly spiritual quality, signified by common faith in Jesus Christ and the unhindered work of the Holy Spirit among all who are so committed. Unity is an essential attribute of the invisibility of the Church: but in its visible state the Church must not consider diversity to be the same as disunity.

A similar justification for denominational divisions arises from the wholly sociological concept of the Church. This view, which is presently declining in favour among theologians, has played a prominent rôle in the history of thought on the Church in this century. According to Paul Tillich, for example, it is sufficient to 'define the Church as that sociological reality in which the holy is supposed to be presented',[6] but more than this is not allowed.

[4] *Convictions* (L. Hodgson, ed.), p. 55.
[5] *The Church: Its Worship and Sacraments*, p. 18.   [6] *The Interpretation of History*, p. 220.

In practice among those who hold this view, the word 'Church' is generally replaced by 'churches', which are 'groups of Christians formed to organize their lives with help from God through a relationship determined by faith in Jesus Christ'.[7] Furthermore, a church is usually described more in terms of its function than of its nature. As a leading exponent of this idea, Shailer Mathews, says: 'An institution which seeks to make men more brotherly by inculcating the ethical message of Jesus and his faith in the God of love will furnish the material for a new society.'[8] Christians of this persuasion would generally agree to the dictum: 'The Church must die to be born again as the Holy Spirit of a righteous social order.'[9]

This is the characteristic understanding of the Church by those who are vaguely designated as theological 'liberals'. The Church is primarily a society of Christians acting as an ethical leaven within society as a whole. It is not, according to this view, 'an organic historical entity,' writes C. C. Morrison with irony, 'but a social contract, and Rousseau and Hobbes are its prophets'.[10] Individual freedom of faith and democratic government are basic in its principles, and no indispensable connexion between one's personal faith and his membership in the Church is recognized. Such, briefly, is how the problem has been regarded by Christian liberalism of this century. Being so obsessed with the application of Jesus' ethical teaching to immediate social problems many liberals, observes W. A. Brown, have simply substituted the 'social gospel' for the doctrine of the Church.[11]

Upon this concept of the Church, or 'churches', it is both anomalous and fruitless to base an unfavourable criticism of the divided state of the Church as a whole. A Church consisting of large numbers of churches of voluntarily organized members must inevitably have divisions; for since the essence of the Church is a purely sociological quality, it must conform largely to the society of which it is a part. Christians in these church units feel a common bond with all other Christians, a feeling which may satisfy them as an expression of true unity; but no theological significance may be attached to such a feeling, in the sense that

---

[7] S. Mathews, *The Church and the Christian*, p. 12.
[8] *Jesus on Social Institutions*, p. 138.
[9] John Lewis, quoted by M. Chaning-Pearce, *The Terrible Crystal*, p. 21.
[10] In *Christendom*, II.2(1937).283.
[11] In *Liberal Theology* (H. P. Van Dusen, ed.), pp. 142f.

it expresses a given unity belonging to the Church's very essence, a unity which is disregarded or threatened by denominational churches.

Those who regard the Church's unity as a thoroughly spiritual and invisible quality, and those who consider the Church to be a collection of variegated churches, are not the only ones who fail to be distressed by the existing state of division. There are some who positively welcome these divisions as a necessary and desirable characteristic of the Church. Admitting that it sounds paradoxical, W. Elert urges that the very strength of the Church depends upon these divisions in theology and practice.[12] He argues that where there are no theological and ecclesiastical divisions the faith of Christians becomes complacent in its self-sufficiency. The tension which is sustained by opposing doctrines keeps the Church in a healthy state of unrest, for it demands that beliefs be constantly proved and checked. Stated in paraphrase, his view is: let us continue in division, that faith, or at least theology, may abound. When this idea is proposed as a rejection of thorough-going uniformity of belief in the Church, it commends itself to those who will not equate uniformity with unity. Even in the areas of the Church where true unity of faith and fellowship is most genuinely realized, there are differences in theological interpretation. But these do not necessarily threaten the unity of the Church so long as they are not allowed to disrupt the love and fellowship of those who belong to Christ.

The danger of Elert's position is that it is easily perverted, being changed from a defence against theological stagnation to a pragmatic rationalization of divisions based upon issues which are not strictly theological. Differences in theology have certainly stimulated the intellectual activity of Christians, but they have also been used as wedges to drive people apart, making cleavages which are partly theological in nature and partly social and moral. Moreover, when problems of theology cease to be living ones, when they become petrified as unalterable dogmas to which assent must be given as a condition for recognized membership in the Church, and when they defy all challenges made by opposing interpretations, it can hardly be claimed that the welfare of the Church is being served by such divisions, nor that its unity is not being jeopardized.

[12] *Der christliche Glaube*, p. 534.

Confronted by the apparently irreconcilable theological and ecclesiastical differences existing between the major segments of the divided Church, some persons have been satisfied to explain the lack of outward unity by what is called the 'branch theory'. According to this view, which commends itself to many fair-minded Christians, the *one* Church of Christ is a tree having different branches which, though distinct, are still part of the whole. This theory has been applied specifically to those sections of the Church which are deemed to be 'Catholic' in orders and tradition, as when a theological committee of the Church of Sweden declared: 'That the Church developed into three chief forms: Orthodox, Roman, and Evangelic Catholicism, with their different varieties, we do not believe to be against the will of God but in accordance with His plan, because it was necessary that Christianity should reveal its boundless riches in different forms.'[13] However, the figure of the 'branches' lends itself so well to a defence of all denominational divisions that it has also been applied to Christian bodies outside the 'Catholic' tradition, referring to a great many branches rather than only three.[14]

Logical as the 'branch theory' may seem to be, it has been opposed vigorously by those who have a less accommodating idea of unity. This theory, contends W. A. Visser 't Hooft, 'stands for a conception of tolerance which owes its origins, not to the Bible, but to modern humanitarianism. Its weakness is that it isolates the question of *unity* from the question of *truth*.'[15] In other words, it does not take seriously enough the belief that the unity of the Church consists of other factors than common faith in Jesus Christ. 'What is our standing ground', asks Barth, 'if we take the familiar line of ascribing to the Roman, the Greek, the Lutheran, the Reformed, the Anglican and other churches their special attributes and functions within an imagined organic totality? However well this may sound, it is not theology, it is mere sociology or philosophy of history.'[16] Where Church unity is concerned, therefore, it is believed by many authorities that the

---

[13] *Convictions* (L. Hodgson, ed.), p. 156.
[14] cf. the figure used in Hooker's *Ecclesiastical Polity*: '. . . as the main body of the sea being one, yet within divers precincts hath divers names; so the Catholic Church is in like sort divided into a number of distinct Societies, every one of which is termed a Church within itself'; quoted by G. K. A. Bell, *Christian Unity*.
[15] *The Church and Its Function in Society*, p. 92; cf. A. C. Headlam, *The Doctrine of the Church and Christian Reunion, p.* 215.
[16] *The Church and the Churches*, p. 27.

existing schisms are to be judged, though not necessarily explained, on the basis of theology rather than sociology. And the theological understanding of the unity of the Church does not seem to allow for the claims of the 'branch theory'.

In discussing these divisions, we are under the obligation of taking a critical view of the problem of sectarianism. The numerous sects of Christianity have frequently been ignored in treatises in the nature and unity of the Church, because it is ostensibly assumed by certain theologians that they stand wholly outside the Church. Talks on unity and reunion are greatly complicated when the sectarian issue is introduced, because for every article of faith or practice which an ecumenical group may hold to belong to the *esse* of the Church, there is at least one sect which disavows that article. The difficulty of such discussion is further aggravated by the fact that there is no universally accepted definition of a 'sect' which can be efficiently employed. The renowned distinctions made by Ernst Troeltsch between the 'Church-type' and the 'sect-type' of Christian organization have served the purpose of definition fairly well during the decades since *Die Soziallehren* was published. However, it has lately become the fashion to take a rather condescending view of Troeltsch's distinctions; for it is now clear that the 'Church' and 'sect' he described were not actual religious bodies, but abstractions of a rather too well defined nature.[17] Thus it is easy to point to many denominations which include elements of both the 'Church-type' and the 'sect-type', but which still do not conform sufficiently to either type to be classed with the one or the other.[18]

After his intensive study of American sectarianism, E. T. Clark concluded that 'it is scarcely possible to define the church or the sect' beyond the generalization that 'a narrow dogmatism is perhaps the most nearly universal characteristic of the typical sectarian spirit'.[19] The very caution exercised by Clark, following so intensive an investigation, bears witness to the fact, already patent in the work of Troeltsch, that a sociological description of various sects cannot sufficiently define either what a sect or the sectarian spirit is. But the sociological observations do help us to

[17] cf. D. Bonhöffer, *Sanctorum communio*.
[18] cf. R. H. Bainton in *Christendom*, XI.3(1946).382.
[19] *The Small Sects in America* (Revised edn.), p. 21.

understand the nature of sectarianism and provide a basis for theological thought on the problem.

The exclusiveness of the sect, whether doctrinal or social, is its most noticeable feature. This is described very aptly—though unintentionally!—by one who purports to be describing the Church: he calls it 'the smaller company of regenerate persons who in any given community unite themselves voluntarily together in accordance with Christ's laws for the purpose of securing the complete establishment of his Kingdom in themselves and in the world'.[20] The emphasis upon fixed boundaries, moral perfectionism, and voluntary membership is typical of the sect, as usually conceived in sociological terms. To these may be added the elements of hostility to 'the world' and a tendency to withdraw from the social community into the private life of the smaller group. As G. van der Leeuw points out, the sect does not break away from the Church as much as it breaks away from the social community, for it has a disdain for society, and 'a secret yearning for the dissolution of each and every community, for the return to solitude in the presence of God'.[21] Members of the sect burn with such a passion for the present realization of everything promised in the Gospel, whether moral saintliness or possession of the Kingdom of God, that they cannot abide the 'worldliness' and indifference of the institutional Church.

This attitude is well illustrated in Reinhold Niebuhr's comments on David's reluctance to build the temple because of his sense of unworthiness (1 Chronicles 28^{20}–29^{1}): 'Let the temple be built by the purity of youth. It has not yet involved itself in the conflicts of life. . . . This is a moral solution. It seeks to find someone good enough to build the temple of God. In terms of modern analogy, it is the sectarian solution. The sectarian church usually protests that the members of the orthodox church are not worthy to belong to it. The sect therefore builds a new church with wholly regenerate members.'[22] And because this moral fervour is always strongest in the first generation of the sect, so that in ensuing generations the radical demands become steadily weakened and the sect itself tends toward an institutional status, there is nothing to stop new sects from branching off the old ones,

---

[20] A. H. Strong; quoted by S. Mathews, *The Church and the Christian*, p. 7.
[21] *Religion in Essence and Manifestation*, pp. 261-4.
[22] *Beyond Tragedy*, p. 56.

thereby contributing to the further fragmentation of the whole Christian Church.

Beneath these sociological manifestations of the sects are to be found the intrinsic ideas which constitute sectarianism. From the standpoint of the New Testament, Gloege finds that the distinctive feature of the sect (*hairesis*) is that its fellowship arises as a result of the autonomous action of men, whereas the *ekklēsia* is the fellowship which comes alive only by the calling (*klēsis*) of God.[23] While such may well have been true in the first century, however, it would be uncharitable and untrue to assert that in our own time none of the members of sects think of their fellowship as a result of the divine calling.

There is another element of sectarianism regarding which a certain degree of consensus has been reached by theologians in recent times. In essence it is much more than extreme moralism expressed by separation from both the rest of the Church and the social community as a whole. Real sectarianism, according to P. T. Forsyth, shows the monopolizing tendency to claim exclusive autonomy for some part of the Church for the overt purpose of arrogating to that part the sole right to be the custodian of Christian truth.[24] More tersely stated by C. C. Morrison: '*A sect is a part of the body of Christ which exercises by itself and for itself those functions which belong to the unity of the whole body.*'[25] In the light of this distinction, sectarianism involves far more than is customarily attached to the word, and it is not to be observed solely in those bodies which are ordinarily called sects. Sectarianism stands in direct opposition to true catholicism, for it is divisive rather than unifying, exclusive rather than inclusive. It is not recognizable by signs of numerical size, type of worship, or moral behaviour, so much as by the positivism of its claim to truth. So, as Brunner sees it, 'the "sect" idea is not primarily a sociological conception or an idea of Church order, but it is a dogmatic conception'.[26] Judged in reference to such a definition, it may well be seen that the very denomination which, according to the sociological definitions of Troeltsch, is the opposite of the sect-type, namely the Roman Catholic, is one of those which is thoroughly characterized by the sectarian spirit.

[23] *Reich Gottes und Kirche im Neuen Testament*, p. 346n.
[24] *The Church and the Sacraments*, p. 37.
[25] *What is Christianity?* p. 280.   [26] *The Divine Imperative*, p. 542.

It would only add to an already existing state of verbal confusion to urge that the so-called 'Catholic' denominations, because of their dogmatic exclusiveness, be called the truly sectarian, and this is not recommended. Viewed from the standpoint under discussion, however, any denomination which, for example, will welcome the reunion of splintered parts of the Church only upon its own terms is surely manifesting the divisive spirit of the sect.

Returning to the more conventional, though indistinct, concept of the sect, we find a very suggestive theological explanation for sectarianism in a proposal of Prenter's. He asserts that sectarianism, like other attempts to realize pure theocracy, originates from a 'too direct and undialectical conception of the unity between Christ and His Church'.[27] Because the relationship of Christ to the Church is thought to be immediate and uninterrupted by sin, since the members of the sect are perfectly regenerate, it follows that the teachings of Jesus, as the very will of God, are considered to be effective for the Church as definite laws which can be satisfactorily fulfilled. Otherwise stated, the belief is that the life of the sectarian community can and does express the perfect will of God which is revealed in Jesus Christ. And inasmuch as the rest of the 'world' is obviously unregenerate and sinful, the separation of the sect from its social *milieu* is inevitable. Such separation indicates a substantially Pelagian doctrine of sin. It is due, continues Prenter, 'to an under-estimation of the sinfulness of the members of the Church, an under-estimation which again is due to a false conception of the unity of the Head and the body, a direct unity of nature instead of the broken unity of faith and repentance'.[28] Where the sinfulness of persons, even of persons who are Christian, is not seen as a reality, divinity is considered a present possession; then there arises continually the danger that this unrecognized sinfulness will change into the most unregenerate and unchristian arrogance. Because this does often happen in those groups which are conventionally known as sects, as well as in institutional churches which have the sectarian spirit, Brunner can say with justification that 'the ecclesiasticism of the sects is ecclesiasticism in its extremest and worst form, the will to create the pure Church'.[29]

However accurate and revealing these current thoughts about

[27] Files of Commission I, W.C.C., Geneva.   [28] ibid.
[29] *The Divine Imperative*, p. 563.

the nature of sectarianism may be, they do not answer conclusively the critical question of whether, or how, the many Christian sects belong to the one Church, the Body of Christ. This is a problem of first magnitude in the present time, for despite the momentous movement toward ecumenical reunion and the significant progress which has been made in that direction, the numerical strength and vigour of those sectarian bodies which will have no part in ecumenical conversations are on the increase. Attitudes toward this problem range from the narrowest exclusiveness to the broadest inclusiveness; but neither the simple answer that *no* sects are part of the Church, nor the equally simple answer that *all* of them belong to the Church, is satisfactory.

Few Protestants would pass the former judgement unconditionally, although many would agree with H. Burn-Murdoch, an Anglican, when he says that *baptized* members of sects belong to the Church but that the sects themselves cannot be called the Church in any way.[30]

Taking the opposing view, A. Lecerf writes: 'The severe judgement that we have passed on sects must not be interpreted as implying their exclusion from the universal Church, nor even from historic Protestantism. That which is carnal, and even demoniac, in them must not make us forget that, in other respects, however irregular their methods, they work for the conquest of souls by Jesus Christ. . . . Even when they anathematize the Church, the latter must not cease to place the ideal unity of the mystical body of Christ above the narrowness and inconsistencies of certain of its living members.'[31]

Which of these is nearer the truth? Again we are confronted by the perplexing problems of visibility, limits and standards of the Church, which defy ultimate solution. And it is profitless to condemn either the man who would set up a rigid doctrinal wall around the Church any more than the man who would gladly include within the Church all persons and groups which at least claim to belong to the Christian tradition. The only possible answer to the difficulty, and it is not a working solution either, is that each of the several views of the nature of the Church, emphasizing either doctrinal, moral, sacramental, or hierarchical principles, carries with it a distinctive attitude toward sectarianism; and until there can be wider agreement on these fundamental

[30] *Church, Continuity and Unity*, p. 46.   [31] *An Introduction to Reformed Dogmatics*, p. 360.

factors of the Church's nature, we are in no position to formulate a synoptic policy regarding sects.

Recognition of the seriousness of this impasse has brought many contemporary theologians to the belief that, so long as there are any divisions in the Church, the whole Church is in a state of schism.[32] It is not as though the true Church remains undisturbed and unaffected when a section of it departs to form a new denomination. That very fact of separation and division, declares A. Richardson, throws all the denominations of the Church into the same condition of schism, and no one has the right to throw the first stone.[33] It is difficult to see how any attempts toward a better realization of the unity of the Church in the world can begin without an acknowledgement of this general state of schism.

We have already seen how the 'branch theory' of the Church looks upon the divisions of the Church, at least to a certain extent, as being justifiable, if not inherent in the Church's nature. Schism is admitted as a fact, but not attributed to sinfulness. As F. Ménégoz described the debate over this issue of the sinfulness of schism, a problem which was alive at the Lausanne Conference, 1927, neither Lutherans nor Calvinists, much less the Orthodoxists would ever regard their historical resistance to papal supremacy as a manifestation of their sin.[34] A few years prior to this conference, Headlam had declared that sin is implicit in all schism, but that it 'lies with those who are morally responsible for having caused the division'.[35] This principle is probably valid as a standard for judging historical divisions, and it serves to satisfy the conscience of those who treasure the faith and courage of their denominational founders and will not attribute their reforms and separations to sin. The ostensible fault in Headlam's thesis is that no one ought to be confident in deciding which side of a particular schismatic division is morally responsible and which is innocent, since responsibility usually lodges with both.

Some theologians in more recent years have been inclined to equate Christian disunity with unqualified sinfulness. 'In fact,

[32] This idea was developed and urged by A. C. Headlam, *The Doctrine of the Church and Christian Reunion*, p. 223; cf. O. C. Quick, *The Christian Sacraments*, p. 147: 'We conclude then that, the "visible" Church being manifestly divided, all bodies professing Christianity belong to it imperfectly and in varying degrees.'
[33] In *La Sainte Église Universelle*, p. 160.
[34] *Convictions* (L. Hodgson, ed.), p. 15.
[35] *The Doctrine of the Church and Christian Reunion*, p. 223.

we have no right to explain the multiplicity of the Churches at all,' observes Barth; 'We have to deal with it as we deal with sin.'[36] The apparent converse of this idea would be that no divisions at all would rend the seamless robe of the Church in a hypothetical state of sinlessness. Unless schism is the consequence of sin, therefore, we must assume the correctness of the 'branch theory', or ideas similar to it, namely, that such divisions are intended by God for the Church. But those who have an uneasy conscience about the lack of outward and real unity in the Church cannot admit this alternative. 'A divided Church in the New Testament sense of the word Church is something illogical and incomprehensible—as illogical and incomprehensible as human sin.'[37] It is this appeal to the New Testament, notably in the prayer 'that they all may be one' (John 17[21]), and in the affirmation that 'there is one Body and one Spirit' (Ephesians 4[4]), that a basis has been found for regarding all sectarian divisions of the Church as the fruit of sin. This interpretation of the essence of disunity commends itself to modern thought on the nature of the Church, despite the protestations of those who subordinate empirical unity to a vague and chimeric spiritual unity or see only the richness of a variety of gifts in the scattered and separated denominations. And this interpretation also indicates unmistakably the obstinate and formidable factors which must be reckoned with in all efforts to achieve reunion.

II. WHY THE CHURCH IS ONE

The idea that the Church is fundamentally and constitutionally a unity is accepted as virtually axiomatic by most Christians. Unity is the first of the four basic and interrelated attributes traditionally acknowledged for the Church: as the Church is holy, catholic, and apostolic, so it is also one. In spite of the obvious divisions in the Body of Christ, the theological cleavages, the racial and national barriers, which to varying degrees negate the loving fellowship of those who belong to Christ, it is still a firmly held belief that there cannot be two or more Churches of Christ, however many denominations or 'churches' there may be. 'The Church is one as certainly as God is only one,' writes Barth:

[36] *The Church and the Churches*, p. 29.
[37] J. E. L. Newbigin, *The Reunion of the Church*, p. 24.

'It is the Body of Christ on earth, of which there can be but one. It is an absurdity that there should be more than one, opposing Churches.'[38] If there is any article of the doctrine of the nature of the Church which may be seen to have the full support of Christians, it is this belief in unity.

'Unity' is an ambiguous term, however, and we should be aware of the two-fold meaning it has for the Church. This is explained rather clearly by Gloege, when he distinguishes between the 'uniqueness' (*Einzigkeit*) and the corporate 'oneness' (*Einheitlichkeit*) of the Church.[39] The former testifies to the fact that there is but one Church. The latter expresses the unified spirit which pervades the membership of the Church, the oneness of all in the Body of Christ. While both concepts are included in the one word, 'unity', therefore, they are still to be borne in mind as separate meanings.

In their report to the Amsterdam Assembly, 1948, the members of Section I testified to the givenness and indestructibility of the unity of the Church. 'God has given to His people in Jesus Christ a unity which is His creation and not our achievement.... We have been drawn together to discover that, notwithstanding our divisions, we are one in Jesus Christ.'[40] This statement of faith expresses a consensus which has persisted from ancient times through the present generation without noticeable diminution. But is it a self-evident, or demonstrable, fact that this unity is a reality? Seen as a whole by any outsider, of course, the Church shows little evidence of being either one or at one among its members. Often this ostensible disunity may be articulately expressed by Christians who have no intention of claiming a unity which includes those sections of the Church which are objectionable to them. But no theologian can hope to present the case for unity by reference to the disunited appearance which the denominations present.

The appeal must be made instead to the original witness of the New Testament and to consistency with the faith concerning the Church which this witness has fostered. First, the Bible speaks specifically and repeatedly of the oneness of the *ekklēsia*, the Body which is as much a unity as Christ Himself is. Secondly, upon this

---

[38] *Die Theologie und die Kirche*, p. 289.
[39] *Reich Gottes und Kirche im Neuen Testament*, p. 407n.
[40] *The Universal Church in God's Design* (W.C.C.), p. 211.

scriptural basis has been established the Christian faith that the Church continues to possess the mark of true and essential unity. Theological evidence, as distinguished from empirical evidence, is drawn from these two sources. And Christian thought in recent years has been directed more and more toward a deeper understanding of the concept of unity which these sources reveal.

One of the most oft-quoted passages which affirms the divine intention that the Church should be one is John 17[21], the part of the long prayer ascribed to Jesus which reads: '. . . that they may all be one; even as thou, Father, art in me, and I in thee, that they also may be in us, so that the world may believe that thou hast sent me.' The implication of this petition reaches farther than the expression of the Lord's wish for the Church. It says a great deal in a few words about the nature of this unity and says it very plainly. In the paraphrase by A. Loisy: 'Christian unity is not merely a unity of purpose and a unity of means employed to effect this purpose, it is, rather, a vital organic union, not only similar to, but veritably identical with, the union of the Father and the incarnate Son.'[41] From the standpoint of Christian faith, no higher concept of the bond of unity among members of the Church than this, that they should represent on earth the unity existing between the Son and the Father, is possible. This is the profound mystery of the oneness of the Church, as inconceivable in its fullness as the manner of unity of the Holy Trinity. It is because the unity has such a supersensible basis in the divine nature that we must speak of it as being 'given' by God, rather than created by man, and as being 'preserved' by the Holy Spirit. To cite the appropriate parable of L. S. Thornton: 'The unity of the Body is a living unity created and sustained by the one Spirit. The drenched soil holds together, whereas if left dry it would crumble apart into dust.'[42] The sole unifying power, which issues in the experience of *koinōnia* and binds together those who are by faith united in Christ, is that same divine relationship of the Trinity.

Such metaphysical language, being difficult to grasp, is also difficult to hold in check. The exaltation of the Church is indeed lofty, being compared to the very Godhead as a unity in the Spirit. But such comparison, according to the context of this

---
[41] Quoted by E. C. Hoskyns, *The Fourth Gospel*, p. 505.
[42] *The Common Life in the Body of Christ*, p. 94.

passage of John, is not intended to mean identification of the Church with the Son and the Father. The added words, 'so that the world may believe that thou hast sent me,' declare the purpose of the Church in the world and indicate that those who have faith in Christ are subordinate to Him even when in union with Him and with one another. This maintenance of distance between the Lord and the individual, demanding obedience of the latter, is, according to Hoskyns, the root distinction between the meaning of faith in the Fourth Gospel and the esoteric mysticism of Gnostic and Neo-Platonic thought, according to which the identification of the Church with its Lord would have been made complete.[43] In this part of the Johannine prayer, we do not find Christ and the Church merging into an indistinguishable identity of being. Rather, we find a teaching on the nature of Christian unity which, more than any other, gives a clue to the mystery of the oneness of persons in the Church, and hence of the uniqueness of the Church.

For the minds of many Christians today, this exalted testimony to the nature of unity seems to be a rather vague speculation with little apparent relevance to the Church as they know it. However, theologians who have been giving the most thought to the problem are increasingly disposed to take the teaching with all due seriousness. They see behind the outer divisions of the Church a given unity which men can indeed obscure, but never destroy, since it is the work of God.[44] This is not a peculiarly 'Catholic' notion of the Church, as some might say, for it is proclaimed by the same Gospel which all Christians accept. As W. A. Visser 't Hooft explains: 'The Reformers do not teach the disembodied unity of a church in the clouds, which some people persist in regarding as a typically protestant notion. They call us to be the Church, one, holy, catholic, and apostolic, in which we believe, but which must not remain invisible in the world.'[45] The Church's unity is not that of an organization, but of an organism.

The organic union of the *ekklēsia* in the New Testament is a familiar theme, expressed clearly in various figures of speech, and emphasized positively throughout. These figures and their interpretations have already been treated in Chapter Three.

---

[43] *The Fourth Gospel*, p. 506.
[44] cf. A. Richardson in *La Sainte Église Universelle*, p. 143.
[45] *The Wretchedness and Greatness of the Church*, p. 57.

Here we should only recall that the figures of the Vine, the Temple or Building, the Bride of Christ and the Body of Christ imply not just the relationship of the Church to its Lord, but also the unified relationship of all Christians. It is the basic function of the Christ not only to bring persons into faithful and filial relation to God through Himself, but also to create among them all the life of the New Humanity which is the Church. '*As reconciler Christ is both the vertical and the horizontal bond of unity of the Church*,' concludes S. Hanson.[46]

We meet this concept especially in the various usages of the Body of Christ in the Epistles, which were written in the face of flagrant divisions, to urge the necessity of recognizing the organic unity of the Church. 'Is Christ divided?' demands Paul.[47] Because there is one loaf of which all partake, are not all one Body?[48] By one Spirit all are baptized into the one Body of Christ,[49] so that, though many, all are individually members of one another, suffering and rejoicing together in each other's pain and honour.[50] Thus is apprehended the unity of persons in the Body, a kind of unity to which there can be no permissible alternative. Whatever natural diversities of temperament and belief may be necessary within the fellowship of the *ekklēsia*, the following allow no multiplicity: one Body, one Spirit, one hope, one Lord, one faith, one baptism, one God and Father.[51]

It is true, as Johnston remarks, that this fundamental unity of the Body is an ideal conception, the only one which could be held before the schismatic Christians of the first century or the twentieth century, as a terrible reminder of the sin of division and the need for 'continual growth into Christ, greater obedience, fuller contact with the source of their life'.[52] That the concept reflects the ideal, however, does not indicate that it is an unreal illusion, since 'ideal' in this sense does not mean a philosophical concept of the Church in its perfection, but the Church as it *is* essentially when no longer obscured by the veil of human imperfection. 'We do not have to create unity,' writes F. J. Taylor, 'but to remove the barriers to its expression which have been erected by human sin in the course of history.'[53]

The fact that the unity of the Church is 'given' or created by

---

[46] *The Unity of the Church in the New Testament*, p. 119.   [47] 1 Corinthians 1^{13}.
[48] 1 Corinthians 10^{17}.   [49] ibid., 12^{13}.   [50] ibid., 12^{26}.   [51] Ephesians 4$^{4-5}$.
[52] *The Doctrine of the Church in the New Testament*, p. 95.   [53] *The Church of God*, p. 106.

God in the very constituting of the Body of Christ need not and should not deceive men into thinking that they have no responsibility for the Church's unity. On the contrary, the Christians' responsibility on behalf of unity is very great, for it is their task to *express* the unity, rather than to create or achieve it.[54] This is why it is not accurate in the ecumenical movement to speak of 'building the unity of the Church' or of 'unifying the churches', except in so far as order and organization are concerned. The proper word in this world-wide movement is 'reunion'—the reassembling of the divided and scattered hosts of the People of God into the state of mutual recognition, common faith, *koinōnia*, and love. These are the expressions of unity, not the tools and materials by which it is made. In the light of this existing, though repressed, unity of the Church, the keynote of divided Christians is the dictum: Become what you are, not what you hope to be. Unless there lies deeply embedded in the faith of Christians this conception of unity as a fundamental gift of God to be expressed and used, rather than as a goal to be attained, the prospects for a Church which maintains 'the unity of the Spirit in the bond of peace'[55] are most discouraging.

Admitting the given, essential unity, however, we are still faced with the staggering problem of *how* to express the Church's oneness in spite of the numerous major and minor schisms within the Church in the world. In the present discussion it is unfortunately necessary to avoid becoming involved in specific schemes for reunion on regional, national, and ecumenical levels. These have lately become so complicated by the many differences of polity and doctrine and other factors, that any general remarks which might be made or cited here would be of little or no value. This is not to disparage the immense importance of the practical planning needed to make the Church's unity more manifest in the experience of Christians, but only to indicate that even a bare minimum discussion of this problem lies outside the scope of this study.

What the trend toward reunion among Protestants, at least, in the past forty years has shown us is, that the unity of the Church cannot be considered in isolation from its catholicity. To speak of unity is so much a part of speaking of catholicity that the two concepts are mutually complementary. Both have their common

---

[54] cf. N. Micklem, *What Is the Faith?* p. 211.   [55] Ephesians 4[3].

point of reference in Jesus Christ. The one Christ, in unity with the Father and with His disciples, is the Head of the one Body: He is the Lord of the multitudes who live in a state of division from one another, but who are yet one in Him. Moreover, the work of salvation which He has wrought, and to which the Church bears witness, extends that unity to the whole of mankind. The Church is called 'catholic' or 'universal', therefore, because it is the projection of Christ to the entire human race. As Adolph Schlatter puts it, just as God's creation, love, and judgement apply to all men and women of all time, so the saving work of Christ is for all. His work is the Gospel of the Word, and so far as the Word is spread in time and space, there is the Church.[56]

In order to explain what they mean by the catholicity of the Church, some modern theologians have felt that the fourfold definition laid down by Cyril of Jerusalem in 347 cannot be improved upon.[57] This analysis, ancient as it is, well comprehends most of what has been said about the meaning of catholicity in our own time, and it may be used as a pattern for discussion to elucidate the relationship of catholicity to unity.

(a) The first dimension is the one most commonly associated with the idea of catholicity, namely *the extension of the Church throughout the world*. Theologians who have rediscovered the use of the word 'catholic' in recent years have generally understood that it is not just synonymous with 'world-wide', but that it includes the latter among other meanings. The point need not be pressed that within the past hundred years this meaning of catholicity has become more real than ever before, from both the numerical and geographical considerations. In distant areas where missionaries have planted the seed of faith, it has taken root and sprouted forth as indigenous communities of the one universal Church. As H. Kraemer has shown, these new Christians have found that the biblical conception of the nature of the Church is perfectly valid for them in their own cultures, and that so long as 'the impelling and primary notice is to express the Gospel and its invariable essence', they can draw upon their own cultural heritage and still have full experience of the universal oneness of the Body of Christ.[58] In fact, upon these missionary

---

[56] '*Die Grenzen der kirchlichen Gemeinschaft*' in *Deutsche Theologie* (1935), pp. 185f.
[57] *Catecheses* xviii.23; cf. A. G. Hebert, *The Form of the Church*, pp. 91-7; F. J. Taylor, *The Church of God*, pp. 114-26.
[58] *The Christian Message in a Non-Christian World*, pp. 420f.

frontiers the demand for, and experience of, true unity are more emphasized than elsewhere, and the so-called 'younger churches' have been setting the pace in the movements toward Christian reunion.[59]

(b) *The wholeness of the Christian faith* is the second aspect of catholicity, as well as a vital factor of unity. This may be interpreted variously, depending upon the understanding of faith held by one person or another. Where directly opposite and contradicting views of certain doctrines are in conflict, of course, this element of catholicity is not being manifest. But the faith itself, which is also catholic, is the whole Gospel of Jesus Christ, and, as Hebert remarks, not 'the sum-total of beliefs held by all Christians everywhere and always'.[60]

Systematic uniformity of doctrine is not necessary to the Church's catholicity, but the faithful proclamation of the one Gospel is. The surest test of the Church's claim to catholicity, asserts D. T. Jenkins, is whether it preaches the resurrection of Jesus Christ, since this carries with it the fullest implications of the New Testament faith, and is therefore the most authentic sign of the apostolicity of its message.[61]

Judged by theologians of differing positions, this test is either too rigorous or too lax. C. J. Cadoux believes that there is no satisfactory minimum standard of doctrine to be applied as a test of catholicity, and he represents a view that is widely held in liberal circles.[62] But A. C. Headlam, speaking for another large section of the Church, recommends universal acceptance of the Nicene Creed as the common expression of faith.[63] The whole history of the Church has demonstrated how difficult it is for Christians to agree on what is indispensable and essential to the fullness of the Gospel. Complete agreement has not yet been reached by any means. But since the beginning of the Church it has been the hope of Christians that agreements shall become increasingly universal, 'until we all attain to the unity of the faith and of the knowledge of the Son of God'.[64]

(c) Concern for *the unifying of 'all sorts and conditions of men'* is the third dimension of the Church's catholicity. This may be expressed in two ways: by perfecting the actual unity of all

---

[59] cf. J. E. L. Newbigin, *The Reunion of the Church*, p. 20.   [60] *The Form of the Church*, p. 92.
[61] *The Nature of Catholicity*, p. 67.
[62] In *Essays Congregational and Catholic* (A. Peel ed.) p. 63.
[63] *The Doctrine of the Church and Christian Reunion*, p. 238.   [64] Ephesians 4^{13}.

Christians, and by continually reaching out to include the whole of mankind. It is self-evident in the New Testament that, while there are differences of gifts and functions in the Church, there are no differences of worth or persons. 'There is neither Jew nor Greek, there is neither slave nor free, there is neither male nor female; for you are all one in Christ Jesus.'[65] So far as Christ is concerned, the distinctions of race, culture, social prestige, sex, and all other natural differences are swept away as being irrelevant to the fundamental unity which binds Christians to Him and in Him.

The Church, moreover, is potentially wide enough to claim and include every man and woman. 'One aspect of the Church's holiness upon earth', observes O. C. Quick, 'consists precisely in the fact that it exists primarily for the sake of those who do not yet belong to it.'[66] This is the effect of the universality of Jesus Christ, which makes it absolutely necessary that the Church be a missionary Church under all circumstances. The Church stands before God on behalf of the whole of mankind, declares Paul Althaus, and not just for its own members,[67] assuming responsibility for those who are not yet members of it. Since this aspect of catholicity is at present so imperfectly realized by the Church, it must be considered ultimately as an eschatological manifestation of the Church, as the condition existing when the Church is finally consummated in the Kingdom of God.

(*d*) In the last place, the Church is catholic because it is *the 'universal physician,' which is capable of healing every sin of soul and body*. This is a part of the Church's nature which is easily and often overlooked, or else is relegated to a secondary position of importance. And yet, if the Church truly is to represent Christ in the world in order to draw all men unto Him, its concern is not merely for the numerical wholeness of the race but also for the qualitative wholeness of every person. Christian unity is most seriously thwarted by the divorce between religious faith and the secular interests of life, a divorce which unhappily characterizes the 'split-personality' of numerous Christians today. The idea

---

[65] Galatians 3[27]. Since the Greek *eis*, 'one,' is here masculine, it is plausible and clarifying to render the clause, 'you are all *one man* in Christ Jesus,' Christ representing the corporate unity of the Body; cf. S. Hanson, *The Unity of the Church in the New Testament*. Against this, cf. G. S. Duncan, *The Epistle of Paul to the Galatians*, p. 124; 'Each man stands on the same level as his neighbour.'
[66] *The Christian Sacraments*, p. 126.
[67] *Die christliche Wahrheit*, II.313.

of belonging to the one Body of Christ cannot be taken with sufficient seriousness unless it be strengthened by the complementary idea that one belongs to the Body in the entirety of his life. By this is meant, in the words of O. S. Tomkins: 'That unity of all human living, a balanced wholeness of work, craftsmanship, family life, community life, scholarship, games, art, bound together in a living and joyful sacrifice laid before God in worship, by union with the Word made Flesh and in the power of the Holy Spirit.'[68] All this is encompassed by the saving work of Christ, and can become actualized in the common life of the Church.

These four dimensions of catholicity do not have any claim to reality unless they are seen as manifestations of the universal Christ, who lives in the one Church. A Church which is divided constitutionally and by necessity of divine will cannot be a Church which is truly catholic; and, as Christians are steadily rediscovering, there is no such Church. 'The Church's Catholicity is the carrying into effect of its Unity,' writes Hebert.[69] Therefore, wherever Christians live in a state of separation from one another; wherever one denomination, be it ever so large, claims full sufficiency for itself; above all, wherever access to the Lord's Table is denied by one Christian group to another: in all these situations and others of like kind, the catholicity of the Church is being overtly denied and the unity in Christ is rendered ineffective. The primary tasks of Christians in the present and coming generations is to find the means of recovering and expressing the unity which God gave to the Church when He created it through Jesus Christ.

Since this full unity has never been thoroughly realized, however, being from the time of the apostles a hoped-for expression of unity rather than a present possession, the question remains open, whether complete unity can be realized in history, or whether it belongs to the eschatological destiny of the Church. It is not sufficient to discuss the Church's unity without bearing in mind how relevant to it is the expectation of ultimate consummation in the Kingdom of God. 'If the given unity of the Church is essentially eschatological,' writes T. F. Torrance, 'then the validity of all that she does is conditioned by the *Parousia* and cannot be made to repose upon any primitive structure of unity already complete in the naturally historical realm or upon

[68] *The Wholeness of the Church*, p. 71.   [69] *The Form of the Church*, p. 98.

any continuity in the fallen world out of which we are redeemed'.[70] However successful our efforts at outward reunion may be, however genuine the spiritual union of all Christians, however real the unity of the Church with Christ—these all have an ultimate point of reference which is transcendent and eschatological. It is eschatology which gives to the Church its form of unity, remarks G. Gloege, since unity is bound to the Christian hope for the fulfilment of God's rule.[71] So we must seek the continuation of this discussion in the problem of the relation of the Church to the Kingdom of God.

[70] In *Scottish Journal of Theology* II.3(1949).244.
[71] *Reich Gottes und Kirche im Neuen Testament*, p. 415.

CHAPTER EIGHT

THE CHURCH AND ESCHATOLOGY

I. THE CHRISTIAN AND THE 'LAST THINGS'

BECAUSE the Church's nature cannot be fully known when considered in the light of its earthly manifestations in the community, and because every essential mark of the Church in the world is shown to be imperfectly expressed, the question inevitably arises, whether the Church can look forward in hope of an ultimate perfecting of all its latent possibilities. In order to seek an adequate answer to this question, theologians of this century have been analysing every word of the Bible which concerns the 'last things' and the Kingdom of God. It is common knowledge now that New Testament scholarship has uncovered and re-emphasized the rich deposit of eschatological ideas which permeated the religious atmosphere of the first-century Church and found various modes of expression in the Bible. The words of Jesus, the background of contemporary Jewish apocalypticism, and the striking interpretations of Paul and the other New Testament writers all combine to present a vast body of material for study and exposition It is hardly surprising that so many conflicting conclusions have been reached by scholars and theologians who have struggled with the task, for the sources themselves are full of variety and often are enigmatic. In this chapter we shall consider some of the major forms of eschatological ideas which have been put forward in the past thirty years as attempts to reach a clear understanding of the truth of eschatology, and we shall notice especially how each of these forms pertains to the nature and destiny of the Church.

The doctrine of the Kingdom of God is one which has played an increasingly great rôle in recent theology, as more and more light is being shed upon its meaning. That the Kingdom was primary in the message of Jesus and in the expectation of the first Christians can hardly be doubted. But for all the efforts of modern biblical scholarship, it is far from evident that theologians have been able to interpret the Kingdom in such a way as to make it again the vital element of Christian faith which it then was. 'It is time for our Christianity to examine itself and see whether we really still have faith in the Kingdom of God, or whether we merely retain it as a matter of traditional phraseology,' writes Albert Schweitzer.[1] For it is true that, widely as the term is employed by Christians, only a relatively small number of persons think of the Kingdom realistically in terms of the biblical usage and make it the basis for their hope. While multitudes pray, 'Thy Kingdom come,' very few consider their prayer to be an eschatological petition.

The reason for this divorce of word from idea is, according to Schweitzer, that Protestantism in particular has concentrated its faith upon the direct redemption of the individual through Christ, rather than including within this concept of redemption the fulfilment and perfecting of the People of God within His Kingdom.[2] At the same time, belief in the Kingdom of God, being held as an isolated doctrine, has not included belief in personal redemption through Christ, but has been corrupted by utopianism on the one hand and by apocalypticism on the other. As a result, both the redemptive and eschatological aspects of faith have been rendered weak and incomplete, in contrast to the strong unity of these aspects in the faith of the early Church. If such ancient faith is to be considered normative for our own today, we must conclude with Schweitzer that 'to be a Christian means to be possessed and dominated by a hope of the Kingdom of God'.[3]

But the problem of how to articulate such a hope so that it shall be both consistent with the New Testament and intelligible to our modern mode of thinking is a most perplexing one. Thought on the problem is a continuing process, as Folke Holmström has shown in his study of Continental theology until 1935.[4] From the Ritschlian idea of the Kingdom as a progressing moral order within history with its emphasis upon building the Kingdom on earth, theologians moved abruptly to the antithetical position, championed by J. Weiss, that the Kingdom involves nothing of the present order of the world but is purely eschatological and non-historical, the ultimate gift of God rather than the construction of human piety and morality. More recently, however, the

[1] *The Mysticism of Paul the Apostle*, p. 385.   [2] ibid., p. 382.
[3] ibid., p. 384.   [4] *Das eschatologische Denken der Gegenwart*, pp. 15-25.

trend has been to seek a synthesis between these two extremes, which can account for both the divine revelation in the Incarnation of the Son of God and the divine action within the sphere of history. In the course of this development, the relevance of the Church to the Kingdom has either been ignored or rejected to a large extent, depending upon the varying concepts of both Church and Kingdom. Within the last twenty years, however, a kind of consensus has been attained, concludes O. Linton, in which the Church is recognized as an inseparable part of the whole eschatological problem.[5]

The specific nature of this development of thought will be treated more fully in the following discussion. But one more preliminary observation must be made, and that concerns the problem of time and eternity. This problem can be treated philosophically as well as theologically, and it is important not to confuse the two methods of approach, for the speculations of philosophy concerning the end (*telos*) of history may ignore completely the Christian belief in God's Kingdom. As Paul Althaus reminds us, eschatology is a far different thing from teleology.[6] So we guard against temptations to rely upon teleological ideas which have nothing to do with the biblical category of fulfilment. In a like manner, we must avoid the easy solution of Platonism, which eventually annuls the meaning of time by regarding the culmination of history as the single simultaneous moment of eternity, for this is neither a biblical nor a Christian concept.[7] The results of philosophical reflection upon the problem have definite value for us, but only when they do not stand in opposition to the distinctive thought of the Bible.

II. THOROUGHGOING ESCHATOLOGY

It has been said that the recognition of the eschatological character of the Gospel of Jesus is the Copernican fact for modern theology.[8] It is hardly to be questioned that this recognition, made at the turn of the present century, has exercised the most extensive influence upon both the study of the New Testament and dogmatic

---

[5] *Das Problem der Urkirche in der neueren Forschung*, p. 150.
[6] *Die letzten Dinge*, 3. Aufl., p. 77f.
[7] cf. Reinhold Niebuhr, *Faith and History*, p. 269; J. E. L. Newbigin, *The Reunion of the Church*, p. 75.
[8] F. Heiler; quoted by F. M. Braun, *Neues Licht auf der Kirche*, p. 163.

theology. But this influence has never had such a radical effect upon biblical interpretation as it had in the years immediately following the initial discovery by Weiss that all of Jesus' sayings and parables concerning the Kingdom of God referred to His expectation that the Kingdom would come quickly and apocalyptically. The chief emphasis of Jesus' message was seen to lie in the warning that the Kingdom was just 'at hand', the axe already was laid at the root of the tree. Taking into account the historical conditions in which Jesus lived, and the prevailing kind of messianic thought which occupied the Jews at the time, fraught as it was with apocalyptic images derived from the books of Daniel and Enoch, the scholars who followed J. Weiss and Schweitzer used this eschatological emphasis as a key for interpreting the whole mission of Jesus, including His ethical teaching, His parables, His self-consciousness and sacrifice.

Further elaboration upon this familiar line of thought is unnecessary at this place, just because it is so familiar. But our concern is, rather, to know what kind of understanding of the Church is possible within the context of this thoroughgoing eschatology. Could there really have been a place for the *ekklēsia* as a concrete community if all of Jesus' thought was concentrated on the imminent and catastrophic coming of the Kingdom?[9] Would it not conform to the logic of this radical eschatology to exclude the Church altogether?

Linton points out that for the earlier protagonists of this school there was no question about the Church at all: Jesus' eschatology and the existence of the Church stood in absolute separation and opposition.[10] Because this was true, asserts C. Damour, the historical fact that the Church did take form is simply to be understood as meaning that the Church assumed the place of Jesus' eschatology, not fulfilling the hope of the Kingdom but displacing it with a temporal order.[11] Against the argument that Jesus, as the Messiah, would naturally require a messianic people about Him, which would in effect constitute the Church, it is argued that such people would be needed only on the 'last day'. Thus Schweitzer, even when he assumes the authenticity of the 'Thou art Peter' passage in Matthew 16^{18},

[9] That the Kingdom had a fully apocalyptic, Jewish sense for Jesus is attested by K. L. Schmidt, Article *Basileia*, *TWNT*, I.586.
[10] *Das Problem der Urkirche in der neueren Forschung*, p. 121.
[11] *Die Epochen des Protestantismus*, p. 6.

declares that Jesus is referring, not to the Church on earth, but to the community of saints, which is to be manifest at the coming of the Son of Man, according to the prophecies of Enoch.[12]

In the light of this view, therefore, the Church is either adjudged to be extraneous to the purposes of Jesus, or else it is necessarily conceived as a purely eschatological entity with no significance for the present. Since all of Jesus' teaching plainly refers to the future consummation, concludes Wilhelm Michaelis, it is just as wrong to say that the Church was founded by Jesus as to say that the Kingdom of God was then a present possession.[13] Jesus expected the end to come soon with disastrous effect upon the temporal order of mankind. Would He have thought of building a Church, knowing that in a short time it would have to be scattered and destroyed?

Such an exclusion of the Church from the intention of Jesus is unavoidable when the Gospels are read from the point of view of radical eschatology. However, Michaelis reminds us that Jesus' teaching was wholly conditioned by His own time, namely the time before Easter and Pentecost.[14] These two momentous events, while not the Parousia of fulfilment themselves, annulled and broke through the unity of the eschatological content of Jesus' preaching. After Pentecost there could be no question about the reality of the *ekklēsia*, for it had taken form in the power of the Holy Spirit and in singleness of faith in the risen Lord. It was just when the Christians were obliged to reckon with the fact of Jesus' resurrection and to reflect upon its significance that they transformed the eschatological outlook which He had taught them. Then the Fourth Gospel, written with the post-resurrection point of view,[15] spoke of the unity of believing persons with the Son, who is in unity with the Father; and it emphasized, not the Kingdom of God, but the quality of eternal life. Then Paul sought to explain the existence of the Elect people between the resurrection and the return of Christ by teaching that they shared in the new life of resurrection with Christ during their state of expectation.[16] By this Paul intended to show that the community of the Elect already enjoyed the supernatural spiritual powers even before the general resurrection of the dead on the last day.

[12] *The Mysticism of Paul the Apostle*, p. 103.
[13] *Täufer, Jesus, Urgemeinde*, pp. 80, 105.
[14] ibid., pp. 81, 129.   [15] W. Michaelis, *Täufer, Jesus, Urgemeinde*, p. 84.
[16] cf. A. Schweitzer, *The Mysticism of Paul the Apostle*, pp. 109f.

This Pauline mysticism, adds Schweitzer, 'is therefore nothing else than the doctrine of the making manifest, in consequence of the death and resurrection of Jesus, of the pre-existent Church (the Community of God)'.[17] On the basis of this sense of unity in participation with Christ rest Paul's concepts of 'being in Christ' and of the quasi-physical corporeity of the Body of Christ. Paul's doctrine is not an emptying of the eschatological message of Jesus, therefore, but a modification of it to fit the post-resurrection situation. But in view of the existing *ekklēsia*, which is the mystical Body of Christ, Paul's idea of the Kingdom of God is quite different from that which the thoroughgoing eschatologists believe to have been Jesus' own. 'Inasmuch as believers have died and risen again with Christ, and possess the Spirit, they are already partakers of the Kingdom of God, although they will not be made manifest as such until the Kingdom begins'.[18] Thus Schweitzer perceives that already in Paul's understanding the Kingdom has a dialectical relationship to the Church, being in some way present and yet lying in the future or beyond.

A vigorous and uncompromising defence of the views of Weiss and Schweitzer has lately been set forth by Martin Werner,[19] but in the field of New Testament exegesis as a whole it is generally felt that thoroughgoing eschatology, despite its many insights, has failed to vindicate itself as an adequate clue to the meaning of the Kingdom of God.[20] Much less has it served to provide a satisfactory basis for an eschatological understanding of the Church, which has now existed for so many centuries since the great 'disillusionment' of Jesus and the first Christians. If it has been argued that the building of the Church in the face of imminent catastrophe would have been utter nonsense to Jesus and the disciples, it can be argued with equal weight that the very reverse is true, namely, as Linton insists, that they considered the Church to be a rock, a place of security and refuge, to which

---

[17] W Michaelis, *Täufer, Jesus, Urgemeinde*, p. 116.
[18] *The Mysticism of Paul the Apostle*, p. 120.
[19] *Die Entstehung des christlichen Dogmas*, especially pp. 43ff.
[20] cf. V. Taylor, *Jesus and His Sacrifice*, p. 9; C. J. Cadoux, *The Historic Mission of Jesus*, p. 6; C. H. Dodd, *The Parables of the Kingdom*, p. 49; W. Michaelis, *Der Herr verzieht nicht die Verheissung*, p. 72. F. C. Grant accuses the thoroughgoing eschatologists of a 'fundamental insincerity' in their treatment of the Gospels, for rather than accounting for all the recorded and accepted sayings of Jesus, they picked their texts to support their one-sided interpretation of his whole teaching on the Kingdom; *The Gospel of the Kingdom*, p. viii.

persons could flee when the floods of disaster rose.[21] But by regarding the Church as dissociated from, and even in opposition to, the eschatological meaning of the Kingdom, this school of thought not only strips the Church of any theological significance, but also takes away from the eschatological thought and teaching of Jesus an element which many scholars now believe to have been implicit in it.

Moreover, when thoroughgoing eschatology is employed not just as a principle of exegesis but as a principle for continuing Christianity, it easily leads to adventist and millenarian fanaticism, which in general considers the Church to be nothing more than a meaningless 'parenthesis' or 'interruption' between apocalyptic prophecies and ultimate consummation after the second coming of Christ.[22] While being grateful for guidance in understanding Jesus' eschatological outlook, therefore, theologians are not disposed to make the principle of radical eschatology a norm for interpreting the New Testament as a whole in respect to the faith and hope of the Church.

III. REALIZED ESCHATOLOGY

'Whereas Jewish eschatology looked to the close of the historical process as the necessary fulfilment upon which the meaning of history depends,' writes C. H. Dodd, 'Christianity found the fulfilment of history in an actual series of events within history—namely the life, death, and resurrection of Jesus Christ, and the emergence of the Church as the bearer of His Spirit. History, indeed, still goes on, and at long last it will have an ending. But meanwhile, the true *eschaton*, the event in which its meaning is conclusively revealed, has become an object of experience.'[23]

The conviction that eschatology has already been realized in Jesus Christ and no longer need be the object of Christian expectation has been articulated and defended most completely by Dodd. Obviously his view stands at the opposite extreme from that of the thoroughgoing eschatologists. Yet both views derive from the study of the same passages of Scripture. To reproduce the opposing arguments, with sufficient references to the New

---

[21] *Das Problem der Urkirche in der neueren Forschung*, p. 180.
[22] cf. the argument against this kind of 'Dispensationalism' by O. T. Allis, *Prophecy and the Church*, pp. 10f.
[23] In *The Kingdom of God and History*, p. 23.

Testament, is not possible here, however valuable such an exposition would be. But Dodd is convinced that, despite Jesus' references to the *coming* Kingdom, 'the sayings which declare the Kingdom of God to have come are explicit and unequivocal'.[24] It was not the disciples or the evangelists, but 'Jesus Himself who first interpreted His own ministry, death, and resurrection as the breaking-in of the Kingdom of God'.[25]

Five essential characteristics of the eschatological thought of the Bible are shown by Dodd to have been transferred from mere hope and brought to realization in the historical appearance of Jesus:[26]

(a) Jesus' coming is the 'fullness of time' (*kairos*) in which the prophets said the Day of the Lord would dawn.
(b) 'The arm of the Lord is made bare' in the many 'mighty acts' which Jesus performs among the people.
(c) The powers of evil are overcome and cast out.
(d) The Judgement takes place in the presence of Christ, in whose Light men can recognize their sinful darkness.
(e) Eternal life is realized in the experience of those who believe the resurrection of Jesus Christ.

Dodd does not stand alone in recognizing the New Testament witness to the perfect realization of these elements of the 'last days' or the 'new age' in Christ.[27] He finds that full justice to the principle of 'realized eschatology' is first done in the epistles of Paul, who believed that the supernatural order of life was a present fact of experience.[28] In the Fourth Gospel, also, Dodd sees the story of Jesus told from the following point of view: 'The episode of the life, death, and resurrection of Jesus is history, but it is *Endgeschichte*, eschatological history, history with its full meaning revealed.'[29] Further evidence for the dominant position of this faith he finds in the interpretation given to the Sacrament of the Eucharist, both in the primitive Church and in the modern practice of Eastern Orthodoxy. 'In its origin and in its governing idea', he says of the Eucharist, 'it may be described as a sacrament

---

[24] *The Parables of the Kingdom*, p. 49.
[25] In *The Kingdom of God and History*, p. 32.
[26] *The Apostolic Preaching and Its Developments*, pp. 85f.
[27] cf. H.-D. Wendland, *Die Eschatologie des Reiches Gottes bei Jesus*, p. 177; P. S. Minear, *Eyes of Faith*, p. 89.
[28] *The Apostolic Preaching and Its Developments*, p. 65.
[29] In *The Kingdom of God and History*, p. 31.

THE CHURCH AND ESCHATOLOGY 219

of realized eschatology.'[30] In the bread and wine, broken, blessed, and distributed, there is a re-enactment of the events in which Jesus Himself took part as the suffering Messiah. Rudolph Otto concurs heartily with this sacramental idea and insists that the Last Supper was just as much an eschatological sign for Jesus as it was for the disciples, and as it should be in present Christian belief.[31]

On the basis of this evidence, Dodd asserts that the coming of Jesus was the true fulfilment of the eschatological hope and the advent of the Kingdom of God. 'The Kingdom of God is not something yet to come. It came with Jesus Christ, and in its coming was perceived to be eternal in its quality. That eternal quality is manifested in time by the continuous life of the Church, centred in the Sacrament in which the crisis of the death and resurrection of Christ is perpetually made present.'[32] The presence of the Kingdom in Jesus Christ is not limited to those who knew him in the flesh, but is known and experienced equally in the lives of all who constitute the *ekklēsia*. Although he seems to come very close to it, Dodd does not fall into the Roman Catholic position of identifying the hierarchical Church with the Kingdom of God. He is careful to point out that the Church in this relationship is not 'an exclusive body with a limited membership', but the universal entity which is 'ideally identified with the whole human race as "redeemed" through Christ ... the unity of all mankind in Christ'.[33]

In this idea of the Kingdom and the Church, Dodd is in agreement with some other Protestant theologians who have been dissatisfied with the doctrine that the Kingdom is wholly in the future and has no present reality in the Church. Taking a view of the Church which is similar to Dodd's, P. Tillich declares: '*The realization of the Kingdom of God within history is determined by the history of the Church.*'[34] He feels that all ideas of the Kingdom as a transcendent order only deprive history of meaning and negate the concept of salvation; hence the Kingdom is real in so far as

---

[30] *The Parables of the Kingdom*, p. 204.
[31] *The Kingdom of God and the Son of Man*, pp. 328f.; cf. Kattenbusch, in *Festgabe für Harnack*, pp. 172f.
[32] In *The Kingdom of God and History*, p. 35.
[33] *The Bible Today*, pp. 71f.
[34] In *The Kingdom of God and History*, pp. 120-6; cf. N. S. F. Ferré, *Return to Christianity*, p. 44: 'Yet in so far as the Church is the Church it is the Kingdom present on earth.'

it is embodied in the Church, which is not only historical, but is the 'bearer' of all history.

A corresponding attitude toward realized eschatology in the Church is held by E. Sommerlath, although he is more inclined to think of the visible Church than 'redeemed mankind' as being coincident with the Kingdom of God.[35] Because the New Testament, as he reads it, expresses the equality of each, because each has a supernatural and supertemporal origin, and because in each the presence of Jesus Christ is manifest, the visible Church and the visible Kingdom are virtually the same, he concludes.

Are we to assume, then, that the present Church is the consummation of the Kingdom itself? Will there, or will there not be an 'end' which shall fulfil and perfect all that may be lacking in the present? These are the crucial questions of Christian eschatology. But while Sommerlath and others admit that such an end will come, Dodd remains consistent with this thesis that eschatology has been realized fully in Jesus. He agrees with Paul that the Kingdom has been realized as an 'earnest' (*arrhabon*), but believes this 'first instalment' to be qualitatively equivalent to the fullness of the Kingdom.[36] 'There will be an end when the Church, or redeemed humanity, has grown into the stature of the fullness of Christ. But there will be nothing in the end which is not already given implicitly to the Church,'[37] writes Dodd in respect to the thought of Paul. Therefore, his explanation of the prayer, 'Thy Kingdom come,' which is usually thought to have a future eschatological reference,[38] shows that it means we seek the manifestation of the Reign of God in *this* present situation of life, for 'the future can bring with it nothing to supersede that revelation of the Kingdom of God'.[39]

English-speaking Protestants in particular have given a warm reception to Dodd's interpretation of eschatology, for many of them feel that he has solved the riddle of the Kingdom of God in Jesus' own preaching without emptying the eschatological sayings of their real meaning or yielding to the humanistic temptation of calling a righteous social order the realization of the

---

[35] *Zeitschrift für systematische Theologie* XVI(1939):569f; cf. T. O. Wedel, *The Coming Great Church*, p. 85: 'In the light of a Biblical doctrine of the Church, one generalization seems to be warranted. The Church is the Kingdom of God in history.'
[36] *The Apostolic Preaching and Its Developments*, p. 65.
[37] In *The Kingdom of God and History*, p. 28.
[38] cf. S. Hanson, *The Unity of the Church in the New Testament*, p. 38.
[39] In *The Kingdom of God and History*, p. 36.

Kingdom. John Knox, for example, while rejecting Dodd's idea that Jesus Himself thought of the Kingdom as being realized in His own life and ministry, supports the idea that 'the whole meaning of eschatology is *for us* fulfilled in the revelation in Christ—that is, in the active presence in Christ as known within the Church—of the eternal order, the kingdom of God'.[40] For Christians who know Jesus Christ in faith, therefore, the Kingdom is always realized as present. 'It *will* come soon because it *is* near,' writes Knox: 'The kingdom, in this absolute sense, did not come soon—it did not come at all—but it is still near. We are each moment under the awful judgement of God and the forgiveness of God is being in each moment freely offered to us.... The time is always being fulfilled: the kingdom of God is always at hand; not as a future event perhaps, but in the profounder sense of an ever-present reality, both within our life and above it, both immanent and transcendent.'[41] Such a reinterpretation of Jesus' teaching represents a modification of Dodd's views but is essentially in harmony with them. The 'eternal righteous sovereignty of God' is realized through Christ for the believing Christian.

Attractive as the theory of 'realized eschatology' may be, there are scholars who feel that it does not do full justice to the words of Jesus which relate clearly to the future coming of the Kingdom,[42] and that when used absolutely as a norm for interpretation it must inevitably result in the dilution of the meaning of the Kingdom as Jesus taught it. It has been pointed out further that this scheme can hardly avoid the consequence of ultimately having to relegate the Kingdom to the realm of myth or symbol.[43] Dodd already has declared explicitly that the Last Judgement may be considered only as a mythological and symbolical statement of Christian teleology.[44] Would it not be consistent, then, to be obliged to consider the idea of a fulfilled Kingdom of God in the same way?

[40] *Christ the Lord*, p. 28.   [41] ibid., p. 30.
[42] C. J. Cadoux, *The Historic Mission of Jesus*, p. 296; W. Michaelis, *Täufer, Jesus, Urgemeinde*, p. 83; E. F. Scott, *The Nature of the Early Church*, pp. 36-40; C. T. Craig, *Journal of Biblical Literature*, LVI(1937).17ff. On strictly linguistic grounds, both J. Y. Campbell, *The Expository Times*, XLVIII(1936).91ff. and K. W. Clark, *Journal of Biblical Literature*, LIX(1940).367-83, have contended that Dodd errs in translating Mark 1¹⁵, 'the Kingdom of God has come,' for they show that *ēggiken* means 'has come near'. For this same reason, among others, Dodd's realized eschatology is rejected by W. G. Kümmel, *Verheissung und Erfüllung*, pp. 10f.
[43] A. N. Wilder, *Eschatology and Ethics in the Teaching of Jesus*, rev. ed., p. 64.
[44] *History and the Gospel*, pp. 168-71.

Although it may be true, as Johnston remarks, that 'realized eschatology' has come to stay,[45] it remains to be seen whether the principle can prove to be a sufficient and satisfying rationale for the New Testament passages concerning the 'last things', and whether it can explain the relationship of the Church to the Kingdom of God.

In so far as 'realized eschatology' evacuates Jesus' teaching of any real relevance for the future consummation, it is related to another school of interpretation which stresses only the present aspect of the Kingdom as a social reality on earth. F. C. Grant maintains that it was the prophetic, non-apocalyptic concept of the Reign of God which Jesus taught, namely, a theocratic order 'to be realized completely upon the soil of Palestine, the holy land'.[46] The Kingdom was conceived by Jesus as a strictly this-worldly order, not as a transcendent or other-worldly one. The value of such teaching for the Church today consists in the stimulus it gives to Christians as they strive to express more and more the will of God in human society. Not only God's initiative, but man's activity in response to God must effect the extension of the Kingdom in the world, until all men are brought into fellowship with one another under the rule of God.[47] The Christian hope, so far as earthly life is concerned, is therefore expressed in terms of the social significance of the Kingdom for the welfare of humanity as it is progressively being realized.[48] And the Church is the vehicle by which God wills the message of social renewal to be proclaimed and exemplified among men. This is the view of the Kingdom of God which is presently dominant among liberal Christians, especially in England and America, and unquestionably it can lay claim to responsibility for much vigorous life in the Church and reform in society. 'Because it is most congenial to our modern mood,' observes J. Knox, this position 'is probably held by the largest number of modern readers' of the Gospels; but from the point of view of exegesis and historical study, it is the least tenable of all consistent views of the Kingdom of God.'[49] This judgement upon the exponents of the non-futuristic understanding of the Kingdom is supported

---

[45] *The Doctrine of the Church in the New Testament*, p. 53.
[46] *The Gospel of the Kingdom*, p. 131.
[47] cf. A. T. Cadoux, *The Theology of Jesus*, pp. 52f.
[48] cf. C. J. Cadoux, *The Historic Mission of Jesus*, p. 349
[49] *Christ the Lord*, p. 26.

alike by those who hold to thoroughgoing eschatology and those who believe that the Kingdom is neither wholly present nor wholly future, but both.

IV. THE KINGDOM PRESENT AND STILL TO COME

Many interpreters of the New Testament can agree with Vincent Taylor when he remarks that 'discussions as to whether the Kingdom is present or future are barren; it is obviously both'.[50] The decisive fact is not the sayings of Jesus by themselves, but the fact of Jesus Himself living in the sphere of history. 'Jesus can only be the coming Messiah if He is the presently real Messiah—and vice versa,' declares H.-D. Wendland.[51] The sayings of Jesus are anything but clear and consistent as they relate to the nature of the Kingdom and the manner of its coming. This fact must be admitted by all students of the Gospels, whatever the kinds of interpretation toward which they are inclined. It is small wonder that so many diverse opinions concerning the Kingdom and its coming have been set forth, for the reader of Jesus' collected words unavoidably encounters what R. Otto calls 'a peculiar double-sidedness, which must appear paradoxical. On the one hand the liveliest feeling of the immediate inbreaking of the supra-mundane future; on the other hand a message which is completely undisturbed by the former fact in its relation to time, the world, and life, which reckons on duration, on continuance in time and in temporal and world affairs, and is related thereto.'[52]

If this double-sidedness is to be taken seriously for present Christian faith, and not simply regarded as a regrettable error in Jesus' thinking, it is not very difficult for the individual believer to grasp the meaning of his own and the total Church's relationship to the Kingdom which Jesus proclaimed. As John Baillie explains it: 'The fullness of the transfigured life can indeed only be enjoyed in the transfigured community, yet even now it is possible to some extent to envisage ourselves proleptically as members of that community.'[53] His words are cautious, to be sure, but not without reason, for there is a tension existing

---

[50] *Jesus and His Sacrifice*, p. 9.
[51] *Die Eschatologie des Reiches Gottes bei Jesus*, p. 177. So Kümmel asserts that Jesus really regarded the Reign of God as present in Himself, but still looked for the coming of full salvation for mankind in the future; *Verheissung und Erfüllung*, p. 93.
[52] *The Kingdom of God and the Son of Man*, p. 62.   [53] *And the Life Everlasting*, p. 134.

between the Kingdom as present in Jesus Christ and His Church, and that which is still to be consummated by the final act which God shall perform. If this tension characterizes the true state of the Church in relation to the Kingdom of God, it would be just as erroneous to over-emphasize the unimaginable remoteness of the Kingdom's perfect realization as it would be to stress too much the finality of the Church as its present and full manifestation.

A similar idea of this tension is expressed by Brunner in a somewhat different manner. 'The ultimate, absolute end, that is, the Kingdom of God, begins in this community, in the Church,' he writes. But the fact that it is 'beginning' and not 'completion' is to be underlined. 'The Church is the earthly, historical veil which conceals the "Kingdom", or, to change the metaphor, she is already "the Kingdom" in "the form of a servant".'[54] This can only imply that Christians within the Church should live in an attitude of thankfulness for the kind of life which has been granted them due to the coming of Christ and the effect of the Holy Spirit in giving righteousness, peace, and joy.[55] As the 'veil' which conceals the Kingdom, the Church trusts that God Himself will draw it away to reveal the perfect Kingdom, of which Christians in this life have but a foretaste. While the Church already experiences something of the fruit of the Spirit, therefore, Paul reminds us that 'flesh and blood cannot inherit the Kingdom of God'.[56]

Such a view of biblical eschatology is consonant with the doctrine of the two-fold life of the Church: like the Christian himself, the Church partakes of life in two worlds in virtue of its relation to Christ, and so it may be considered in the light of the one world or the other. This can be grasped only on faith, to be sure, just as any appreciation at all of eschatology and God's Kingdom must be a matter of faith. Those who treat the Church's eschatological hope as though it were just a myth are merely viewing the issue from the natural, human side. As Mascall writes: 'While in the natural order the eschatological language of the New Testament refers for the Christian, as for everyone else, merely to future events of cataclysmic importance, in the supernatural order which is the possession of the Christian through

---

[54] *The Divine Imperative*, p. 526; cf. R. N. Flew, *Jesus and His Church*, p. 32: 'The kingdom has come in the person of Jesus. Its blessings can be enjoyed now, through faith. But it is not fully come. The final consummation is delayed.'
[55] *Romans* 14^{17}.   [56] 1 *Corinthians* 15^{50}.

his rebirth into Christ it describes the very nature of his present experience.'[57] When this is understood, he continues, 'the disastrous antithesis between the two interpretations of the New Testament eschatology' is avoided, the life of the Church is taken seriously, and history is not eviscerated by a denial that eschatology refers to the event when God's will and work shall be consummated.

But what can we say of the *time* of this consummation? Is it not enough that the Christian should wait in faith and hope, rather than to speculate about 'the times or seasons'? 'But of that day or that hour no one knows, not even the angels in heaven, nor the Son, but only the Father.'[58]

We will not speak here of attempts to set the date of the Parousia, which have often been made by fanatical adventists, but rather of the problem of *time* itself as it relates to the *eschaton* —though not as a philosophical concept. For there is a great difference of thought among theologians today with regard to the problem of whether the Kingdom in its fullness is to be within historical time or in the realm of eternity. And upon one's decision respecting this problem depends his understanding and evaluation of the Christian life and the history of the Church.

As we have seen, those who are content to believe that eschatology has been *fully* realized are not really concerned over this matter any more. Tillich does not deny the possibility of either an infra-historical end nor a supra-historical end, for he thinks that both belong to the Christian belief. However, he holds that, unless we realize that we can speak of the end only in symbols, and only in negative terms at that, we easily fall into the common error of 'transcendent Utopianism'.[59] By this Utopianism he means the belief that in some future age the destructive power of the demonic elements of the world will be destroyed. For those, therefore, who believe that the overpowering and subduing of evil power, and even of death, are a characteristic of the Kingdom, as S. Hanson does,[60] the teaching of Tillich amounts to a negation of the New Testament concept of the Kingdom. In the same discussion, Tillich explains that Christ is the centre of history;

---

[57] *Christ, the Christian and the Church*, p. 107.
[58] Mark 13^{32}.
[59] In *The Kingdom of God and History*, pp. 126f.
[60] The *Unity of the Church in the New Testament*, p. 98.

and therefore the ultimate meaning of history—i.e. its eschatological meaning—consists only of the preparation for or the reception of this centre.[61] This seems very plausible. But then it may be asked, on the basis of Jesus' own words about the Kingdom, whether there is not a consummation beyond the preparation for and reception of Christ. And to this question, some theologians would give the affirmative answer.

The proclamation of Jesus testifies against the foregoing scheme, according to the interpretation of Flew. He points out that Jesus spoke of the coming of the Son of Man, not meaning by this the coming of the Kingdom, which is already present in Himself, but 'the last act of God's Kingly Rule in history, the final consummation of the Kingdom, the supreme end of God's purpose for mankind'.[62] These terms were not meant to be mere symbols of a Utopian imagination, but words descriptive of what shall really *happen* in the history of the world. In reasserting this biblical view, he receives strong support from theologians such as Newbigin, who writes: 'I have the impression that the recent re-emphasis upon the eschatological character of the whole New Testament has been achieved at the cost of removing the whole group of ideas which we call eschatological from the realm of reality to that of symbol.'[63] The idea of a merely symbolic *eschaton* is attractive to those in whose view all time is pure simultaneity with God, but this is not the biblical idea of time at all, continues Newbigin; for history has movement toward a real end, according to the Bible, toward the Judgement and consummation, and this movement is real to God Himself. 'The whole time-process is but the working out of His eternal purpose. Its end will come when His purpose is accomplished.'[64]

These men are convinced that such a 'naïve' conception of time as the New Testament displays does not lessen the certainty that God is transcendent. Positively, this concept gives meaning to the fundamental Christian elements of ethics, intercessory prayer, life of the Church, and hope of the Judgement and the Kingdom, which all become illusory when no real end in time is anticipated. Christian ethics is thus an *Interimsethik*, but valid no matter how long the interim may be before the end.[65] Prayer for others is possible, because it is believed that God acts in the

---

[61] op. cit., p. 122. [62] *Jesus and His Church*, p. 32.
[63] *The Reunion of the Church*, p. 73. [64] ibid., p. 75. [65] Flew, op. cit., p. 33.

time of human experience. What happens now in the course of the Church's history, as it carries the Gospel to increasing numbers of persons, is a visible pledge of the Kingdom of God, of which the Church has a foretaste, and is a matter of concern to God.[66] And the life of suffering and sin which we now live, though 'not worth comparing with the glory that is to be revealed',[67] possesses meaning only because we can anticipate a real Kingdom of unity in love, wherein the full meaning of life, which was disclosed in Jesus of Nazareth, shall be wholly realized. Such are the implications of the eschatological view which sees the life of the Kingdom partly manifest in the present, but looks toward a fulfilment within the context of historical time.

This interpretation of eschatology, which appropriates the faith of the early Church and urges its acceptance in the contemporary Church, assumes that the primitive state of hopeful expectancy can be maintained in the present experience of Christians, and that the hope is all the more justifiable because it looks for a real, not a symbolic, end to history. Newbigin assures us that the Christians' participation in new life in Christ is not so complete as to preclude any further hope, nor is such hope to be adjudged a mere longing for 'a far-off vindication, at the end of history, of faith's stubborn stand within history'.[68] What is anticipated by the Church, and what gives significance to the ethical life and sacramental worship of the Church, is just the belief that there will be a consummation in glory of the life which we now know only in part.

But did the primitive Church, and should we, think of the consummation of life in the Kingdom in such temporal terms as these? The course of the development of eschatological thinking among certain Continental theologians has led toward a very different idea of the 'time' of the consummation, namely a supra-temporal concept. It is argued that we must always resist the temptation to be too optimistic about the possibilities of fulfilment within the scope of historical time, since between the time in which we live and the eternity which is of God there is an 'infinite qualitative distinction' (Kierkegaard).[69] Having to do all our theological thinking in constant awareness of this distinction, we

[66] cf. F. J. Taylor, *The Church of God*, p. 199.   [67] Romans 8^{18}.
[68] *The Reunion of the Church*, p. 77.
[69] cf. Barth, Preface to 2nd edition of *Der Römerbrief*.

are wrong to think of historical, calendar time as being capable of embracing so transcendent a dimension as the Kingdom of God, just as we err if we say that the historical life of the Church is an expression of this Kingdom in the world.

Wendland describes with clarity how the temporal-eternal aspect of the Christian eschatology is to be understood.[70] The end of world history will be a real end, and that end is the Last Judgement. This is no more a 'symbol' of what is to happen than the Incarnation was a symbol. 'The parousia of the Lord is the end of history and of this age at a particular time and hour, toward which the world's history tends. At the same time of course the parousia completely shatters the form of this world and the structure of secular history. We must, therefore, think of the end of history neither "idealistically" as a timeless eternity which abides above the world, nor as a purely temporal event within the historical process; in neither case could we speak of the Last Judgement or of the end of history.' When we speak of the Kingdom of God, then, in connexion with this end of history, it is not enough that we think in terms of the end-time (*Endzeit*) only, but that we think of what is supra-temporal and eternal (*überzeitlich-ewig*), for the final form of the Kingdom embraces both.[71] The history of the Church is not deprived of meaning, because the Church arose as a result of the coming of the kingly rule of God in the words and work of Jesus Christ,[72] and the Church has since then served as a bridge between His resurrection and His coming again.[73] The miracle of the coming of the Kingdom of God in the Incarnation accounted for the life in the 'new creation' to which the New Testament bears witness. And the same miraculous action of God is to be discerned in the fulfilment of the Kingdom at the end of history. This matter may be expressed more generally, according to Wendland, in the equation, 'Christology is eschatology. Eschatology is christology.'[74] With regard to both the Incarnation and the *eschaton* the problem of time is the same, since the temporal and the supra-temporal are involved in each.

In spite of his recognition that the Kingdom of God is ultimately characterized by *Überzeitlichkeit*, however, Wendland does not

---

[70] In *The Kingdom of God and History*, pp. 164f.
[71] *Die Eschatologie des Reiches Gottes bei Jesus*, p. 45.
[72] ibid., p. 249.   [73] ibid., p. 178.   [74] ibid., p. 247f.

THE CHURCH AND ESCHATOLOGY 229

apply the principle of the 'infinite qualitive distinction' between time and eternity without some reservation. He is concerned to appreciate the critical importance of the transcendence of the Kingdom, without at the same time forfeiting what is of value in the course of human life and history, subject as these are to sin and error. A similar understanding of this eschatological tension is manifest in the writing of Niebuhr, who asserts unequivocally that the end of history has meaning for the Christian only with respect to the life, death, and resurrection of Jesus Christ.[75] But he rejects with equal vigour the concept of eschatology which speaks only in transcendent language and that which it opposes as wholly immanent and historical. 'When followed consistently,' he observes, 'the biblical faith must be fruitful of genuine renewals of life in history, in both the individual and collective existence of man.'[76] This is one side of the tension. On the opposite side is that fulfilment in the Kingdom, the *telos* or goal of history, which is not within history itself, and in the light of which the Church must always guard against the sin of insinuating its temporal and historical evils into the final sanctity.[77] Both Wendland and Niebuhr, then, are perfectly aware of the transcendent element of eschatology and are not deluded by any hopes for a this-worldly consummation. However, they are still disposed to protect the concept that the Kingdom is effective, however partially and incompletely, in the history of men.

A most singular contribution to current thought on the problem of eschatology has been made by R. Bultmann, whose name is associated with the mythological interpretation of the words of Jesus. Bultmann does not recognize any real presence of the Kingdom in the literal sense, but he still stresses the *effect* of the wholly transcendent Kingdom upon the individual person, who at every hour of life must make a decision for or against the holy will of God. 'The real significance of "the Kingdom of God" for the message of Jesus does not in any sense depend on the dramatic events attending its coming, nor on any circumstances which the imagination can conceive. It interests him not at all as a describable state of existence, but rather as the transcendent event, which signifies for man the ultimate Either-Or, which constrains him to decision.'[78] As Bultmann understands Jesus' thought, the

---

[75] *Faith and History*, p. 157. [76] ibid., p. 244.
[77] ibid., p. 267. [78] *Jesus and the Word*, p. 40f.

Kingdom as a real order of persons does not and cannot exist. It is the supra-temporal life of God Himself which is meant by the 'Kingdom', and all parabolic references to it, all theological concepts of its nature, are merely symbol and myth. But this fact, he contends, does not remove the Kingdom from reality—indeed, it is the ultimate reality itself. And each man, as he is confronted by this reality in faith, must respond, must decide, must act in the light of its divine demands upon him: 'Man now stands under the necessity of decision . . . his "Now" is always for him the last hour, in which his decision against the world and for God is demanded.'[79]

While Bultmann speaks of the 'present' and the 'future' in respect to the problem of eschatology, his concept of the Kingdom shows that these temporal words are not used in their literal sense. The 'presence' of the Kingdom and the 'future' are alike God's timeless will as it impinges upon man.

For an exposition of eschatology in terms of absolute transcendence we may turn to the writings of Karl Barth. Here we find the exclusive distinction between the time of history and calendar, in which man is confined, and the time which is the province of revelation, fulfilment, and God. Barth makes no simple contrast between 'vulgar time' and eternity as such, but he speaks of pre-temporality as the 'pure time' of God,[80] as well as of post-temporality and supra-temporality, wherein God has His being. While human creatures are confined to the contingencies of the temporal world, God has perfect freedom from the bounds of time, and His ultimate purposes demand the same freedom. Even though God, in virtue of His love for men, has broken into temporality by His revelation in Christ, this is no indication that we are to look within historical time for the Kingdom of God which He proclaimed. 'The Kingdom of God has not "broken forth" upon the earth, not even the tiniest fragment of it; and yet it has been *proclaimed*; it has not come, not even in its most sublime form; and yet, it is *nigh at hand*. The Kingdom of God remains a matter of faith, and most of all is the revelation of it in Jesus Christ a matter of faith.'[81] God acts in history, to be sure, but He does not become conditioned by history because He remains above and beyond historical time.

---

[79] *Jesus and the Word*, p. 131. [80] cf. *Die kirchliche Dogmatik*, II.1.701.
[81] *The Epistle to the Romans*, p. 102.

THE CHURCH AND ESCHATOLOGY   231

When we consider such eschatological events as the resurrection of the dead, the coming of Christ, and the Kingdom of God, we must make no compromise with the temptation to think in the category of historical time, nor is the philosophical concept of eternity the proper category. 'Here it cannot be altogether forgotten and overlooked that the eternity, of which others perhaps also speak, is the eternity of *God*,' asserts Barth, 'that is to say, the *rule*, the *Kingdom* of God, His absolute *transcendence* as Creator, Redeemer, and King of things, of history.'[82] So when a Christian deals with the *end* of history, it is really the end and not just a symbol; it is 'a reality so radically superior to all happenings and all temporality, that in speaking of the finiteness of history and the finiteness of time, he is also speaking of that upon which all time and all happening is *based*'.[83] By this he does not mean the termination of the historical process, as though calendar time should one day stop and leave eternity by itself, thereby annihilating all history. Time is not dissolved by eternity, but it is *marked* by it as finite, and this is a great difference.[84] The 'time' toward which the eschatological hope points, then, is not that of finiteness, but of the eternity of God, which is not a continuation of historical time, but a wholly other dimension.

To this other dimension belong the Incarnation and the ultimate fulfilment. Barth stresses the fact that 'the time of the Church, our time' is qualitatively different from the time of revelation in Christ.[85] How then can we consider the Christian hope of fulfilment to be realized already in our own finite time?

These views of Barth have been brought under sharp criticism by many theologians who feel that he does not do real justice to the biblical doctrine of eschatology, and so Barth himself has more recently modified his extreme position. His opponents revolt primarily against what they consider to be a nihilistic attitude toward the world of time in which men live. O. Michel protests that in Barth's teaching there is no hope whatsoever left for the future of man, assuming the ultimate perfection which is part of Christian faith to be beyond the range of human imagination.[86] F. Holmström, who discusses the eschatological ideas of Barth at length, charges Barth with the very thing which he seeks

---

[82] *The Resurrection of the Dead*, p. 111.   [83] ibid., p. 110.   [84] ibid., p. 112.
[85] *Die kirchliche Dogmatik*, I.2.604.
[86] Quoted by Holmström, *Das eschatologische Denken der Gegenwart*, p. 238n.; cf. Michel, *Das Zeugnis des Neuen Testaments von der Gemeinde*, pp. 27-9.

to avoid, namely, displacing the biblical thought of eternity with a philosophical postulate of the Absolute and thereby doing great violence to the meaning of the Christian hope.[87] Whether these attacks be valid or not, it is significant that even Paul Althaus, who does not believe that eschatological fulfilment can be expected within history,[88] parts company with Barth because he feels that Barth's extreme doctrine cannot take adequate account of the Christian's present and real consciousness of salvation and his perception of moral value.

How can Barth reconcile his radical concept of eschatology with the New Testament teaching concerning the last things and the Kingdom of God? And how can he formulate an explanation for the Church which will do justice to the significance of the Church in God's work of salvation? The clue to this reconciliation and formulation is found in the New Testament references to the 'Kingdom of Christ' as distinguished from the Kingdom of God. This distinction, which is explicitly made in Paul's discourse on the ultimate fulfilment of all things in God (1 Corinthians 15$^{22-8}$) and is implied in Colossians 1^{13}, makes it possible for Barth to speak of a waiting *basileia* within history and a consummated one outside history. In the Kingdom of Christ we now stand, but here our present relationship to God is just a provisional one, in anticipation of the relationship in glory which shall come.[89] The Kingdom of Christ is one of transition and struggle against the forces of the world, and it must be so until *all* things of creation have been subjected to the reign of Christ. It is to the state of things which will exist after this that eschatology really pertains. 'Christians must grasp the idea that the last word of the Kingdom of Christ is its end in the *Kingdom of God*, the last word of faith is its end in fulfilment. The *Kingdom of God*, or *fulfilment*, is not, as may so easily be thought, a higher continuation of this life, but just the resurrection of the dead. Faith, that is, to be in the Kingdom of Christ, means to await the *resurrection*.'[90] Until the 'last enemy', death, is destroyed and abolished, the Kingdom of Christ to which the Church is bound, cannot become the eternal Kingdom of God.

---

[87] Quoted by Holmström, *Das eschatologische Denken der Gegenwart*, p. 238n.; cf. C. Van Til, *The New Modernism*, pp. 341-50, where he says Barth's view of time is no different from F. H. Bradley's or M. Heidegger's.
[88] *Die letzten Dinge, 3. Aufl.*, pp. 77-8.
[89] *The Resurrection of the Dead*, p. 176f.   [90] ibid., p. 180.

Following the same thought, and developing the argument more comprehensively than Barth does, O. Cullmann sees in the Kingdom of Christ the solution of the problem of the relation of the Church to the Kingdom of God. In spite of the contrary opinion of K. L. Schmidt, that 'Kingdom of Christ' is the same as 'Kingdom of God' in the New Testament,[91] Cullmann asserts that the Kingdom of Christ and the Kingdom of God are just as little interchangeable as the Church and the Kingdom of God are.[92] The Kingdom of Christ—or the 'kingly rule' (*Königsherrschaft*) of Christ—and the *ekklēsia* are not identical, but they are very closely bound to one another, for they share the same kind of time. This fact distinguishes both from the Kingdom of God, which does not belong to this time. Beyond this temporal distinction may be seen another difference, a spatial one, which identifies the Church. For the Church and the Kingdom of Christ are temporally co-extensive, but not spatially. The Church is the Body of which Christ is the Head. The Church is a part or section of the Kingdom of Christ, therefore. While the purpose of the Kingdom of Christ is to subject all creation to Christ the King, that of the Church is limited to include the earthly fellowship of men and women. Moreover, the Church is the centre of this Kingdom, and is the only point in history where the Kingdom of Christ becomes visible,[93] and so it shall be recognized until all things in history have been conformed to God's purpose.

Cullmann's very neat ordering of the tangled elements of biblical eschatology may seem too facile and too one-sidedly Pauline to be accepted by some scholars.[94] From the theological point of view, however, it is perfectly consonant with the thought of Barth, who once wrote: 'I know that we must bear it in mind that the Church is the existential form of the Kingdom of Christ in the interim between the Ascension and His second coming.'[95]

V. CONCLUSION

In summary, we find in the contemporary Protestant thought on eschatology no uniformity of interpretation, either of the New

[91] Article *Basileia* in *TWNT*, I.581.
[92] *Königsherrschaft Christi und Kirche im Neuen Testament*, p. 11.   [93] ibid., p. 28.
[94] e.g. S. Hanson, *The Unity of the Church in the New Testament*, p. 39; P. Althaus, *Die letzten Dinge*, 5. Aufl., pp. 339f.
[95] *The Church and the Churches*, p. 33.

Testament evidences nor of the theological speculations which are based upon them. The differences stand out sharply: thoroughgoing and apocalyptic eschatology, realized eschatology, and eschatology of the kind which grapples with the problem of present and future, temporal and eternal. The three main types, with their various forms, stand as correctives to one another, reminding theologians that eschatology is a most complex area of Christian belief and is not to be easily simplified. Having considered these types so briefly in the foregoing pages, it is not within our province to choose from among them the one which is most valid and consistent, for any such choice would be subject to the serious criticism of those who espouse the others.

But can we see some area of relatively close agreement among Protestants respecting the place of the Christian Church in the eschatological picture? Perhaps the one real point in which a consensus may be found is the negative one, that the Church is not the completed Kingdom of God. If it were the Kingdom in its perfection, it is impossible to see how eschatology could play any part at all in the Christian faith.

It has come more and more to be thought instead that the Church comes between Christ and the fulfilled Kingdom of God, not as a chasm, but as a living link.[96] The Church lives in a state of crisis and tension between the time of promise and the time of final consummation. During this earthly interim of however long duration, the Church must proclaim the Lord's Word of salvation to every creature and gather those who hear and respond into its loving fellowship. It must labour without slackening, and rejoice when counted worthy to suffer for Christ's sake, knowing that not even death itself can separate it from the love of God which is in Christ Jesus.

[96] M. Goguel, *Le Problème de l'Église*, p. 187.

BIBLIOGRAPHY

(The titles listed below only begin to comprise a comprehensive bibliography on the nature of the Church in recent theological writing, for the volume of publications dealing directly or indirectly with this problem is immense. Therefore, only those books and articles which have been actually used and cited in the foregoing chapters are named here.)

ALLIS, O. T.: *Prophecy and the Church* (London 1945, Philadelphia 1947).
ALTHAUS, Paul: *Die letzten Dinge, Lehrbuch der Eschatologie, 3. Auflage* (Gütersloh 1926), *5. Auflage* (1949).
  Communio sanctorum. Die Gemeinde im lutherischen Kirchengedanke (München 1929).
  Die christliche Wahrheit (Gütersloh 1948).
AMERICAN THEOLOGICAL COMMITTEE: *The Nature of the Church* (Chicago 1945).
ANDERSON, W. K. (Editor): *Protestantism, a Symposium*, 3rd edn. (Nashville 1946).
APPASAMY, A. J.: *The Gospel and India's Heritage* (London 1942).
ASMUSSEN, Hans: 'Kirche augsburgischer Konfession,' *Theologische Existenz Heute*, XVI (1934).
  'Ein kleiner Spiegel für das kirchliche Amt,' *Rechtgläubigkeit und Frömmigkeit*, III (1939).
ASHWORTH, R. A.: 'The Witness of the Churches of the Congregational Order,' *Christendom*, V. 4 (1940), pp. 481-91.
AULÉN, Gustaf: 'The Church in the Light of the New Testament,' *The Universal Church in God's Design* (W.C.C.) (London & New York 1948), pp. 19–30.
  The Faith of the Christian Church (orig., *Den allmänneliga kristna tron*, 4th ed.), (Philadelphia 1948).
  'The "Errors" of Lutheranism,' *Theology* (March 1949), pp. 82-90.
  'The Ministry and Sacraments,' *The Ministry and the Sacraments* (R. Dunkerley, ed.) (London 1937), pp. 157–64.
BAILLIE, D. M.: *God Was in Christ* (London 1948).
BAILLIE, John: *And the Life Everlasting* (London 1934).
  ——(Editor) with H. MARTIN: *Revelation* (London 1937).
BAINTON, Roland H.: 'The Sectarian Theory of the Church,' *Christendom*, XI.3 (1946), pp. 382–7.
BARRETT, C. K.: *The Holy Spirit and the Gospel Tradition* (London 1947).
BARRY, F. R.: *The Relevance of the Church* (London 1935).

BARTH, Karl: '*Die Kirche und die Kultur*,' *Zwischen den Zeiten* (1926), pp. 363-84.
Die Theologie und die Kirche (München 1928).
The Resurrection of the Dead (orig., *Die Auferstehung der Toten*, 1924) (London 1933).
The Epistle to the Romans (orig., *Der Römerbrief*, 6. Auflage, 1928) (London 1933).
'*Gottes Wille und unsere Wünsche*,' *Theologische Existenz Heute*, VII (1934).
The Doctrine of the Word of God (orig., *Die kirchliche Dogmatik*, I. 1, 1932) (London 1936).
The Church and the Churches (Grand Rapids 1936, London 1937).
Chapter in *Revelation* (J. Baillie and H. Martin, Eds.) (London 1937).
The Knowledge of God and the Service of God (London 1938).
The Church and the Political Problem of our Day (London 1939).
Die kirchliche Dogmatik, I. 2, 3. Auflage (Zürich 1945), II. 1 (Zürich 1942).
The Teaching of the Church regarding Baptism (orig., *Die kirchliche Lehre von der Taufe*, 1943) (London 1948).
'The Church—the Living Congregation of the Living Lord Jesus Christ,' *The Universal Church in God's Design* (W.C.C.) (London & New York 1948), pp. 67-76.
BELL, G. K. A. (Editor) with A. DEISSMANN: *Mysterium Christi* (London, 1930).
BERNADIN, J. B.: 'The Church in the New Testament,' *Anglican Theological Review*, XXI (1939), pp. 153-70.
BONHÖFFER, Dietrich: *Sanctorum communio. Eine dogmatische Untersuchung zur Soziologie der Kirche* (Berlin & Frankfurt a.d. Oder 1930).
'*Zur Frage nach der Kirchengemeinschaft*,' *Evangelische Theologie* (1936), pp. 214ff.
Nachfolge (München 1937) (Eng. tr., *The Cost of Discipleship*, London 1949).
BOWMAN, John W.: *The Intention of Jesus* (Philadelphia 1943).
BRAUN, F. M.: *Neues Licht auf der Kirche* (Einsiedeln & Köln 1946).
BRILIOTH, Yngve: *Eucharistic Faith and Practice, Evangelical and Catholic* (London 1930).
BROWN, W. A.: Chapter in *Liberal Theology* (H. P. Van Dusen, ed.) (New York 1942).
BRUNNER, Emil: *The Word and the World* (London 1931).
The Mediator (orig., *Der Mittler*, 1927) (London 1934, Philadelphia 1947).
The Divine Imperative (orig., *Das Gebot und die Ordnungen*, 1932) (London 1937, Philadelphia 1947).
The Divine-Human Encounter (orig., *Wahrheit als Begegnung*, 1938) (Philadelphia 1943, London 1944).
Revelation and Reason (orig., *Offenbarung und Vernunft*, 1941) (Philadelphia 1946, London 1947).

BUBER, Martin: *I and Thou* (orig., *Ich und Du*, 1923) (Edinburgh 1937).
BULTMANN, Rudolph: *Jesus and the Word* (orig. *Jesus*, 1929) (New York 1934).
'Die Frage nach der Echtheit von Matthäus 16$^{17-19}$,' *Theologische Blätter* XX (1941), pp. 265ff.
Theologie des Neuen Testaments, 1. Lieferung (Tübingen 1948).
BUNDY, Walter E.: *The Religion of Jesus* (Indianapolis 1929).
BURN-MURDOCH, H.: *Church, Continuity and Unity* (Cambridge 1945).
CADBURY, H. J.: 'The Society of Friends,' *The Nature of the Church*, American Theological Committee (Chicago 1945), pp. 77–83.
CADOUX, A. T.: *The Theology of Jesus* (London 1940).
CADOUX, C. J.: *The Historic Mission of Jesus* (London 1941).
Essays Congregational and Catholic (A. Peel, ed.), (London 1931).
CAMPBELL, J. Y.: 'KOINŌNIA and Its Cognates in the New Testament,' *Journal of Biblical Literature*, LI (1932), pp. 352–80.
'The Kingdom of God has come,' *The Expository Times*, XLVIII (1936), pp. 91–4.
'The Origin and Meaning of the Christian Use of the Word EKKLĒSIA,' *Journal of Theological Studies*, XLIX (1948), pp. 130–42.
CARVER, W. O.: 'Baptist Churches,' *The Nature of the Church*, American Theological Committee (Chicago 1945), pp. 63–72.
CAVE, Sydney: *The Doctrines of the Christian Faith* (London 1931).
CHANING-PEARCE, M.: *The Terrible Crystal* (London 1940).
CHAVASSE, Claude: *The Bride of Christ* (London 1940).
CLARK, Elmer T.: *The Small Sects in America*, Revised edn. (Nashville 1949).
CLARK, K. W.: 'Realized Eschatology,' *Journal of Biblical Literature*, LIX (1940), pp. 367–83.
CRAIG, Clarence T.: 'Realized Eschatology,' *Journal of Biblical Literature*, LVI (1937), pp. 17ff.
'The Church of the New Testament,' *The Universal Church in God's Design* (W.C.C.) (London & New York 1948), pp. 31–42.
CULLMANN, Oscar: '*La Sainte-Cène dans le Christianisme Primitif*,' *Revue d'histoire et de philosophie religieuses* (1936), pp. 1–22.
Königsherrschaft Christi und Kirche im Neuen Testament (Zürich 1941).
Christus und die Zeit (Zürich 1946) (Eng. tr., *Christ and Time*, Philadelphia 1950).
Die Tauflehre des Neuen Testaments (Zürich 1948).
DAHL, Nils A.: *Das Volk Gottes. Eine Untersuchung zum Kirchenbewusstsein des Urchristentums* (Oslo 1941).
DAMOUR, Carl: *Die Epochen des Protestantismus* (Bern & Leipzig 1935).
DAVIES, R. E.: *The Problem of Authority in the Continental Reformers* (London 1946).
DEHN, Gunther: *Man and Revelation* (London 1936).
DEISSMANN, A. (part-Editor): *Mysterium Christi* (London 1930).

DEMANT, V. A.: Chapter in *Union of Christendom* (K. Mackenzie, ed.) (London 1938).
DILLISTONE, F. W.: *The Holy Spirit in the Life of Today* (London 1946).
'How is the Church Christ's Body?' *Theology Today*, II. 1 (1945), pp. 56-68.
The Word of God and the People of God (London 1948).
DIX, Gregory: 'The Ministry in the Early Church,' *The Apostolic Ministry* (K. E. Kirk, ed.) (London 1946).
DOBSCHÜTZ, E. von: '*Die Kirche im Urchristentum*,' *Zeitschrift für die neutestamentliche Wissenschaft, usw.*, XXVIII (1929), pp. 107-18.
DODD, Charles H.: *The Epistle of Paul to the Romans* (London 1932).
The Parables of the Kingdom (London & New York 1936).
The Apostolic Preaching and Its Developments (London 1936, Chicago 1937).
The Authority of the Bible, Revised edition (London 1938).
History and the Gospel (London & New York 1938).
The Bible Today (Cambridge 1946).
The Johannine Epistles (London 1946).
Chapter in *The Kingdom of God and History, Church, Community and State*, Vol. III (London 1938).
DUN, Angus: 'What Is a Sacrament?', *Christendom*, IV.4 (1939), pp. 502-14.
DUNCAN, G. S.: *The Epistle of Paul to the Galatians* (London 1934).
DUNKERLEY, Roderic (Editor): *The Ministry and the Sacraments* (London 1937).
EASTON, B. S.: 'The Church in the New Testament,' *Anglican Theological Review*, XXII (1940), pp. 157-68.
The Pastoral Epistles (New York 1947).
EHRENBERG, H. (Editor), *Credo Ecclesiam* (Gütersloh 1930).
ELERT, Werner: *Der christliche Glaube* (Berlin 1940).
ELIOT, T. S.: *Collected Poems, 1909-35* (London & New York 1936).
FERRÉ, Nels S. F.: *Swedish Contributions to Modern Theology* (New York 1939).
Return to Christianity (New York 1943).
Chapter in *Protestantism, a Symposium*, 3rd edn. (W. K. Anderson, ed.) (Nashville 1946).
FLEMINGTON, W. F.: *The New Testament Doctrine of Baptism* (London 1948).
FLEW, R. Newton: *Jesus and His Church*, Second edition (London 1943).
'The View of the Methodists,' *The Ministry and the Sacraments* (R. Dunkerley, ed.) (London 1937), pp. 230-43.
FLOROVSKY, G.: 'The Church: Her Nature and Task,' *The Universal Church in God's Design* (W.C.C.) (London & New York 1948), pp. 43-58.
FOAKES-JACKSON, F. J.: *The Acts of the Apostles* (London 1931).
'Primitive Christianity,' *The Beginnings of Christianity*, I. 1. (London 1920), pp. 265-418.

FOERSTER, E.: '*Kirche wider Kirche*,' *Theologische Rundschau* (1932), pp. 131-70.
FORSYTH, P.T.: *The Church and the Sacraments* (London 1917).
FRIDRICHSEN, Anton: '*Église et sacrament dans le Nouveau Testament*,' *Revue d'histoire et de philosophie religieuses*, XVII (1937), pp. 337-56.
GARVIE, A. E.: *The Holy Catholic Church from the Congregational Point of View* (London 1920).
GILMOUR, S. M.: 'The Church in the Letter to the Ephesians,' *Christendom*, VI. 3 (1941), pp. 389-95.
GLOEGE, Gerhard: *Reich Gottes und Kirche im Neuen Testament* (Gütersloh 1929).
GOGUEL, Maurice: 'Church, Baptism and Eucharist in the New Testament,' *The Ministry and the Sacraments* (R. Dunkerley, ed.) (London 1937), pp. 306-25.
Le Problème de l'Église (Paris 1947).
L'Église Primitive (Paris 1947).
GORE, Charles: *The Holy Spirit and the Church* (London 1924).
The Church and the Ministry. New edition revised by C. H. Turner (London 1936).
GOUDGE, H. L.: *The Church of England and Reunion* (London 1938).
GRANT, F. C.: 'The Nature of the Church,' *Anglican Theological Review*, XXI (1939), pp. 190-204.
The Gospel of the Kingdom (New York 1940).
An Introduction to New Testament Thought (New York 1950).
GREGG, J. A. F.: 'One, Holy, Catholic, Apostolic Church,' *The Universal Church in God's Design* (W.C.C.) (London & New York 1948), pp. 59-66.
GRÜTZMACHER, R. D.: '*Die alt- und neuprotestantische Auffassung von der Kirche*,' *Neue kirchliche Zeitschrift*, XXVII (1916), pp. 467-97, 535-72.
GUTBROD, Walter: *Die paulinische Anthropologie* (Stuttgart & Berlin 1934).
HAITJEMA, T. L.: 'The Reformed Doctrine of the Sacraments,' *The Ministry and the Sacraments* (R. Dunkerley, ed.) (London 1937), pp. 165-72.
HANSON, Stig: *The Unity of the Church in the New Testament* (Uppsala 1946).
HARNACK, A. von: '*Der Spruch über Petrus als den Felsen der Kirche*,' *Sitzungsberichte der preussischen Akademie der Wissenschaft* (Berlin 1918), pp. 637-54.
HAUCK, Friedrich: Article '*Koinōnia*,' *Theologisches Wörterbuch zum Neuen Testament* (G. Kittel, ed.), Band III, pp. 808-10.
HAYMAN, Eric: *Worship and the Common Life* (Cambridge 1944).
HEADLAM, A. C.: *The Doctrine of the Church and Christian Reunion* (London 1920).
HEATH, C.: 'The Views of Society of Friends,' *The Ministry and the Sacraments* (R. Dunkerley, ed.) (London 1937), pp. 244-52.

HEBERT, A. G.: *The Throne of David* (London 1941).
The Form of the Church (London 1944).
HEILER, Friedrich: *Im Ringen um die Kirche* (München 1931).
HEIM, Karl: *Der evangelische Glaube und das Denken der Gegenwart*, Band I (Berlin 1931) (Eng. tr., *God Transcendent*, London 1935).
Band III (Berlin 1937).
Spirit and Truth (orig. *Das Wesen des evangelischen Christentums*, 1929) (London 1935).
HENDRY, G. S.: 'The Exposition of Holy Scripture,' *Scottish Journal of Theology*, I. 1 (1948), pp. 29-47.
HERMELINK, H.: 'The Ministry and Sacraments in the Evangelical Churches of Germany Today,' *The Ministry and the Sacraments* (R. Dunkerley, ed.) (London 1937), pp. 146-56.
HICKINBOTHAM, J. P.: 'The Doctrine of the Ministry,' *The Ministry of the Church* (S. Neill, ed.) (London 1947).
HODGSON, L. (Editor): *Convictions* (London 1934).
(Editor): *Faith and Order, Edinburgh 1937* (London & New York 1938).
The Doctrine of the Trinity (London 1943).
HOLL, Karl: '*Der Kirchenbegriff des Paulus in seinem Verhältnis zu dem der Urgemeinde*,' *Sitzungsberichte der preussischen Akademie der Wissenschaft* (Berlin 1921), pp. 920-47.
Gesammelte Aufsätze zur Kirchengeschichte, Band I, II (Tübingen 1927-8).
HOLMSTRÖM, Folke: *Das eschatologische Denken der Gegenwart* (Gütersloh 1936).
HOPWOOD, P. G. S.: *The Religious Experience of the Primitive Church* (Edinburgh 1936).
HORTON, W. M.: 'The Congregational Christian Conception of the Church,' *The Nature of the Church*, American Theological Committee (Chicago 1945), pp. 48-53.
HOSKYNS, E. C.: *The Fourth Gospel*, Second revised edition (London 1947).
JACOBS, C. M.: 'The Ministry and the Sacraments,' *The Ministry and the Sacraments* (R. Dunkerley, ed.) (London 1937), pp. 138-45.
JENKINS, Daniel T.: *The Nature of Catholicity* (London 1942).
The Gift of the Ministry (London 1947).
JOHNSTON, George: *The Doctrine of the Church in the New Testament* (Cambridge 1943).
Files of Commission I, W.C.C., Geneva (unpublished).
JUNCKER, A.: '*Neuere Forschungen zum urchristlichen Kirchenproblem*,' *Neue kirchliche Zeitschrift*, XL (1929), pp. 126-40, 180-213.
KÄSEMANN, Ernst: *Leib und Leib Christi* (Tübingen 1933).
'*Anliegen und Eigenart der paulinischen Abendmahlslehre*,' *Evangelische Theologie* (1947-8), pp. 263ff.
KATTENBUSCH, Ferdinand: '*Der Quellort der Kirchenidee*,' *Festgabe für Harnack* (Tübingen 1921).
'*Der Spruch über Petrus und die Kirche bei Matthäus*,' *Theologische Studien und Kritiken*, XCIV (1922), pp. 96-131.
Die Doppelschichtigkeit in Luthers Kirchenbegriff (Gotha 1928).

KIRK, K. E. (Editor): *The Apostolic Ministry* (London 1946).
KITTEL, G. (Editor): *Theologisches Wörterbuch zum Neuen Testament* (Stuttgart 1933—).
KNOX, John: *Christ the Lord* (Chicago & New York 1945).
'Christianity and the Christian,' *The Christian Answer* (H. P. Van Dusen, ed.) (New York 1945, London 1946), pp. 209–44.
KNOX, W. L.: 'The Authority of the Church,' *Essays Catholic and Critical* (E. G. Selwyn, ed.) (London 1929), pp. 98-116.
St. Paul and the Church of the Gentiles (Cambridge 1939).
KÖHNLEIN, H.: '*La notion de l'Église chez l'Apôtre Paul*,' *Revue d'histoire et de philosophie religieuses*, XVII (1937), pp. 357–77.
KRAEMER, Hendrik: *The Christian Message in a Non-Christian World* (London & New York 1938).
KÜMMEL, Werner G.: *Die Eschatologie der Evangelien* (Leipzig 1936).
Kirchenbegriff und Geschichtsbewusstsein in der Urgemeinde und bei Jesus. (Uppsala and Zürich 1943).
Verheissung und Erfüllung (Basel 1945).
KÜNNETH, W.: '*Das Formproblem der evangelischen Kirche*,' *Luthertum*, XLV (1934), pp. 357-65.
LACEY, T. A.: *The One Body and the One Spirit* (London 1925).
LAUERER, H.: '*Sichtbarkeit der Kirche*,' *Luthertum*, XX (1939), pp. 65–80.
LECERF, Auguste: *An Introduction to Reformed Dogmatics* (London 1949).
LEENHARDT, F. J.: '*Realité et caracterès de l'Église*,' *La Sainte Église Universelle* (Neuchatel 1948), pp. 59–91.
LEWIS, Edwin: 'Constructive Statements,' *The Ministry and the Sacraments* (R. Dunkerley, ed.) (London 1937), pp. 475-91.
A Philosophy of the Christian Revelation (New York 1940, London 1948).
LEWIS, L. C.: 'The Anglican Conception of the Church,' *The Nature of the Church*, American Theological Committee (Chicago 1945), pp. 84–93.
LIETZMANN, Hans: *Messe und Herrenmahl* (Bonn 1926).
LILJE, Hans: '*Die reformatorische Lehre von der Kirche*,' *Allgemeine evangelisch-lutherische Kirchenzeitung* (1935), pp. 914ff.
LINTON, Olof: *Das Problem der Urkirche in der neueren Forschung* (Uppsala 1932).
LOCK, W.: *The Epistle to the Ephesians* (London 1929).
LOHMEYER, Ernst: *Grundlagen paulinischer Theologie* (Tübingen 1929).
'*Vom urchristlichen Abendmahl*,' *Theologische Rundschau* (1937), pp. 168–227, 273–312.
LOISY, Alfred: *The Birth of the Christian Religion* (orig. *La naissance du Christianisme*, 1933) (London 1948).
LOWRIE, Walter: *Problems of Church Unity* (London 1924).
MACGREGOR, G. H. C.: *The Gospel of John* (London 1928).
MACKENZIE, D.: 'Views of Modern Churches: Reformed-American,' *The Ministry and the Sacraments* (R. Dunkerley, ed.) (London 1937), pp. 200-10.
MACKENZIE, K. (Editor): *Union of Christendom* (London 1938).

MANSON, T. W.: *The Teaching of Jesus* (Cambridge 1931).
The Sayings of Jesus (London 1949).
The Church's Ministry (London 1948).
MARTIN, H.: *See* BAILLIE, J.
MASCALL, E. L.: *Christ, the Christian and the Church* (London 1946).
MASON, A. J.: 'Conceptions of the Church in Early Times,' *Essays on the Early History of the Church and the Ministry* (H. B. Swete, ed.) 2nd edn. (London 1921).
MATHEWS, Shailer: *Jesus on Social Institutions* (New York 1928).
The Church and the Christian (New York 1938).
MENOUD, Phillipe-H.: *L'Église et les ministères selon le Nouveau Testament* (Neuchatel 1949).
METHODIST CHURCH: *The Nature of the Christian Church according to the Teaching of the Methodists* (London 1937).
METZGER, B. M.: 'Paul's Vision of the Church,' *Theology Today,* VI (1949), pp. 49–63.
MICHAELIS, W.: *Täufer, Jesus, Urgemeinde* (Gütersloh 1928).
Der Herr verzieht nicht die Verheissung (Bern 1942).
MICHEL, Otto: *Das Zeugnis des Neuen Testaments von der Gemeinde* (Göttingen 1941).
MICKLEM, Nathaniel: *What Is the Faith?* (London 1936).
Congregationalism and the Church Catholic (London 1943).
MINEAR, P. S.: *Eyes of Faith* (Philadelphia 1946, London 1948).
Files of Commission I, W.C.C., Geneva (unpublished).
MOFFATT, James: *The Presbyterian Churches* (London 1928).
The First Epistle of Paul to the Corinthians (London 1938).
MORRISON, Charles C.: 'The Church, Catholic and Protestant,' *Christendom,* II. 2 (1937), pp. 274–89.
What Is Christianity? (Chicago 1940).
MOULE, C. F. D.: 'The Apostolic Commission in the New Testament,' *The Ministry of the Church* (S. Neill, ed.), (London 1947).
MULERT, H.: 'Congregatio sanctorum,' *Harnack-Ehrung* (Leipzig 1921).
NEILL, Stephen (Editor): *The Ministry of the Church* (London 1947).
NEWBIGIN, J. E. L.: *The Reunion of the Church* (London 1948).
'The Duty and Authority of the Church to Preach the Gospel,' *The Church's Witness to God's Design* (London & New York 1948), pp. 19–35.
NIEBUHR, Reinhold: *Beyond Tragedy* (New York 1937, London 1938).
The Nature and Destiny of Man (New York 1941, 1943).
Faith and History (New York & London 1949).
NIESEL, W.: '*Wesen und Gestalt der Kirche nach Calvin,*' *Evangelische Theologie,* III (1936), pp. 308ff.
NYGREN, Anders: '*Vom geistlichen Amt,*' *Zeitschrift für systematische Theologie* (1935), pp. 36–44.
'*Corpus Christi*', *En bok om kyrkan av svenska teologer* (Lund 1943).

OEPKE, Albrecht: Article '*en*', *Theologisches Wörterbuch zum Neuen Testament* (G. Kittel, ed.) Band II, pp. 573f.
'Der Herrenspruch uber die Kirche Mt 16$^{17-19}$ in der neuesten Forschung,' *Studia Theologica*, Band II, Fasc. II (1948), pp. 110-65.
OLDHAM, J. H.: see VISSER 'T HOOFT.
OTTO, Rudolf: *The Kingdom of God and the Son of Man* (orig. *Reichgottes und Menschensohn*, 1934) (London 1938, Grand Rapids 1939).
PEEL, A. (Editor): *Essays Congregational and Catholic* (London 1931).
PERCY, Ernst: *Der Leib Christi (Sōma Christou) in den paulinischen Homologumena und Antilogumena* (Lund 1942).
Die Probleme der Kolosser- und Epheserbriefe (Lund 1946).
PHYTHIAN-ADAMS, W. J.: *The People and the Presence* (London 1942).
The Way of At-one-ment (London 1944).
Files of Commission I, W.C.C., Geneva (unpublished).
PITTENGER, W. N.: 'The Church as the Body of Christ,' *Christendom*, IX.2 (1944), pp. 202-13.
PRENTER, Regin: '*L'Église d'apres le temoinage de la Confession d'Augsbourg*,' in *La Sainte Église Universelle* (Neuchatel 1948), pp. 93-131.
'Catholic and Evangelical,' *The Ecumenical Review*, I. 4 (1949), pp. 382-8.
Files of Commission I, W.C.C., Geneva (unpublished).
QUICK, O. C.: *The Christian Sacraments*, New edn. (London 1932).
'The Doctrine of the Church of England on Sacraments,' *The Ministry and the Sacraments* (R. Dunkerley, ed.) (London 1937), pp. 124-37.
'Validity,' *Faith and Order, Edinburgh 1937* (L. Hodgson, ed.) (London & New York 1938), pp. 324-5.
RALL, H. F.: 'The Church, Given or Gathered?' *Christendom*, IV.2 (1939), pp. 164-75.
RAMSEY, A. M.: *The Gospel and the Catholic Church* (London 1936).
RAVEN, C. E.: *Jesus and the Gospel of Love* (London 1931).
RAWLINSON A. E. J.: *Authority and Freedom* (London 1924).
The Church of England and the Church of Christ (London 1930).
'*Corpus Christi*,' *Mysterium Christi* (G. K. A. Bell and A. Deissmann, eds.) (London 1930), pp. 225-4.
REITZENSTEIN, R.: *Die hellenistischen Mysterienreligionen nach ihren Grundgedanken und Wirkungen* (Leipzig & Berlin 1910).
RENGSTORF, K. H.: Article '*Apostolos*', *Theologisches Wörterbuch zum Neuen Testament* (G. Kittel, ed.), Band I, pp. 397-448.
RICHARDSON, Alan: '*Une interpretation anglicaine de l'Eglise*,' *La Sainte Eglise Universelle* (Neuchatel 1948), pp. 133-74.
RIETSCHEL, Ernst: *Das Problem der unsichtbar-sichtbaren Kirche bei Luther* (Leipzig 1932).
ROBINSON, H. Wheeler: *The Christian Experience of the Holy Spirit* (London 1928).
ROBINSON, T. H.: *The Gospel of Matthew* (London 1928).
ROBINSON, William: *Essays on Christian Unity* (London 1922).

SASSE, H.: Chapter in *Credo Ecclesiam* (H. Ehrenberg, ed.) (Gütersloh 1930).
'Jesus Christ, the Lord,' *Mysterium Christi* (G. K. A. Bell and A. Deissmann, eds.) (London 1930), pp. 93-120.
Files of Commission I, W.C.C., Geneva (unpublished).
SCHLATTER, A.: *Die Geschichte der ersten Christenheit* (Gütersloh 1926).
'Die Grenzen der kirchlichen Gemeinschaft,' *Deutsche Theologie* (1935), pp. 181ff.
SCHLIER, Heinrich: *Christus und die Kirche im Epheserbrief* (Tübingen 1930).
Article '*Kephalē*,' *Theologisches Wörterbuch zum Neuen Testament* (G. Kittel, ed.), Band III, pp. 672-82.
SCHMIDT, K. D.: *Die Bekenntnisse und grundsätzlichen Aeusserungen zur Kirchenfrage des Jahres 1933* (Göttingen 1934).
SCHMIDT, K. L.: '*Die Kirche des Urchristentums*,' *Festgabe für Deissmann* (Tübingen 1927).
Article '*Basileia*,' *Theologisches Wörterbuch zum Neuen Testament* (G. Kittel, ed.), Band I, pp. 579-92.
Article '*Ekklēsia*,' *ibid.*, Band III, pp. 502-39. (Eng. tr. *The Church*, London 1950).
SCHMIDT, Traugott: *Der Leib Christi* (Leipzig und Erlangen 1919).
SCHWEITZER, Albert: *The Mysticism of Paul the Apostle* (orig., *Die Mystik des Apostel Paulus*, 1930) (London 1931).
SCHWEIZER, Eduard: *Das Leben des Herrn in der Gemeinde und ihren Diensten* (Zürich 1946).
SCOTT, C. A. A.: *The Fellowship of the Spirit* (London 1921).
The Church: Its Worship and Sacraments (London 1927).
Christianity According to St. Paul (Cambridge 1939).
SCOTT, E. F.: *The Epistles of Paul to the Colossians, to Philemon and to the Ephesians* (London 1930).
The Nature of the Early Church (New York 1941).
SEESEMANN, H.: *Der Begriff KOINŌNIA im Neuen Testament* (Giessen 1933).
SELWYN, E. G. (Editor): *Essays Catholic and Critical* (London 1929).
SIMPSON, P. Carnegie, *Church Principles* (London 1923).
The Evangelical Church Catholic (London 1934).
SOMMERLATH, Ernst: '*Kirche und Reich Gottes*,' *Zeitschrift für systematische Theologie*, XVI (1939), pp. 562-72.
STÄHLIN, Wilhelm: *The Mystery of God* (London 1937).
STRACHAN, R. H.: *The Fourth Gospel*, 3rd edn. (London 1931).
STRÖM, Å. V.: '*Kyrkan som Kristi kropp*,' *Svensk Exegetisk Årsbok*, VIII (1943), pp. 114-24.
Vetekornet (Stockholm 1944).
Kyrkans Väsen (Stockholm 1948).
SWETE, H. B. (Editor): *Essays in the Early History of the Church and the Ministry*, 2nd edn. (London 1921).
TAYLOR, F. J.: *The Church of God* (London 1946).

TAYLOR, Vincent: *Jesus and His Sacrifice* (London 1937).
TEMPLE, William: *Christian Unity and Church Reunion* (London 1943).
THORNTON, L. S.: *The Incarnate Lord* (London 1928).
The Common Life in the Body of Christ (London 1942).
THURNEYSEN, E.: 'Kirche und Staat,' *Zwischen den Zeiten* (1925), pp. 188–205.
TILLICH, Paul: *The Interpretation of History* (New York 1936).
Chapter in *The Kingdom of God and History. Church, Community and State*, Vol. III (London 1938).
'The World Situation,' *The Christian Answer* (H P. Van Dusen, ed.) (New York 1945, London 1946), pp. 19–71.
The Protestant Era (Chicago 1948).
TOMKINS, Oliver S.: *The Wholeness of the Church* (London 1949).
TORRANCE, T. F.: Review of *Catholicity*, *Scottish Journal of Theology*, II. I (1949), pp. 85-93.
'The Nature and Mission of the Church,' *ibid.*, II.3 (1949), pp. 241–70.
UNDERWOOD, A. C.: 'Views of Modern Churches: Baptist,' *The Ministry and the Sacraments* (R. Dunkerley, ed.) (London 1937), pp. 223-9.
VAN DER LEEUW, G.: *Religion in Essence and Manifestation* (orig. *Phänomenologie der Religion*, 1933) (London 1938).
VAN DUSEN, H. P. (Editor): *Liberal Theology* (New York 1942).
The Christian Answer (Editor), (New York 1945, London 1946).
VAN HOLK, J.: 'The Nature of the Church,' *Christendom*, V.1 (1940), pp. 35–46.
VAN TIL, C.: *The New Modernism* (Philadelphia and London 1946).
VISSER 'T HOOFT, W. A. (with J. H. Oldham): *The Church and Its Function in Society. Church, Community and State*, Vol I (London 1937).
The Wretchedness and Greatness of the Church (London 1944).
WACH, Joachim: *Sociology of Religion* (Chicago 1944, London 1947).
WAHLSTROM, E.: 'The Lutheran Conception of the Church,' *The Nature of the Church*, American Theological Committee (Chicago 1945), pp. 39-47.
'A Book about the Church,' *Christendom*, XIII.2 (1948), pp. 232-6.
Files of Commission I, W.C.C., Geneva (unpublished).
WEDEL, T. O.: *The Coming Great Church* (New York 1945, London 1947).
WENDLAND, H.-D.: *Die Eschatologie des Reiches Gottes bei Jesus* (Gütersloh 1931).
Chapter in *The Kingdom of God and History: Church, Community and State*, Vol. III (London 1938).
'*Geistleibliche Gestalt der Kirche*,' *Luthertum* (1939), pp. 230–42.
WENNFORS, I.: Files of Commission I, W.C.C., Geneva (unpublished)
WERNER, Martin: *Die Entstehung des christlichen Dogmas* (Bern & Leipzig 1941).

WHALE, J. S.: *Christian Doctrine* (Cambridge 1941).
'The Views of the Congregational Church,' *The Ministry and the Sacraments* (R. Dunkerley, ed.) (London 1937), pp. 211-8.

WILDER, Amos N.: *Eschatology and Ethics in the Teaching of Jesus*, Revised edn. (New York 1950).

WILL, Robert: '*La conception protestante de l'Église considérée comme le corpus Christi*,' *Revue d'histoire et de philosophie religieuses*, XII (1932), pp. 465-94.
'*Christianisme et Église*,' *Le Problème de l'Église* (M. Goguel, ed.) (Paris 1947).

WINDISCH, H.: '*Urchristentum*,' *Theologische Rundschau* (1933), pp. 186-200, 239-58, 289-301, 319-34.

WORLD COUNCIL OF CHURCHES: Files of Commission I, Geneva (unpublished).
The Universal Church in God's Design (London & New York 1948).
The Church's Witness to God's Design (London & New York 1948).

ZÄNKER, O.: Chapter in *Credo Ecclesiam* (H. Ehrenberg, ed.) (Gütersloh 1930).

INDEX OF NAMES

Allis, O. T., 217n.
Althaus, P., 31n., 129, 134, 144, 162n., 186, 208, 213, 232n., 233n.
Anderson, W. K., 183n.
Appasamy, A. J., 23n.
Aquinas, Thomas, 122
Arseniew, N., 121n.
Ashworth, R. A., 173
Asmussen, H., 138n., 149
Augustine, 120, 179
Aulén, G., 41n., 62, 90–1, 110, 130, 137n., 161, 165n., 166, 173n., 176, 186, 189

Baillie, D. M., 12n., 49, 52–3
Baillie, J., 178n., 187n., 223
Bainton, R. H., 194n.
Barrett, C. K., 35n., 44
Barry, F. R., 11n.
Barth, K., 5, 38, 43, 50–1, 61, 63n., 64, 76n., 91, 107, 110n., 111n., 112, 116n., 121n., 130, 145, 156, 162n., 172, 175n., 177, 179, 181, 182n., 186–7, 200, 227n., 230–1, 232–3
Bell, G. K. A., 39n., 49n., 70n., 73n., 76n., 193n.
Bernadin, J. B., 24n.
Boegner, M., 27n.
Bonhöffer, D., 20, 21, 35n., 45n., 60, 62, 90–1, 100, 128, 169, 171, 186, 194n.
Bowman, J. W., 55n.
Bradley, F. H., 232n.
Braun, F. M., 33n., 213n.
Brilioth, Y., 65, 125n.
Brown, W. A., 191
Brunner, E., 19, 61, 64, 83, 100, 108–9, 111, 129, 138, 147, 150, 163, 171, 176, 181, 187, 196, 224
Buber, M., 61
Bultmann, R., 15n., 30, 31n., 40, 47n., 58n., 69, 69n., 75, 86, 229–30
Bundy, W. E., 22n., 23
Burn-Murdoch, H., 153n., 185, 198

Cadbury, H. J., 135n.
Cadoux, A. T., 34n., 222n.
Cadoux, C. J., 31n., 172n., 207, 216n., 221n., 222n.
Calvin, J., 109, 113n., 114, 120, 164, 173n., 174, 179, 185

Campbell, J. Y., 7–8, 29, 53nn., 57, 221n.
Carver, W. O., 170
Cave, S., 58n., 139
Chaning-Pearce, M., 191n.
Chavasse, C., 68, 80, 81n., 82, 96
Clark, E. T., 194
Clark, K. W., 221n.
Craig, C. T., 9n., 25n., 91, 221n.
Cullmann, O., 15, 24n., 28n., 34n., 35nn., 46n., 47, 84n., 130n., 233
Cyprian, 185–7
Cyril of Jerusalem, 206

Dahl, N. A., 11, 24n., 35n.
Damour, C., 138, 167, 214
Davies, R. E., 113
Dehn, G., 100
Deissmann, A., 39n., 49n., 70n., 73, 76n.
Demant, V. A., 185
Dillistone, F. W., 4, 9n., 58n., 59, 85n., 89, 102–3
Dix, G., 151–2, 155
Dobschütz, E. von, 2n., 23–4
Dodd, C. H., 14–15, 39, 50, 53n., 56, 71, 76n., 87, 110, 145, 216n., 217–21
Dun, A., 121n., 127
Duncan, G. S., 52, 208n.
Dunkerley, R., 22n., 35n., 78n., 96n., 116n., 117n., 121n., 123n., 124n., 127n., 131n., 133n., 140n., 147n., 149n., 173n.

Easton, B. S., 19n., 23, 31n., 84, 152, 183
Ehrenberg, H., 2n. 24n., 163n.
Elert, W., 131n., 185, 192
Eliot, T. S., 63–4

Ferré, N. S. F., 176n., 183, 186n., 219n.
Flemington, W. F., 46n., 130
Flew, R. N., 9n., 10, 11n., 16, 21, 23, 27n., 33n., 34n., 42, 43n., 48n., 55n., 87n., 121n., 124, 173n., 224n., 226
Florovsky, G., 134n.
Foakes-Jackson, F. J., 31n., 43n., 46
Foerster, E., 27n., 101n., 186
Forsyth, P. T., 88, 98, 131, 158, 196
Fridrichsen, A., 27n.

GARVIE, A. E., 11n.
Gerke, F., 12n.
Gilmour, S. M., 83
Gloege, G., 35n., 68n., 82, 166n., 186n., 189, 196, 201, 210
Goguel, M., 14n., 22, 31n., 35n., 73, 76, 78n., 130n., 164, 234n.
Goodspeed, E. J., 56, 86n., 94
Gore, C., 33n., 34n., 151–2
Goudge, H. L., 24, 183n.
Grant, F. C., 10n., 40, 54n., 216n., 222
Gregg, J. A. F., 95
Grützmacher, R. D., 27n.
Gutbrod, W., 69n.

HAITJEMA, T. L., 146
Hanson, S., 70n., 72, 94, 204, 208n., 225, 233n.
Harnack, A. von, 31–2, 151
Hauck, F., 53n., 57
Hayman, E., 66, 96
Headlam, A. C., 12n., 151, 154, 193n., 199, 207
Heath, C., 141n.
Hebert, A. G., 10n., 12n., 41n., 48n., 59, 60, 152, 206n., 209
Heidegger, M., 232n.
Heiler, F., 27n., 101, 151, 213n.
Heim, K., 26, 29, 61, 80n., 138, 145–6, 179n.
Hendry, G. S., 158
Hermelink, H., 12n., 134
Hickinbotham, J. P., 154n.
Hobbes, T., 191
Hodgson, L., 39, 41n., 42, 44n., 51, 85n., 89n., 125n., 139n., 140n., 143n., 149n., 157, 165n., 187n., 190n., 193n., 199n.
Holl, K., 31n., 134n., 158
Holmström, F., 212, 231
Holtzmann, H. J., 92
Hooker, R., 193n.
Hopwood, P. G. S., 6n., 8, 16, 17, 34n., 54, 55n.
Horton, W. M., 96
Hoskyns, E. C., 42n., 76n., 79n., 151n., 202n.

JACOBS, C. M., 127n., 134
Jenkins, D. T., 148, 157n., 207
Johansson, N., 72n.
Johnston, G., 1n., 6n., 7n., 24, 28n., 31n., 35, 73, 77n., 78n., 83, 87, 92, 99, 204, 222
Juncker, A., 34n.

KÄSEMANN, E., 68n., 69, 71n., 77, 85, 87n.
Kattenbusch, F., 7n., 31, 33n., 34n., 63n., 88n., 145, 219n.

Kierkegaard, S., 227
Kirk, K. E., 101n., 151n., 153, 155n.
Kittel, G., 7n.
Knox, J., 62, 72n., 96, 221, 222
Knox, W. L., 68n., 77n., 84, 94, 111n., 118n.
Köhnlein, H., 70n.
Kümmel, W. G., 7n., 12n., 21n., 31n., 221n., 223n.
Künneth, W., 164
Kraemer, H., 206

LACEY, T. A., 12, 23n., 80n., 84n., 91, 104, 118
Laurerer, H., 163
Lecerf, A., 139, 198
Leenhardt, F. J., 9n., 33n., 34n., 98
Lewis, E., 35, 96, 111n., 131, 157, 176
Lewis, J., 191n.
Lewis, L. C., 166
Lietzmann, H., 35n., 151
Lilje, H., 161
Linton, O., 213, 216
Lock, W., 94
Lohmeyer, E., 16, 28n., 32n., 34n., 47, 51, 62, 125n.
Loisy, A., 5, 6, 8, 14, 69, 202
Lowrie, W., 146, 168
Luther, M., 100, 113n., 120, 134n., 137–8, 144, 162, 163, 173n., 174, 186

MACGREGOR, G. H. C., 42n.
Mackenzie, D., 124
Mackenzie, K., 185n.
Manson, T. W., 12n., 30n., 31n., 32, 97, 151n., 158
Manson, W., 121n.
Martin, H., 178n., 187n.
Mascall, E. L., 167n., 224
Mason, A. J., 20
Mathews, S., 191, 195n.
Melanchthon, P., 109, 135, 138
Ménégoz, F., 89, 199
Menoud, P.-H., 47n., 66
Metzger, B. M., 77
Michaelis, W., 215, 216n., 221n.
Michel, O., 10n., 34n., 68–9, 71, 231
Micklem, N., 41, 107, 112n., 116, 132, 135, 159, 161, 165–6, 182n., 205n.
Minear, P. S., 24, 121n., 169, 182n., 218n.
Moffatt, J., 48n., 52, 55, 68n., 73–5, 81, 86n., 157n.
Morrison, C. C., 26, 71, 88, 167, 173–4, 187, 191, 196
Moule, C. F. D., 154
Mulert, H., 137
Müller, K., 151

INDEX OF NAMES

Neill, S., 154n., 155
Neufield, H., 121n.
Newbigin, J. E. L., 47, 48n., 93, 98n., 99, 114, 117, 122n., 134n., 157n., 187, 200n., 207n., 213n., 226–7
Niebuhr, Reinhold, 99, 143, 195, 213n., 229
Niemöller, M., 136
Niesel, W., 138n., 167n.
Nygren, A., 72n., 90, 147

Oepke, A., 32n., 34n., 86n.
Otto, R., 13n., 33n., 34n., 219, 223

Peel, A., 172n., 207n.
Percy, E., 68n., 70n., 72n., 77n., 81n.
Phythian-Adams, W. J., 77, 96, 101n. 102–3, 128–9, 140n., 143, 155n., 179, 182, 187
Pittenger, W. N., 84n., 104n.
Plato, 68
Prenter, R., 137, 141, 158, 189, 197

Quick, O. C., 96, 121n., 123n., 125n., 132, 134n., 140, 153, 199n., 208.

Rall, H. F., 175, 187
Ramsey, A. M., 12n., 17, 35n., 58n., 68, 72n.
Raven, C. E., 170
Rawlinson, A. E. J., 68, 70–1, 76n., 118, 166
Reitzenstein, R., 69
Rengstorf, K. H., 151n.
Richardson, A., 46, 199, 203n.
Rietshel, E., 100n., 163, 172n.
Ritschl, A., 38
Robinson, H. W., 41n., 44n., 49, 52, 54–5, 75, 96
Robinson, J. A., 151
Robinson, T. H., 33n.
Robinson, W., 96, 116n., 121n.
Rousseau, J., 191

Sasse, H., 2n., 24, 39, 49n., 89, 164n.
Scheel, O., 186n.
Schlatter, A., 58, 186n., 206
Schleiermacher, F., 170
Schlier, H., 69, 70n., 77, 81n., 84–5, 92
Schmidt, K. D., 136n.
Schmidt, K. L., 7n., 31, 32, 34n., 62, 77, 82n., 83, 92, 163n., 214n., 233
Schmidt, T., 68n., 69n.
Schweitzer, A., 16, 34n., 77n., 85n., 87, 212, 214, 215n., 216
Schweizer, E., 75, 146n., 147, 161
Scott, C. A. A., 10, 18n., 55, 72n., 77n., 84, 126, 190

Scott, E. F., 2n., 9, 22, 75n., 77n., 80n., 81n., 84n., 94, 221n.
Seesemann, H., 55
Selwyn, E. G., 111n., 118n.
Simpson, P. C., 126, 157, 165
Sohm, R., 151
Sommerlath, E., 220
Spörri, T., 186n.
Spener, P. J., 163n.
Stählin, W., 126, 167, 175
Strachan, R. H., 42n.
Streeter, B. H., 151
Ström, Å. V., 7n., 28, 92, 148n.
Strong A. H., 195n.
Swete, H. B., 20n.

Taylor, F. J., 89, 184, 204, 206n., 227n.
Taylor, V., 216n., 223, 227n.
Temple, W., 64n.
Thornton, L. S., 35n., 41n., 54–7, 63, 71, 74–6, 81–2, 89n., 94n., 94–6, 101, 104, 185, 202
Thurneysen, E., 175
Tillich, P., 162n., 174, 190, 219, 225
Tomkins, O. S., 209
Torrance, T. F., 91, 93, 98, 209
Troeltsch, E., 171, 194, 196
Turner, C. H., 152n.

Underwood, A. C., 133

Van der Leeuw, G., 195
Van Dusen, H. P., 62n., 96n., 162n., 191n.
Van Holk, L. J., 25
Van Til, C., 179, 182n., 232n.
Vasady, B., 121n.
Visser 't Hooft, W. A., 12n., 19n., 193, 203

Wach, J., 163n., 168
Wahlstrom, E., 80n., 90n., 162
Wedel, T. O., 45, 48, 156, 166, 220n.
Weiss, J., 212, 214, 216
Wendland, H. D., 34n., 93, 218n., 223, 228–9
Wennfors, I., 91
Werner, M., 216
Wesley, J., 173
Whale, J. S., 96, 123, 140
Wikenhauser, A., 72n.
Wilder, A. N., 221n.
Will, R., 27n., 89, 96, 121n., 166
Windisch, H., 32n., 34n.

Zänker, O., 163n., 187
Zwingli, H., 113n., 127

INDEX OF SUBJECTS

ANGLICANISM. *See* England, Church of.

BAPTISM, 5, 46–7, 70, 75–6, 86–7, 89, 120–3, 127–33, 139, 141, 149, 172, 185
Baptist Churches, 116, 129–32, 170–1
Body of Christ, 45, 51–2, 54, 66–104, 116–19, 148–56, 164, 166–9, 186, 189, 198–210, 216, 233
Bride of Christ, 80–2, 96, 204

CHURCHES OF CHRIST, 132
Congregational Churches, 88

Deutsche Christen, 136, 169

ELECTION, 179–183, 215
England, Church of, 91, 96, 122, 125, 134, 136, 143, 150–7, 166, 179, 193
Eschatology, 12–16, 22–3, 28, 30, 32, 33, 34, 44, 47, 86, 87, 124, 211–34
Eucharist. *See* Holy Communion.

FAITH AND ORDER, WORLD CONFERENCE ON, 85, 115, 117, 121, 140, 141, 143
Friends, Society of. *See* Quakers.

GNOSTICISM, 68–72, 94, 203

HOLLAND, CHURCH OF, 115
Holy Communion, 50, 56–7, 65, 70–1, 73, 120–7, 133–41, 218

ISRAEL, 3–14, 18–25, 33, 72, 179–80, 183

JUDAISM, 2, 3, 4, 9, 10, 18, 80, 180, 183

KINGDOM OF GOD, 5, 12, 17, 23–4, 30–4, 44, 47, 133, 176, 195, 208–10, 233–4
Koinōnia, 53–66, 82, 98–103, 133, 167, 174, 185, 187

LORD'S SUPPER. *See* Holy Communion.
Love (*agapē*), 45, 58, 64, 65, 104, 176–8, 180, 181, 187, 234
Lutheran Church, 130–7, 157, 166–74, 186, 189, 193, 199

METHODIST CHURCH, 37, 115, 124
Ministry, 97, 107–9, 142–59

ORTHODOX CHURCH, 116, 132–4, 150, 152, 189, 193, 199, 218

PENTECOST, 9, 35–6, 41–6, 128, 156, 215
People of God. *See* Israel.
Personification, 71, 87
Presbyterian Church. *See* Reformed Tradition.

QUAKERS, 65, 96, 133, 139–41, 149

REFORMED TRADITION, 66, 96–7, 115, 124–5, 136, 146, 157, 167–74, 179, 189, 193, 199–201
Remnant, 11, 12, 14, 36, 180
Revelation, 23–4, 26, 99, 105–12, 176–8
Roman Catholic Church, 28–9, 33, 63, 98–9, 113, 126, 130, 137, 138, 147, 152, 167, 171, 189, 193, 196, 219

SALVATION, 132–3, 160, 169, 172–87
Salvation Army, 133, 139
Scotland, Church of, 85
Sectarianism, 10, 171, 193–9
South India, Church of, 122
Sweden, Church of, 152

WORD OF GOD, 48, 80, 97, 105–26, 133–41, 146–9, 156, 158, 159, 167, 171, 177, 184, 206
World Council of Churches, 184, 201

www.ingramcontent.com/pod-product-compliance
Lightning Source LLC
Chambersburg PA
CBHW050346230426
43663CB00010B/2015